☐   The New Deal and the Last Hurrah

☐ The New Deal and ☐ the Last Hurrah

☐ Pittsburgh Machine Politics

Bruce M. Stave

☐ UNIVERSITY OF PITTSBURGH PRESS

For my father, B. R. S., who knew
the clubhouses of another city,
and
Sondra Terrie, a wife more resourceful than
the most resourceful of political bosses

Grateful acknowledgment is made to the following:

Little, Brown and Company for permission to reprint material from *The Last Hurrah* by Edwin O'Connor, by permission of Atlantic-Little, Brown and Co. Copyright © 1956 by Edwin O'Connor.

Government Affairs Institute for permission to adapt the map of Pittsburgh from Richard Scammon, *America Votes*, vol. 5 (Pittsburgh, 1964), p. 345.

Mid-America for permission to reprint with adaptations the material in Chapter 2, which originally appeared as "The 'La Follette Revolution' and the Pittsburgh Vote, 1932" in *Mid-America*, XLIX (October 1967), 244–51.

Pennsylvania Historical Society for permission to reprint with adaptations the material in Chapter 7, which originally appeared as "The New Deal, the Last Hurrah, and the Building of an Urban Political Machine: Pittsburgh Committeemen, A Case Study" in *Pennsylvania History*, XXXIII (October 1966), 460–83.

JS
1298
.57

☐ Contents

☐ Maps

☐ Tables

☐ Preface

☐ On April 20, 1969, long after traditional opinion maintained that the New Deal had assisted in destroying America's urban political machines, *The Pittsburgh Press* published the headline "DEMOCRATS FEAR LAST HURRAH." This study investigates the origins of the Pittsburgh Democratic machine, which, after three and a half decades in power, was finally fearing "the Last Hurrah." These origins were rooted deeply in the New Deal; rather than enfeebling machine politics in Pittsburgh, the New Deal invigorated a previously impotent Democratic organization. The interplay of politics and federal work relief did much to further the power of the Democratic organization in its initial stages of growth. Roosevelt's welfare state did not undermine the bosses; instead it facilitated the transfer of urban political power from Republicans to Democrats. For more than three decades, the organization consolidated its control over patronage; its grass-roots voting support increased as well. The existence of boss politics in other cities during the post-New Deal years indicates that news of the death of the urban political machine had been prematurely reported.

Wherever possible and appropriate, noncomputerized quantitative methodology, such as voting return analysis and collective biography, has been employed to study the workings of the Pittsburgh machine. For his encouragement in this direction, as well as for his advice on substantive matters, I am indebted to Prof. Samuel P. Hays of the University of Pittsburgh, who has seen this work through from its inception as a doctoral dissertation. I also profited from the reading given my manuscript in its initial stage by John M. Allswang of California State College at Los Angeles.

ix

I am most grateful for the assistance given me by the staffs of the Carnegie Library of Pittsburgh, especially the Pennsylvania Division and the Microfilm Room; the Franklin D. Roosevelt Library in Hyde Park, New York; the library of the Health and Welfare Association of Allegheny County; the library of the Washington and Jefferson College; the National Archives Library in Washington, D.C.; the Archives of Industrial Society, University of Pittsburgh; and the libraries of the University of Pittsburgh, the University of Bridgeport, and the University of Michigan.

Without the cooperation of the political leaders, as well as the anonymous 103 New Deal committeemen or their relatives who were interviewed, this study would have suffered immeasurably. In addition, Frank Comis and others on the staff of the Allegheny County Board of Elections deserve my warmest thanks for leading me to the treasure trove of election-return books stored in the board's attic. It was with the gracious aid of Mrs. Rosemary Plesset of the Allegheny County Democratic Committee Headquarters that I gained entrance into the party's files kept by the late David L. Lawrence during the depression years.

I would also like to thank the Fulbright Foundation in India for granting me a lectureship during the 1968–1969 academic year. Moving from urban America with all its megalopolitan distractions to rural India with its few, provided me with an enormously interesting and educational experience and allowed me the time to revise for publication this manuscript about the urban America I had temporarily left.

The encouragement of Frederick A. Hetzel, Director of the University of Pittsburgh Press, to pursue this project to its completion and the thorough and painstaking editing of Mrs. Louise Craft place the author in great debt to his publisher. The greatest debt, however, is owed to my wife, Sondra Astor Stave, whose services as editor, computer, cartographer, indexer, and general sounding board were beyond the call of wifely duty, but totally in character. I am solely responsible for errors of fact and interpretation.

☐ **The New Deal and the Last Hurrah**

ABBREVIATIONS IN FOOTNOTES

ACDCH	Allegheny County Democratic Committee Headquarters
Courier	*Pittsburgh Courier*
DNC	Democratic National Committee
FDRL	Franklin D. Roosevelt Library
Leg. Jour.	Commonwealth of Pennsylvania, *Legislative Journal*
Mun. Rec.	City of Pittsburgh, *Municipal Record*
NA	National Archives
NYT	*New York Times*
OF	Official Files
PD, CL	Pennsylvania Division, Carnegie Library
PG	*Pittsburgh Post-Gazette*
PPF	President's Personal Files
Press	*The Pittsburgh Press*
ST	*Pittsburgh Sun-Telegraph*
W & J	Washington and Jefferson College

2

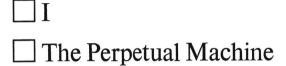

☐ I
☐ The Perpetual Machine

He had no high opinion of the intelligence of the electorate, but experience had taught him that it quite adequately grasped the fact that all successful political activity was based on quid pro quo. *In light of benefits to be conferred, he thought it unlikely that those who came to him this morning would consider themselves as uncommitted on election day. . . .*

Edwin O'Connor, The Last Hurrah

☐ The rise of the modern political machine was advanced by the quickening pace of economic expansion and urban growth during the decades following the United States' emergence from the Civil War. America bore witness to the growth of an institution that would cast an indelible mark on its political character. Corporate entrepreneurs, seeking privileges, charters, and franchises, turned to the politicians for aid; they were not disappointed. Immigrants searched for security from the uncertainties of a new world; the local politician answered their need. The urban boom placed on the official municipal governments demands that could not be met. The big city political machines could, and did, meet the new challenge.

A multitude of reasons have been offered to explain the rise of the urban political machine. Business, in return for the politician's favors, supplied the funds that enabled the machine to operate. The immigrant, in reciprocation for the politician's largess, returned the vote as his *quid pro quo,* the favor for the vote. Apathy on the part of the average citizen, according to James Bryce, permitted the machine to romp merrily through urban America, leaving behind a trail of corruption and democratic decay. A much more recent analyst, Seymour Mandelbaum, contends that in the case of New York City the fragmentation of that city's communication and transportation network called forth the prototype William Marcy Tweed to unite the splintered metropolis. Some have seen the separation of powers and the myriad number of local offices as providing the machine with the opportunity of making order from chaos. When Lincoln Steffens asked Tammany Boss Richard Croker, "Why must there be a boss, when we've got a mayor and a council," Croker replied:

"That's why. . . . It's because there's a mayor *and* a council *and* judges and—a hundred other men to deal with. A government is nothing but a business with a lot of officials who check and cross check one another and who come and go, there this year, out the next. A business man wants to do business with one man and one who is always there to remember to carry out the business."[1]

Samuel P. Hays, one observer of Pittsburgh politics, maintains that the machine provided a vehicle of political expression to those groups in urban society which in no other way could exert an effective voice in government control. Through the machine numerous ward communities and lower-and-middle-income groups could join to influence municipal policy. Hays has written:

Their private occupational and social life did not naturally involve these groups in larger city-wide activities in the same way as the upper class was involved; hence they lacked access to privately organized economic and social power on which they could construct political power. The "machine" filled this organizational gap.[2]

Whereas Hays believes that the machine tied together the interests of

1. Samuel P. Orth, *The Boss and the Machine: A Chronicle of Politicians and Party Organization* (New Haven, 1919), pp. 33, 38, 55, 58, 61; Fred I. Greenstein, "The Changing Pattern of Urban Party Politics," *The Annals*, 353 (May 1964), 4; James Bryce, *The American Commonwealth*, vol. III (New York, 1924), pp. 103, 124–25; Seymour Mandelbaum, *Boss Tweed's New York* (New York, 1965); William B. Munroe, "The Boss in Politics—Asset or Liability," *The Annals*, 169 (Sept. 1933), 14; Lincoln Steffens, *The Autobiography of Lincoln Steffens* (New York, 1931), p. 236.
2. Samuel P. Hays, "The Politics of Reform in Municipal Government in the Progressive Era," *Pacific Northwest Quarterly*, LV (Oct. 1964), reprinted in Alexander B. Callow, Jr., ed., *American Urban History: An Interpretive Reader with Commentaries* (New York, 1969), p. 429.

various neighborhoods and income groups, Richard Wade maintains that reform groups such as the ubiquitous Committees of One Hundred did the same for the Protestant middle-class reformers living in the outer wards of the city. These citizens, having taken advantage of the urban transportation revolution, had moved from the inner core of the city to the more spacious and scattered outlying neighborhoods. There they joined forces in "reform associations," in contrast with the boss and his organization who represented the political desires of the densely populated inner city inhabited by immigrant groups. The machine "was simply the political expression of inner city life," and "reform was a movement of the periphery against the center."[3]

Hays and Wade, who disagree as to the class origins of the reformers, also differ with regard to another important distinction. Wade, in an attempt to connect contemporary inner-core and outer-city conflict with a similar urban polarization during the progressive era, emphasizes the reformers' residence as the launching pad for good government. He sees the residential composition of the inner city only as the basis for the political machine. Hays, however, sees the institutional activity of the central city as the roots of reform and points to the occupational and social life of the reformers, centered in the inner city, as the catalyst for reform. Nevertheless, both observers would agree that reformers attacked the lower-class ethnic groups as often as their ostensible target—corruption.

Although the reformers found it difficult to communicate with the lower classes, especially with the immigrant, the political machine did not. When speaking about the hoards of immigrants flooding the gates of New York City, Croker said, "There is not a mugwump in the city who would shake hands with them." However, the machine politicians shook hands —and did much more. And the immigrant, thankful to the party worker for learning his ways as well as teaching him about America's strange customs, gravitated to the boss and his machine rather than to the reformer. Suspicious of the mugwump, who reminded him of his upper-class, autocratic rulers in Europe, and interested more in a job and the

3. Richard C. Wade, "Urbanization," in C. Vann Woodward, ed., *The Comparative Approach to American History* (New York, 1968), pp. 196–97. For an application of Wade's model to a single city, Cincinnati, see Zane L. Miller, *Boss Cox's Cincinnati: Urban Politics in the Progressive Era* (New York, 1968). A critique of this residential approach can be found in Joel A. Tarr, review of *Boss Cox's Cincinnati,* by Miller, the *American Historical Review,* LXXIV (Apr. 1969), 1380–81.

next meal for his family than in citizenship, efficiency, and good government, the immigrant aligned with the ward politicians, who believed as did Boston's boss James M. Curley that "reform administrations suffer from a diarrhea of promises and a constipation of performance." Even as late as the 1930s, an observer of the foreign born in McKeesport, Pennsylvania, could remark: "It is almost impossible to convince the average foreigner that the Mayor, the ward politician or the local representative in either state or federal legislation cannot set aside laws to grant a favor to anyone loyal to the party."[4]

Politics, in addition to serving as a means to obtain material assistance, stood as a way station in the immigrants' sojourn into the mainstream of American life. The fictional Irish boss Frank Skeffington, hero of Edwin O'Connor's *The Last Hurrah*, remarked to his young nephew, "I had no education to speak of, a good many roads were closed to our people, and politics seemed to be the easiest way out." Oscar Handlin points out that for other newcomers the way out may have been through sports or racketeering as well as politics; but for so many of the real-life Irish, like the fictional Skeffington, the political way was the first step on the status ladder, when so many other occupations were closed to them. The sign "Irish need not apply" did not hang over the door of the local political clubhouse.[5]

The Irish comprised the most active group in Pittsburgh's grass-roots politics during the New Deal and after. They were carrying on a long and

4. Ralph G. Martin, *The Bosses* (New York, 1964), p. 33; Richard Hofstadter, *The Age of Reform* (New York, 1960), pp. 181–86; Oscar Handlin, *The Uprooted* (Boston, 1951), pp. 209–13; Alexander B. Callow, Jr., *The Tweed Ring* (New York, 1966), pp. 69–71, 262–65, 299; Elmer E. Cornwell, Jr., "Bosses, Machines, and Ethnic Groups," *The Annals*, 353 (May 1964), 30; Robert E. Burns, "An Irrepressible Politician," *Review of Politics*, XX (Apr. 1958), 252–57; Mary E. Hurlbutt, *New Americans in Allegheny County: A Cultural Study* (New York, 1937), p. 82, also in Philip Klein, *A Social Study of Pittsburgh* (New York, 1937), p. 257. For the view that bosses, machines, and their immigrant followings were not as estranged from reformers and reform legislation as traditionally believed, see J. Joseph Huthmacher's two articles, "Urban Liberalism and the Age of Reform," *Mississippi Valley Historical Review*, XLIX (Sept. 1962), 231–41, and "Charles Evans Hughes and Charles Francis Murphy: The Metamorphosis of Progressivism," *New York History*, XLVI (Jan. 1965), 25–40. Nancy Joan Weiss adopts the same view in *Charles Francis Murphy, 1858–1924: Respectability and Responsibility in Tammany Politics* (Northampton, Massachusetts, 1968). Miller in *Boss Cox's Cincinnati* relates that the boss's acceptance of municipal reform led some to conclude that "a boss [was] not necessarily a public enemy" (p. 94).

5. Edwin O'Connor, *The Last Hurrah* (New York, 1956), p. 62; Handlin, *The Uprooted*, pp. 251–52; Cornwell, "Bosses, Machines, and Ethnic Groups," p. 33.

tried American political tradition: Tim Sullivan's Lower East Side Manhattan political organization, an amalgam of party regularity, social-welfare liberalism, and organized vice, typified the Irish political machines that had begun to emerge in the 1890s. Hinky Dink Kenna and Bathhouse John Coughlin, and later Pat Nash and Ed Kelly, ruled Chicago; Tom Pendergast controlled Kansas City until his sensational downfall; Frank Hague was the law in Jersey City and Bernard McFeely ruled the roost in Hoboken; the O'Connells reigned over New York's state capital, Albany.[6]

One observer hypothesizes that the machine governments resulted from a merger of rural Irish custom and urban politics. First, there was a certain indifference to Yankee proprieties: stealing an election reflected the corrupt eighteenth-century Irish politics. Secondly, the Irish had a tradition of regarding the formal government (England) as illegitimate and the informal one (Ireland) as bearing the imprimatur of righteousness. In America, the machine stood as the informal government. Thirdly, the Irish immigrants arrived with political experience; many had been part of the Catholic emancipation movement and Daniel O'Connell's Catholic Association, a democratic political party. Finally, the social structure of the Irish village, ruled by a stern oligarchy of elders, in which a person's position was generally likely to improve with time, mirrored the essentials of a Tammany. The narrow boundaries of peasant Ireland were similar to small precinct confines.[7] In addition, the Irish, having English as their native tongue, had an immediate advantage over many immigrants in American urban politics.

Although, traditionally, the Irish have been the most active ethnic group in politics, many other nationalities have been represented. And even though the ethnic bloc has not always been active in the organizational sense, its vote is often sought by the boss—who just may be Irish himself. On one weekend in 1941 Chicago's boss Ed Kelly told a luncheon meeting honoring Antanas Smetona, who was then president of Lithuania, how the Lithuanians were a liberty-loving, democratic people. He later went on to celebrate Polish Constitution Day by noting: "Po-

6. William V. Shannon, *The American Irish: A Political and Social Portrait* (New York, 1963), pp. 139–40. For the role of the Irish in Pittsburgh politics, see Chapter 7.

7. Daniel Patrick Moynihan in Nathan Glazer and Daniel Patrick Moynihan, *Beyond the Melting Pot* (Cambridge, Mass., 1963), pp. 223–29.

land will rise again. There is an immortal tradition of stamina and fierce determination in the Polish people. . . ." An hour after that he spoke to a meeting of the (Jewish) Workmen's Circle, telling the members: "Just as the talmud and its great teachings are eternal—so too is the hebrew spirit constant and undying. . . ." In polyglot Chicago, as in other urban areas, this strategy was good sense—and good politics.[8]

While the immigrant groups and their children allied themselves with the boss and his machine, others in the urban community found his kind of politics anathematic. Resentment often resounded against the vote frauds, the protection given to vice and gambling, and the "honest graft." However, attacks on the organization are often more of a rhetorical gesture than a serious criticism, especially during hotly contested primary battles. Exemplary of such rhetoric is a statement made by an antiorganization Democratic candidate as he declared himself for the 1938 Pennsylvania gubernatorial nomination. Charles Margiotti, rejected by the regular organization, told the public, "Boss rule destroys political parties, disenfranchises the people, and saps the life blood from democracy."[9]

Sociologist Robert K. Merton, trying to avoid a normative judgment regarding political machines and attempting to take what he calls a functional approach, gives perhaps the best explanation for the existence of the boss and his machine. Merton notes that although the political machine has generally been held responsible for violating certain moral codes, it has endured because it has performed a positive function, which at the time could not have been adequately fulfilled by other existing patterns and structures: it has satisfied a basic latent function; has cut across the bureaucratic red tape that imprisons most local city governments, as well as state and federal authority; it has humanized the cold procedures of the law for the immigrant; and, as Croker noted, it has permitted the businessman to do business with one man, rather than a slew of petty officials. Historians might also do well to mark Merton's hypothesis regarding the short-lived existence of the many reform movements. He remarks, "Any attempt to eliminate an existing social structure without providing an adequate alternative structure for fulfilling the function

8. Speeches of Kelly, President's Personal Files 3166 (hereafter cited as PPF), Franklin D. Roosevelt Library (hereafter cited as FDRL), Hyde Park, N.Y.
9. Speeches of Attorney General Margiotti, Primary Election Speeches, 1938, Files of Allegheny County Democratic Committee Headquarters (hereafter cited as ACDCH), Pittsburgh, Pa.

previously fulfilled by the abolished organization is doomed to failure."[10] The endurance of the Pittsburgh political machine well after the end of the New Deal lends support to Merton's thesis.

The internal structure of the machine encourages its perpetuation. Ed Flynn, boss of the Bronx and one of the more literate of his breed, explained that "it is not only a machine; it is an army. And in any organization, as in the army, there must be discipline." David L. Lawrence, then Pennsylvania Democratic state chairman and leader of the Pittsburgh political organization, used the same metaphor when, on the eve of the 1936 Roosevelt landslide, he told his party workers: "For the past two months our heavy artillery has been pounding the Republican entrenchments. . . . The barrage has been laid down. Tomorrow we go over the top. Tomorrow all of you, representing the infantry of our party, carry the battle to the polling places." Others have made an analogy between the political machine and a streamlined medievalism. Observing the tight hierarchy enveloping Pennsylvania's Democratic machine, they have compared the precinct captains, ward chairmen, county leaders, and state chairmen to the serfs, vassals, and overlords of medieval Europe; for each owed allegiance to the man above him in the hierarchy.[11]

At the apex of this disciplined party organization is the boss—or "leader." The terms, used interchangeably here, are often dependent on one's attitude toward the man, the organization, or the party in question. Pennsylvania's Joe Guffey, whom historian Arthur M. Schlesinger, Jr., perhaps mistakenly, cites as the first of the liberal bosses, claimed that he had the answer to the question, "When does a leader of the people become a boss of a political machine?" The New Deal senator quipped, "When he's on top." However, Guffey actually hated to be called a boss. His successor to control of the Keystone State's Democratic party, David L. Lawrence, claimed that although his opponents tried to tag him Boss, that epithet never latched on to him. "That's why I was able to win public office. It was only used at election time, and the people didn't be-

---

10. Robert K. Merton, *Social Theory and Social Structure* (Glencoe, Ill., 1957), pp. 71–82. For a sophisticated elaboration of the functional approach to the study of the political machine, see Eric L. McKitrick, "The Study of Corruption," in Richard Hofstadter and Seymour Martin Lipset, eds., *Sociology and History: Methods* (New York, 1968), pp. 358–70.

11. Edward J. Flynn, *You're the Boss: The Practice of American Politics* (New York, 1962), p. 30; speeches of Lawrence, File, 1936, ACDCH; Joseph Alsop and Robert Kintner, "The Guffey," *Saturday Evening Post*, CCX (Apr. 16, 1938), 16.

lieve it to any great extent," remarked the four-time mayor of Pittsburgh and governor of Pennsylvania, who may have been doing some wishful thinking.[12]

Although, like the term *boss*, the word *machine* may conjure up sinister images, it could easily refer to a regular party organization that functions with exceptional efficiency, resembling a mechanical device in the smoothness and precision of its operations. It offers services and favors—legal and extralegal—and in return expects votes and sometimes funds. To the lower-income constituent the favor may be paying a gas bill that is overdue, aiding in the naturalization of a relative, providing a ton of coal, presenting a food basket at Christmas, or finding a job for somebody out of work. For the better-heeled citizen adjusting a tax assessment, changing a zoning code, or fixing a traffic summons may be enough to build an obligation on the part of the voter to the local politician. Nevertheless, as one student of machine politics points out, "the party organization is strongest where the needs of the voters are most compelling." This correlation may be one reason why the poorest of America's urban areas are generally the most controlled. Supporting this theory is a statement made during the depression by a ward leader to his workers, "If your people are not indebted to you, we cannot expect you to control your division."[13]

The Great Depression of the 1930s made the needs of the voters more compelling than usual. Since individuals at all levels of the economy felt its impact, the political job became more important than ever. The files of the Allegheny County Democratic Committee Headquarters reveal the hundreds upon hundreds of requests for patronage received during the dark days of the 1930s by this local organization. For many election

12. Arthur M. Schlesinger, Jr., *The Politics of Upheaval*, vol. III, *The Age of Roosevelt* (Boston, 1960), p. 442; clipping from *New York Daily News*, Guffey Scrapbooks, Pennsylvania Division, Carnegie Library, Pittsburgh, Pa.; interview with Emma Guffey Miller, Apr. 27, 1964; interview with Lawrence, Apr. 14, 1964; *Pittsburgh Post-Gazette* (hereafter cited as *PG*), Jan. 9, 1963. For portraits of the old-time bosses, see Harold Zink, *City Bosses in the United States: A Study of 20 Municipal Bosses* (Durham, North Carolina, 1930).
13. Harold Zink, *Government of Cities in the United States* (New York, 1948), p. 197; Edward F. Cook and G. Edward Janosik, *Guide to Pennsylvania Politics* (New York, 1957), pp. 47–48; Harold F. Gosnell, *Machine Politics: Chicago Model* (Chicago, 1937); interviews with Pittsburgh's New Deal committeemen; J. T. Salter, *Boss Rule: Portraits in City Politics* (New York, 1935), p. 17; David H. Kurtzman, "Methods of Controlling Votes in Philadelphia" (Ph.D. diss., Dept. of Political Science, University of Pennsylvania, 1935), p. 23.

time meant more than casting a ballot; it meant work—and being paid by the party for that work. The plight of thousands was reflected by one Pittsburgh woman when she wrote to Dave Lawrence in 1935:

> I am writing to ask your consideration for work on the return board in the November election. . . . Since Tom's illness a year ago, I have been employed at Kaufmann's [a large department store], but was laid off in September. Though Tom has been entirely well these last two years, he has been unable like many others, to get any kind of work, though at present he is with the Highways—as you know—yet he is only earning $80 or $85 a month. That much, Mr. Lawrence I am truly thankful for, but it really isn't much to meet the expenses of a home and pay rent, which we must do now, as we had to let our home . . . go back to the owner. We couldn't possibly keep up payments. Tom also has carfare and lunch expenses, and until he gets something better, I am so willing to help, in anyway to get along without further debts. *Mr. Lawrence, I know you are pestered to death with everyone's financial condition,* but I assure [sic] any consideration you give me, either on the Return board or any other position you have to offer, and I assure you I would not be afraid of any kind of work —I will appreciate the kindness as I always have done your many kindnesses in the past" (emphasis added).[14]

Others wrote for themselves, for their relatives, for the widow on the street who had five children and no means of support. They asked for jobs, for contributions, and even for business from the government. An insurance firm, which had lost its state business, commented that it had always supported the state administration "and we feel we should be entitled to some of this business." A local church solicited a contribution for its summer raffle and carnival. When the county chairman donated ten dollars, he added, "I am also enclosing a slate card of the regular Democratic candidates which we wish you would use on the booth." There always appeared the *quid pro quo*.[15]

Within the organization, as well as between it and the voter, the *quid pro quo* served as the nexus of all relations. When organization headquarters refused to endorse a candidate of a district Democratic club, the

14. Letter to Lawrence, Oct. 10, 1935, Return-Board File, General Election, 1935, ACDCH.
15. Letter to David Lawrence, Primary Congratulatory Letter File, 1938, ACDCH; letter to James P. Kirk, July 15, 1939, answer, Aug. 17, 1939, Primary Public File, 1939, ibid.

district leader warned: "After all, for our Democratic organization to remain in power it will be necessary to satisfy individuals through courtesies and consideration to our desires. To be specific, if the populace of our district is to continue to support the Democratic Party, *they must have something in return for their support*" (emphasis added). Another party worker, who had received something, was ready to reciprocate: "I appreciated to the highest the job you got for me. You may rest assured that I will show how much in time to come in any way you can use me. You can count on my full support in the coming election. . . ."[16]

Delivering these favors, the precinct captains or committeemen worked as liaison between the organization and the voter. The Bronx's Ed Flynn noted: "As with any machine it is the motor which keeps it going. The component parts of the political machine are the active workers within the party. It is the least complicated of mechanisms and its foundations are the election district captains." These grass-roots politicians, standing as living symbols of politics, put the voter in personal contact with the sources of political power. If the favor was needed, they were the ones to approach; on election day they did the approaching.[17]

Emphasizing the importance during the depression of personal contact between party and voter, one Philadelphia ward leader commented: "If I have got a man in my ward who does not know every man by his name who lives in his division, who does not know when the man is in trouble, who does not know when there is want and privation visiting a household —if he sees one man moving out and another moving in and he does not know it, he is no good to me." In the extreme, votes were cast for or against the local party worker, rather than the candidate. A Pittsburgh New Deal committeeman explained: "The secret of a good committeeman is to help people—grab the opportunity and help. I'd pull up alongside a woman shopping and take her shopping bags. It helps; you must be willing. In that manner you obligate the voters." Then he sorrowfully added: "It can work in reverse. One family voted against FDR because they disliked me!"[18]

16. Letter to James P. Kirk, Feb. 4, 1935, File, 1938, ACDCH; letter to Kirk, undated, General Election, General File, 1939, ibid.

17. Flynn, *You're the Boss*, p. 35.

18. Kurtzman, "Controlling Votes in Philadelphia," p. 30; interview with Pittsburgh committeeman, 11W14. (To maintain anonymity of committeemen, they are listed by ward and district—hence, 11W14 is read 11th Ward, 14th District.)

A study of the 1956 presidential vote in Gary, Indiana, showed that in areas where the committeemen of both parties had the highest personal contact with their constituents, there was an increase in each candidate's expected vote. Generally, the highest gains came in areas of an uneasy majority for either party, for there the grass-roots activity was most intense. This discovery prompted the authors of the study to find— perhaps what common sense would ordinarily tell us—that the efforts of party organization are particularly important where election outcomes are easily affected.[19]

A similar survey of the Detroit-Wayne County area in Michigan concluded that a strong grass-roots party organization could increase or decrease a candidate's vote, depending on whether the candidate's or the opposition's organization was more active. However, it noted that precinct organization appeared more important for the minority party since the majority party controlled the official government whose agencies could mobilize the vote for it; the minority party had to go it alone. Yet in 1956 only 10 percent of a cross section of citizens surveyed nationally reported being contacted personally by precinct workers; and even when considering only nonsouthern cities of over one hundred thousand, the figure was a good deal less than 20 percent.[20]

The necessity of grass-roots contact between party and voter received its due during one election campaign when Allegheny County's Democratic Committee Headquarters trumpeted the need for a local campaign headquarters in every ward, borough, and township. The Democratic leadership suggested the securing of the most "prominent and central location as possible. Our experience has been that where our leaders have mustered such a headquarters in the past, we have gotten results because it is at least a rallying point for the Democratic workers and Democratic voters as well." Likewise, an endorsement for a neighborhood druggist's candidacy as alderman in Pittsburgh's Seventeenth Ward il-

19. Phillips Cutright and Peter H. Rossi, "Grass Roots Politicians and the Vote," *American Sociological Review*, XXIII (Apr. 1958), 171–79. The authors employed questionnaires set up to measure the parties' campaign activity as a determinant of the vote by establishing what variables the vote should have been based on (candidate appeal, socio-economic composition of the precinct, etc.). They then correlated the actual vote to party activity using a multiple-regression equation.

20. Daniel Katz and Samuel J. Eldersveld, "The Impact of Local Party Activity Upon the Electorate," *Public Opinion Quarterly*, XXV (spring, 1961); Greenstein, "Urban Party Politics," pp. 8–9. Since the three studies mentioned deal with presidential elections, their application to local elections may be questionable.

lustrates the inherent local nature of politics and its connection to community service. The candidate's advocate proclaimed:

> For the span of 20 years, the drugstore which he owned . . . was a veritable haven for the sick people of his neighborhood and never was anyone turned away for lack of money. Not only was the merchandise of his drug store at the disposal of the poor, but also whatever other favors he could render outside the ken of his economic sphere were given without the least bit of stint.

The local committeeman, as well as the candidate, has to be well integrated into his community. As the study of Gary, Indiana, points out: "the effective party worker is one who is embedded in the social life of the area he serves. He knows personally many of the residents, is similar to them in group memberships, and actively seeks to reinforce the bonds of acquaintanceship and friendship in the interim between elections and especially at election time."[21]

Election activity, probably the primary function of the committeeman, has not changed in decades. Lord Bryce's observations of pretwentieth-century district and ward committees related that "at election times they have . . . to superintend the canvass, to procure and distribute tickets at the polls . . . , to allot money for various election services, to see that voters are brought up to the poll. . . . ." This description is little different from that of a Pittsburgh New Deal committeeman, who remarked, "I knocked on doors to get out the vote; I collected money from people for the campaigns; I served as a judge of elections." To James Reichley, a student of Philadelphia government, the main function of the committeeman is to get the faithful of his party to the polls. They are faithful not because he has told them to be, but for economic and social reasons. Hence, the precinct worker is not a boss, but merely a means of transportation.[22]

According to Harold F. Gosnell, an expert in "machine politics: Chicago model," whether he be boss or means of transportation, the ideal

21. Letter, B. B. McGinnis, Allegheny County chairman, to local area chairmen, Sept. 20, 1939, Primary Election File, ACDCH; letter to David Lawrence, July 8, 1937, Primary Election, General File, 1937, ibid.; Cutright and Rossi, "Grass Roots Politicians," pp. 171–79.

22. Bryce, *American Commonwealth*, vol. III, p. 83; interview with committeeman, 4W9; James Reichley, *The Art of Government: Reform and Organization Politics in Philadelphia* (New York, 1959), p. 95.

precinct committeeman reflects these traits: he makes friends easily; he works hard and steadily; he gives absolute obedience; he is intelligent; he is satisfied with a subordinate role; he is not too demanding for himself; he doesn't ask many questions. A combination of faithful sheep dog and patent-medicine salesman, the committeeman always has to be ready to corral the vote and provide the favor. He probably believes, as did Joe Guffey, that "ours isn't a machine; it's an organization for service."[23]

Guffey and his counterpart, Dave Lawrence, both leaders of Pennsylvania's Democratic organization during the Roosevelt era, are exemplary of the influence that the family plays in the motivation to enter politics. In his autobiography Guffey wrote that his father used to quip, "The Guffeys in all generations were Democrats and Presbyterians, and took their whiskey straight." At one time there were thirty-two Guffeys of voting age in the same precinct, all Democrats, and his uncle, James McClurg Guffey, was prominent in national Democratic affairs as well as in Pennsylvania's. Lawrence, in the same manner, remarked: "My family was always Democratic. My grandfather was in politics. My father was a Democrat. They always talked politics at home." This background led him to the law office of the local Democratic leader, where he clerked after graduation from high school at the age of fourteen. From then on, it was a lifetime of politics for the ardent Irishman.[24]

Pittsburgh's precinct workers have entered politics for a variety of reasons. Traditional family involvement has served as motivation for many grass-roots politicians, as well as for their leaders. A New Deal committeeman from the Nineteenth Ward commented that his father had been a Democratic committeeman for about twenty-five years: "When he quit, I was elected. My father was a great believer in William Jennings Bryan and Wilson." For some, like a Fifth Ward party worker, who never held a payroll job, politics meant power and status. He reminisced: "It fascinated me—the glamour, I guess. It seems only those in politics did well. They had cars; they controlled jobs." Others entered because they were already popular in their neighborhoods. Many had gained local reputations as football or baseball players, just as their New Deal political prototype, James A. Farley, had. One, who had mastered English better

23. Gosnell, *Machine Politics*, p. 68; Alsop and Kintner, "The Guffey," p. 16.
24. Joseph F. Guffey, *Seventy Years on the Red Fire Wagon* (privately publ., 1952), p. 9; interview with Lawrence, Apr. 14, 1964.

than his neighbors, stated his reason for becoming involved: "People couldn't speak English well. I'd help interpret English. They asked me to represent them." Others desired neighborhood improvements and chose the person they thought best suited to represent them. "I started in 1934 when my neighbors wanted an alley in the rear where we lived. They thought I would work at it best," remembered a Fifteenth-Ward precinct official.[25]

Before any other motivation, however, loomed the desire for a patronage job. George Washington Plunkitt, Tammany's turn-of-the-century philosopher, once proclaimed: "Men aren't in politics for nothin'. They want to get something out of it." In Pittsburgh the public payroll, as well as the federal relief agencies such as WPA, provided an occupational refuge for the city's Democratic committeemen as their party consolidated its hold on the area's political life. A New Deal party worker in the Twentieth Ward may have overstated the case, but not by much, when he offhandedly remarked, "We all got into politics to get a job because we were unemployed." The hardships of the depression decade put a premium on the political job. However, in the case of many seekers of bread and bacon, the quest for remunerative work led them to run for district committeeman in the hope of obtaining a payroll job; and their hopes were often realized.[26]

According to David Kurtzman, an observer during the early 1930s of Philadelphia's Republican machine politics, "underlying all methods of vote control [is] the public payroll. By means of influence over the public payroll the organization can control the votes of the 'jobholders,' and those of their friends and relatives." He also noted that, in addition, the local government workers helped finance political campaigns through the process of macing, that is, assessments on their salaries from which "contributions" were made to the party coffers.[27]

The value of patronage to the party organization was also attested to in the later 1956 study of Gary, Indiana. The authors of the study noted in statistical terms that the party gained additional support from those precincts led by patronaged committeemen and lost votes in areas where the committeemen were not employed by the local government. How-

25. Interviews with committeemen, 19W21, 5W2, 29W1; James A. Farley, *Behind the Ballots* (New York, 1938), p. 19; interviews with committeemen, 2W2, 15W1.
26. William L. Riordan, *Plunkett of Tammany Hall* (New York, 1948), p. 51; interview with committeemen, 20W10.
27. Kurtzman, "Controlling Votes in Philadelphia," pp. 81, 139.

ever, they also pointed out the difficulty involved in ascertaining whether the better precinct workers were rewarded with city jobs or whether those precinct workers with city jobs were more committed to their precinct work.[28]

The latter instance seems to be substantiated by a survey of two cities, one partisan in its politics and the other nonpartisan. The second municipality was governed by a city-manager plan, had set up nonpartisan election rules, and had little local patronage. In the partisan community the investigator found among the committeemen a higher level of political activity, thus giving the precinct official the image of "economic man." Statistically, whereas in the partisan city 32 percent of the committeemen held patronage jobs, only 3 percent held such jobs in the nonpartisan city. Whereas 41 percent of the committeemen in the partisan city received requests for aid, only 1 percent in the nonpartisan did (83 percent in the latter city as opposed to 34 percent in the former received no requests at all in a thirty-day period). Whereas 63 percent of the partisan committeemen made daily contact with ten or more persons, only 15 percent of the nonpartisans did. Of the partisan precinct officials 34 percent interceded actively for the voter regarding relief, jobs, and legal trouble, in contrast to only 2 percent of the nonpartisans. At primary time 37 percent of the partisans went door to door talking to voters, whereas only 13 percent of the nonpartisans did. In addition, the committeeman's job in the partisan community, where it was attached to patronage, was apparently more highly valued than in the nonpartisan municipality. Sixty-one percent of the partisan committeemen faced a challenge for the office, whereas only 24 percent of the nonpartisans met with competition in the primary election.[29]

The necessity of working with the urban political machines throughout

28. Cutright and Rossi, "Grass Roots Politicians," p. 178.
29. Phillips Cutright, "Activities of Precinct Committeemen in Partisan and Non-Partisan Communities," *Western Political Quarterly,* XVII (Mar. 1964), 93–108. Edward N. Costikyan, former New York County Democratic leader, attests to the value of patronage for the local party leader. Although he claims that the party would disappear if it had to depend on jobholders, Costikyan maintains that for the local leader patronage brings prestige and shows his acceptability to his superior party and public officeholders. He also notes that in some areas of New York City during the early 1960s, 50 to 100 constituents arrived each week at a clubhouse for help from their leader. When Costikyan's area was comprised of 60 percent tenements, 5 to 10 people a week made requests of him; as the district changed, becoming 80 percent middle, upper-middle, and luxury housing, the number dwindled to 1 or 2 per week. Costikyan, *Behind Closed Doors: Politics in the Public Interest* (New York, 1966), pp. 263–68, 88.

the nation was fully realized in the plans of master politician Franklin Delano Roosevelt. He needed no statistical study to establish the fact that patronage made political friends and oiled the machinery that manufactured votes. As Richard Hofstadter has noted in comparing the progressive era with that of the New Deal, the former was filled with crusades against bossism and attempts to change political machinery across the United States. Franklin Roosevelt and his New Deal, on the other hand, made no such efforts and cooperated with the big city political organizations. However, many major political machines opposed Roosevelt during his struggle for the 1932 Democratic presidential nomination. Tammany, which had met Roosevelt's wrath in New York State, envisioned him as a reformer and stomped for Al Smith; Pendergast, in Kansas City, Missouri, beat the drums for Jim Reed; Frank Hague's New Jersey organization staunchly supported Smith; and Chicago's Nash-Kelly machine trumpeted the virtues of a native son, Melvin A. Traylor. Although Pennsylvania's state leader, Joe Guffey, was in the forefront of the Roosevelt cadres, the only well-known urban boss to support Roosevelt was Mayor James Michael Curley, of Boston—prototype for *The Last Hurrah*'s Skeffington. Curley raised over fifty thousand dollars in 1932 for FDR's losing Massachusetts primary fight and almost single-handedly fought the state organization, which supported Smith.[30]

Once the New York governor won the nomination, the machines rallied to his side—and Roosevelt gladly accepted them. Just after the 1932 convention Jim Farley extended the olive branch to Tammany by attending a Tammany rally. Then, while vacationing in Atlantic City, New Jersey, Farley received a telephone call from Frank Hague, mayor of Jersey City, who had been the field marshall for Smith and for the stop-Roosevelt movement during the convention. Hague, admitting that he had been whipped in a fair fight, beckoned Roosevelt to open his campaign in New Jersey. The New York governor did, speaking before a mammoth rally at Sea Girt during the month of August. Within a year after FDR's election to office, Hague could write to him, "Your recog-

---

30. Hofstadter, *Age of Reform*, p. 310; Flynn, *You're the Boss*, p. 106; letters, Apr. 26, 28, 1932, Curley Files, PPF 1154, FDRL. Lyle Dorsett contends that although Pendergast was obligated to support Reed at the convention, he was in fact supporting FDR from the beginning. The boss manipulated the Missouri delegation in order to placate Reed while at the same time aiding Roosevelt. Dorsett, *The Pendergast Machine* (New York, 1968), pp. 103–04.

nition of our state organization has been substantially manifested and in return I feel we owe you this pledge of loyalty."[31]

Dealing with the bosses had its advantages for the president. He could use them, when necessary, as leverage on local, state, and national politicians to obtain the passage of desired legislation. "Call up Ed Flynn," he requested of his secretary, Marvin McIntyre, "and tell him to tell Dunnigan that we hope he can pass the Palisades-New York-New Jersey Compact Bill." At another time, when Tennessee's Senator McKellar opposed an important appropriation for the Bureau of the Budget, Roosevelt arranged an interview with Boss Crump of Memphis. The bosses, always keeping an ear to the ground, provided another service to the president when they reported to Washington grass-roots political sentiment. "I am taking the liberty of sending you the results of a Chicago poll made last weekend," wrote Ed Kelly, enclosing a ward-by-ward description of the 1940 Democratic candidate's potential strength.[32]

Yet, dealing with the urban machines also had its liabilities. When Hague's ("I am the Law!") rule became oppressive in Jersey City, citizens of the area complained to the president. One asked the man in the White House: "Are you a genuine lover of liberty? If you are, you will not close your eyes to the conditions prevailing here in Jersey City." Yet the boss reigned supreme in his own bailiwick. Jim Farley remarked in a private memo: "Of course there is nothing we can do about the New Jersey situation. Hague is going to run it his own way. He has been reelected for four years and there is nothing we can do." In addition, local scandal could blemish the national administration's image. When FDR appointed Ed Flynn to the post of minister to Australia in 1942, that boss's alleged involvement in a New York City paving block scandal brought forth protests from all sections of the country, causing the cancellation of the appointment and much embarrassment to the administration.[33]

31. Farley, *Behind the Ballots*, p. 158; letter, Hague to FDR, Nov. 24, 1933, Hague File, PPF 1013, FDRL.

32. Memo, FDR to McIntyre, Mar. 13, 1936, Flynn Files, PPF 1898, FDRL; memo, William D. Hassett to FDR, Mar. 13, 1945, Crump Files, PPF 5962, ibid.; letter, Kelly to FDR, Sept. 13, 1940, Kelly Files, PPF 3166, ibid.

33. Letter, Dan R. Wilborg to FDR, Dec. 15, 1937, attached memo, Farley to McIntyre, Jan. 3, 1938, Official Files 3294 (hereafter cited as OF), FDRL; letters re. Flynn's appointment, OF 5224, 5278, 5235, ibid.; Flynn, *You're the Boss*, pp. 188–92.

The bosses needed Roosevelt as much as he needed them. By 1936 Lorena Hickok, Harry Hopkins's WPA troubleshooter who sojourned throughout the United States, wrote her boss, "If the President is elected, he is not going to be elected because of the help of any of the machines or the efforts of the Democratic politicians, not more than a handful of whom really understand or care about what he is trying to do." She continued:

> Most of the so-called machines are no damned good anyway. The Pendergast machine in Missouri can and will, I believe, deliver Missouri for him. The rest of them—just a lot of spinach. That Kelly-Nash machine in Chicago, for instance. Unless they are actively out against him, I believe it would be entirely possible for the President to carry Chicago, and by a good majority, without them.[34]

It should be remembered, as Flynn points out in his memoir, *You're the Boss*, that the Roosevelt name was political magic throughout the nation. The first Democratic president in twelve years, he supplied the grass-roots parties not only with federal patronage, but with long coattails to which local candidates could attach themselves. Continued support of FDR was a matter of self-preservation, although in many cases the machines gave only lip service to the president. Of those in the forefront of support for his unprecedented third term in 1940, many represented the urban political organizations. The goal of the game of politics is to win, and Roosevelt seemed the most likely candidate to succeed. Even here, in the relationship between president and party, the *quid pro quo* appeared. In many instances, the machine was more than "just a lot of spinach"; it supplied the necessary margin of safety by providing local organization to muster the vote for Roosevelt, while FDR offered the leadership and charisma to bring his party to victory.[35]

Some observers believe that, paradoxically, Roosevelt's success actually brought defeat to the big-city political machines in the years following the depression decade. His New Deal program, these analysts claim, sapped the machine of its most necessary ingredient—the ability to per-

---

34. Letter, Hickok to Hopkins, Sept. 19, 1936, Federal Emergency Relief Administration—Works Progress Administration Narrative Field Reports, Lorena Hickok, chief investigator, Aug. 1933–Nov. 1936, File, Nov. 1, 1935–Nov. 1936, FDRL; interview with Hickok, July 23, 1963.
35. Flynn, *You're the Boss*, pp. 160, 171.

form a service and thereby create an obligation on the part of the voter. This view is perhaps best expressed by a character in Edwin O'Connor's *The Last Hurrah*:

> He [FDR] destroyed the old-time boss. He destroyed him by taking away his source of power. . . . All over the country the bosses have been dying for the past 20 years, thanks to Roosevelt. . . . The old boss was strong simply because he held all the cards. If anybody wanted anything—jobs, favors, cash—he could only go to the boss, the local leader. What Roosevelt did was take the handouts out of local hands. A few things like social security, unemployment insurance, and the like—that's what shifted the gears, sport. No need now to depend on the boss for everything; the Federal government was getting into the act. Otherwise known as social revolution.[36]

The New Deal's welfare legislation was not alone in leading to this alleged decline. The assimilation of ethnic groups no longer dependent on the local politician, the prosperity resulting from World War II, the higher educational level of the populace, and the extension of the merit system, all supposedly mitigated the old-line urban political machine causing its demise.[37]

36. O'Connor, *The Last Hurrah*, p. 330.
37. Historians, political scientists, and journalists have accepted this view. Works propounding this view include: Schlesinger, *Politics of Upheaval*, pp. 441–43; Hofstadter, *Age of Reform*, p. 270; Charles R. Adrian, *Governing Urban America* (New York, 1961), pp. 147–50, and 1st ed., pp. 121–31; Jewell Cass Phillips, *Municipal Government and Administration* (New York, 1960), pp. 208–14; Marian D. Irish and James W. Prothro, *The Politics of American Democracy* (Englewood Cliffs, N.J., 1959), p. 318; Salter, *Boss Rule*, p. 7. A recent acceptance of this thesis can be found in the articles by Lee S. Greene, Elmer E. Cornwell, Jr., and William C. Havard in "City Bosses and Political Machines," *The Annals*, 353 (May 1964). As noted in a following chapter, Robert S. Hirschfield et al., "A Profile of Political Activists in Manhattan," *Western Political Quarterly*, XV (Sept. 1962), 489–506, is a study that lends statistical support to the thesis. However, the nature of Manhattan makes the conclusions questionable as far as their applicability to other urban areas is concerned. Several studies accept the position, but with qualifications: Gosnell, *Machine Politics*, p. 193, written during the depression, saw the strengthening of the local machine as a short-term effect of the New Deal. Weiss, *Charles Francis Murphy*, p. 94, while trumpeting the death knell of machine politics as a result of the New Deal, recognizes that "elections still pit 'reformers' against 'bosses' and some machines still exist." Edward C. Banfield, *Urban Government: A Reader in Administration and Politics*, rev. ed., pp. 165–66, posits that fragments of machines still exist in various stages of deterioration and that a sudden change of conditions, such as a major depression, might return them to full strength in central cities where low-income Negroes, Puerto Ricans, and white hillbillies reside.

Many think that the New Deal changed the face of American politics in other ways. Sociologist William Foote Whyte, observing a "street corner society" of the depression years, commented that the New Deal helped bring about a complete political reorganization. He claimed that the local organizations of ward bosses were supplanted by a more centralized political organization headed by a United States senator, with the representatives next in line, and the ward politicians assuming more subordinate positions. Whyte premised his view on the theory that the wealth of federal patronage, manufactured by agencies such as WPA, remained totally in control of an area's congressman. Yet in Pittsburgh, at least, the reverse was the case: the federal patronage, as it filtered down to the grass-roots level, strengthened the local ward politicians.[38]

Another theory holds that with the advent of the New Deal politics became more ideological; and the old-line bosses, who were more used to working with tangibles rather than intangibles, with jobs rather than issues, felt stranded in a new political world. They were used to dealing less with coalitions than with organizations; and, as Arthur M. Schlesinger, Jr., remarks, "their lines of force moved from national committee to county courthouse, city hall, ward and precinct, without regard to such odd groups as trade unions, nationality clubs or women." Contrary to this theory, however, following Joe Guffey's lead, Flynn, Kelly, and Hague harnessed these new forces and by adopting a liberal stance successfully made the New Deal itself the issue.[39]

Nevertheless, by 1949, *The New Republic* reported the end of the bosses when Frank Hague Eggers, nephew of the seventy-three-year-old Jersey City leader, was defeated in the mayoralty race by John V. Kenny. The magazine commented that the defeat "marks the passing of almost the last of the bosses from the American city scene. Pendergast, Crump, Vare, Curley, Kelly and Nash, the once mighty Tammany, and now

38. William Foote Whyte, *Street Corner Society: The Social Structure of An Italian Slum,* rev. ed. (Chicago, 1955), pp. 194–98; interviews with Pittsburgh committeemen. The Pittsburgh situation apparently also held true for Boss Pendergast's Missouri where "the growing welfare state placed the *source* of handouts and jobs in the Federal government, but did not alter the all important function of local *distribution* of such services" (Dorsett, *The Pendergast Machine,* p. 103). One of the few recent observers to note the sustaining effect of Roosevelt's policies on the urban machines, Dorsett continued, "Indeed, the Pendergast machine (and probably many others) was actually strengthened by the New Deal."

39. Schlesinger, *Politics of Upheaval,* pp. 441–43.

Hague, are no longer names which topple ballot boxes." Yet, the article continued, Kenny frankly admitted that he bucked Boss Hague only because the latter had removed him as machine leader for the Second Ward. "If he had not thrown me out, I probably still would be a member of the machine," the new mayor ironically declared.[40]

In Pittsburgh, where the bosses were better tacticians and where a large army of pay-rollers was organized, every mayor elected between 1933 and 1969 in the previously staunch Republican stronghold was a Democrat; between 1939 and 1969 no Republican won any city offices. In the years between, the Democratic political machine consolidated its strength and became entrenched under the aegis of David L. Lawrence. It did so to the extent that a 1965 insurgent complained that the party's leadership was too old to fight against its younger Republican antagonists.[41]

This organization had its roots in the New Deal, which, according to the general consensus, should have marked the demise of all political machines. How did it arise during the economic and social ferment that marked the depression decade? How did it build and consolidate its strength in terms of party personnel and voting percentages? What follows is the story of the building of an urban political machine.

40. "Spring House Cleaning," *The New Republic,* CXX (May 23, 1949), 7.
41. *PG,* Feb. 16, 1965.

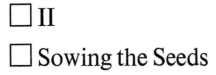

□ II
□ Sowing the Seeds

*I cannot understand why the party is spending so much time and effort
. . . on endeavoring to carry Pennsylvania, the darkest Republican
stronghold of the nation. . . .*
                    William H. Smathers to James Farley, September 13, 1936

□ From the termination of the Civil War to the advent of the New Deal, Pennsylvania was controlled by a Republican political machine. Even during the years of the New Deal's honeymoon with the public, the Republican state party organization battled the Democrats for primacy. Bouncing back from their defeat in the 1934 gubernatorial election, in which the first Democratic chief executive since 1890 was sent to Harrisburg, the Republicans elected their own man in 1938. In the decades that have followed, neither party has been able to achieve a firm and continuous grip on the politics of Pennsylvania.

However, for more than six decades beginning in 1865, the Republican juggernaut had rolled on almost uninterrupted by Democratic interference. As a baseball going from the proverbial Tinker to Evers to Chance, control of the Keystone State's GOP went from Cameron to Quay to Penrose. Simon Cameron, Lincoln's secretary of war and first of the state's bosses, served the party from 1865 to his death in 1877. Cameron failed in his attempt to hand the mantle of leadership to his son, Donald, and Matthew Quay stepped into the void. Consolidating the

24

strength of his inheritance and making the machine more efficient. Quay held on to power until his dying days. In 1904 Senator Boies Penrose picked up the scepter, and after seventeen years he, too, died while still in power. Under Penrose not only was no Democratic governor or senator elected in Pennsylvania, but the state legislature was overwhelmingly Republican and the congressional delegation predominately so.[1]

With Penrose's death in 1921, the clear line of succession was broken. In the eastern part of the state, a Republican troika arose, with the lead horses occasionally pulling this way and that, sometimes in tandem and sometimes not. All shades of Republicanism found representation. Adherents of the big-city machine looked for leadership to William S. Vare, Philadelphia's boss. Conservatives found a rallying point in Bristol textile manufacturer Joseph P. Grundy, the state GOP's financial angel and the president of the Pennsylvania Manufacturers Association. Gifford Pinchot, conservationist, governor, and politician, captured the progressives' imagination. Across the state in smoky Pittsburgh, which was controlled by the Mellon family's interests under the stewardship of William Larimer Mellon, another contender for Republican state leadership arose.

In 1922 Grundy, in an anti-Vare move, supported for governor a triumphant Pinchot. In 1926 Mellon and Grundy allied themselves and Mellon became Republican state chairman. Pinchot, who desired the senatorial nomination, had been at loggerheads with the conservatives and ran a poor third to Vare and a Grundy ally, George Wharton Pepper. Although Vare won the election, a senatorial investigation into campaign expenses ruled that he should not be seated; and in 1929 Pennsylvania's Governor Fisher appointed Grundy to fill out the term. The next year Pinchot ran again. This time the Pittsburgh organization supported him, and he carried every ward in that city, whereas in Philadelphia he lost all forty-eight wards. There, most Republicans supported the Liberal party, a device organized by Vare to help elect the Democratic candidate without voting for him.[2]

In the years before the election of FDR, the political battles of Pennsylvania were fought within the Republican party rather than between the

1. Edward F. Cooke and G. Edward Janosik, *Guide to Pennsylvania Politics* (New York, 1957), pp. 6–8.
2. Cooke and Janosik, *Pennsylvania Politics,* pp. 9–10; Samuel J. Astorino, "The Decline of the Republican Dynasty in Pennsylvania, 1929–1934" (unpubl. Ph.D. diss., University of Pittsburgh, 1962), p. 129.

Republicans and the Democrats. Pennsylvania was thought of as a GOP bastion even after the state's election of a Democratic governor and senator in 1934. Writing to James Farley during the 1936 presidential campaign, a New Jerseyite complained: "I cannot understand why the party is spending so much time and effort . . . on endeavoring to carry Pennsylvania, *the darkest Republican stronghold of the nation*, when one-tenth of the effort exerted in Pennsylvania applied to New Jersey would insure this state for victory" (emphasis added).[3]

During these years of emerging Democratic strength, the myth of the entrenched Republican machine grew in inverse proportion to the GOP's actual power. Perhaps in an attempt to maintain the guise of the underdogs, Democrats continued to complain of the Republican bosses and machines. Owen B. Hunt, chairman of the 1936 Pennsylvania Democratic Speakers Committee, told Farley that the party should capitalize on the public's "resentment at Republican organization methods and it is well to keep that in mind in addressing any appeal to them."[4]

Throughout the New Deal years, Joe Guffey, Pennsylvania's Democratic senator, followed this plan of attack. During the local election in 1935, he told a campaign crowd that the Republican members of the State Senate belonged to the Old Guard machine that had been under the domination of Grundy and Mellon. He declared that for a Roosevelt victory in 1936 these senators, representatives of the local machines, had to be defeated. A year later, in a speech prepared for delivery on the eve of the 1936 election, he noted that Pennsylvania's citizens would show they are not "wooden soldiers under the command of the Republican bosses to be voted and marched as those bosses dictate. The people of Pennsylvania will say that they are free men—they will overthrow the coercion and the payroll pressure of those political and business men who think only in terms of their own selfish interests."[5]

After a hard-fought Democratic primary battle in 1938, in which Guffey's candidate lost, he again leveled his sights on the Republicans.

3. Letter, William H. Smathers to Farley, Sept. 13, 1936, Democratic National Committee File, Official Files 300 (hereafter cited as OF), Franklin D. Roosevelt Library (hereafter cited as FDRL), Hyde Park, N.Y.

4. Hunt to Farley, Sept. 24, 1936, OF 300, FDRL.

5. Speeches of Guffey, Oct. 31, 1935, Greensburg, Pa., and Nov. 2, 1936, speeches and press releases I, 1935 and 1936, Guffey Papers, Washington and Jefferson College (hereafter cited as W & J), Washington, Pa.

Remarking that the GOP's candidates, as in previous years, had been handpicked by the bosses, the Democratic senator stated:

> In more than 40 years of battling for liberal Democrats in Pennsylvania, bosses come and bosses go. I have watched them rise and I have watched them fall—autocrats such as Penrose, Quay and Vare and more recently Grundy and the Mellons. Those party leaders made alliances with railroads, the utilities, the big manufacturers and bankers. In return for their services in breaking strikes, in granting tax exemptions, in extending favors and immunities to great corporations at the expense of the people, they received generous campaign contributions.

Running for reelection in 1940, he continued his theme by proclaiming: "For a generation, the Republican machine in Pennsylvania has been giving a promissory note of good government. That note has never been redeemed." Guffey and other Democrats indulged in this type of campaign rhetoric while building their own machine, which many felt did not "redeem *its* note." Although Philadelphia remained Republican, by the end of the depression decade Pittsburgh was firmly in the grip of the Democracy.[6]

For many years prior to that time, Pittsburgh, like the state, had been a Republican suzerainty. In 1863, two years before Simon Cameron's ascendency to control of Pennsylvania politics, Squire Tommy Steele founded what was to become the Steel City's Republican machine. Unlike Cameron, who failed in his attempt to keep the control of Pennsylvania within the family, Steele passed the gauntlet of Pittsburgh's Republican organization on to his nephew, Christopher Lyman Magee. In alliance with a young contractor, William Flinn, Magee consolidated the Republican hegemony over Pittsburgh politics that lasted, on the surface at least, until the 1930s. He took his job of being a boss seriously, allegedly studying the workings of other machines. When the Tweed ring was broken, Magee is said to have spent months in New York City examining Tammany's mistakes as well as its triumphs.[7]

Lincoln Steffens, through his progressive-tinted spectacles, saw Pittsburgh as "a city ashamed," at best faint praise for a city that he saw in

6. Speeches of Guffey, Oct. 6, 1938, and Oct. 10, 1940, speeches and press releases II and III, Guffey Papers, W & J.

7. George Swetnam, *The Bicentennial History of Pittsburgh and Allegheny County,* vol. I (Pittsburgh, 1955), pp. 209–10; Lincoln Steffens, *The Shame of the Cities* (New York, 1957), pp. 104–05.

a slightly better light than the "corrupt and contented" Philadelphia. According to him, Pittsburgh's graft was divided into the traditional four categories: franchises, public contracts, vice, and public funds. Magee's Duquesne Traction Company easily obtained franchises and controlled the building and running of the city's railways; the construction firm of Booth and Flinn, Ltd., held a monopoly on the municipality's public improvement work. Magee and Flinn controlled the city's government; and not until 1905, when George W. Guthrie, a fusion candidate supported by the Democrats, was elected, did a non-Republican serve as Pittsburgh's mayor. It took more than two decades after Guthrie's tenure for a Democrat to be elected to the office.[8]

Mirroring Pennsylvania, the highlights of Pittsburgh's politics during the first thirty years of the twentieth century were a crazy quilt of Republican politics. From the time of Pinchot's 1922 gubernatorial victory —even after the beginning of the Mellon family's rise to political control—a reform group organized in Pittsburgh. Led by Ralph H. Frank and County Commissioner Charles C. "Buck" McGovern, it acted as a gadfly to the Republican machine. In 1927, when William Larimer Mellon attempted to eliminate McGovern from his post, the latter ran as a candidate of the Independent party and qualified as a minority commissioner.[9] (There are three county commissioners, two of one party and one of the other. Generally, during the era of Republican hegemony, two were Republicans and one, the minority commissioner, Democratic. Nothing, however, prevented an individual from running on a third-party ticket and being elected to the office of minority commissioner.)

To assure their own control over city politics, the Mellons limited each mayor to one term in office. In 1925, when Mayor William A. Magee (Boss Christopher Magee's nephew) made his bid for reelection, they destroyed his chances by freezing his flow of funds and slating Charles Kline for mayor. Kline, however, once in City Hall, was not so easily removed. Taking advantage of William Larimer Mellon's aloofness from the rank and file, the chief executive began building his own organization: Kline vastly increased the patronage power of Republican ward chairmen. This authority gave them far greater prestige than they had had previously and knotted them strongly to Kline. If the local leaders would

8. Steffens, *The Shame of the Cities*, pp. 115–17; Swetnam, *Bicentennial History*, pp. 211–12.
9. Astorino, *Republican Dynasty*, p. 68.

not cooperate with him, he attempted to replace them with his own men, as he successfully did in the city's Third Ward. In addition, tying himself closely to Pittsburgh patronage, Kline made all appointments to city positions. He personally designated to department heads every individual to be appointed, even to the smallest position, giving way only on technical positions such as engineers.[10]

In this manner Kline built up enough support to defeat two other candidates in the Republican mayoralty primary in 1929. One, Richard W. Martin, a common pleas court judge, had the support of the McGovern-Frank reform group; the other, James F. Malone, president of the city council, was backed by Max Leslie, powerful chairman of the Ninth Ward, who had aspirations of becoming the party's boss. Mellon, meanwhile, had diluted his control by supporting two reform measures doomed to defeat—a metropolitan government bill and voting-machine legislation. Having romped over his opponents in the primary, Kline did the same in the November general election against the moribund Democratic party. In office for a second term, he consolidated even further his hold on the city's Republican organization.[11]

However, Kline was forced to leave office under a black cloud of corruption before the end of his official tenure, and the Republican party of Pittsburgh began a descent equal to the Democratic one of the pre-Teddy Roosevelt era. Scandal erupted when in February of 1931 a representative of a wholesale grocery firm wrote in complaint to the city council that awards of city contracts for supplies in his line were being made to high bidders. Council's refusal to hold a public investigation increased public interest in the charges. After Kline made a secret investigation, he dismissed the director of supplies, Bertram L. Succop, for "visible irregularities" and "poor business judgment." However, Kline, himself, was indicted because all contracts were let, at least in theory, by the city's chief executive as well as the head of the proper department. Trick specifications in bids, circumventions of the required advertising of purchases over five hundred dollars, and the appropriation of an allegedly overpriced rug for the mayor's office, all made grist for the scandal mill. Pittsburgh, again, appeared to be "a city ashamed." Both Kline and

10. *Ibid.*, pp. 19, 67, 69; clipping from *Pittsburgh Press* (hereafter cited as *Press*), June 25, 1931, Elections File, Pennsylvania Division, Carnegie Library, Pittsburgh, Pa.

11. Astorino, *Republican Dynasty*, pp. 77, 80, 73.

Succop were found guilty of malfeasance in office, Kline on one count and Succop on twenty-nine. Although his sentence of six months in jail was rescinded on grounds of poor health, Kline left office in early 1933 in disgrace.[12]

In the two years between the first charges and their final resolution, the mayor presided over the final decay of Pittsburgh's Republican party. The results of the 1931 primary for county commissioners evidenced a triumph for the reform element of the Republican party, for Kline's candidate for county commissioner was defeated, as were three of his four candidates for city council. On primary-election day, for the first time in its twenty-six-year history, the State Police was called out to guard against phantom voters. Apparently, however, police protection did not adequately safeguard the new voting machines; reformers charged sabotage, claiming that the buttons from under their candidate's name had been filed off several machines in the city's Third Ward. In other wards election boards were charged with fraud.[13]

During the election campaign that followed, Kline and his political ally Republican State Senator James J. Coyne refused to support the Pinchot reform candidate; nor would they back the progressive Republican Charles M. Barr, who was slated on the Independent ticket, hoping to win the post of minority commissioner. Faced with the dilemma of none of the Republican candidates being their kind of "Republican," Kline and Coyne threw their support to the Democratic candidate—David L. Lawrence. Although the Republicans won, the Republican organization, as well as the hard times, did yeoman service for the Democratic county leaders. Lawrence polled over one hundred and twenty thousand votes, at a time when the average Democratic vote rarely exceeded ten thousand. He bettered Barr in the city of Pittsburgh, but lost the election in Allegheny County's surrounding areas.[14]

The Republican organization's support of Lawrence and his acceptance of such aid raise the question of the relationship between the Pittsburgh Democratic organization and the city's GOP during the long

12. *New York Times* (hereafter cited as *NYT*), Apr. 5, 1931, sec. 2, p. 5; ibid., June 25, 1931, p. 1; ibid., May 8, 1932, sec. 3, p. 6.

13. Ibid., May 15, 1932; ibid., Mar. 27, 1933; ibid., Sept. 8, 1931, p. 13; ibid., Sept. 20, 1931, sec. 3, p. 8; *Press*, Sept. 16, 1931.

14. *NYT*, Nov. 1, 1931, sec. 2, p. 1; ibid., Nov. 5, 1931, p. 2; *Pittsburgh Post-Gazette* (hereafter cited as *PG*), Nov. 4, 1931.

period of Republican hegemony. Across the state Philadelphia's Democratic party had the notorious reputation of being a Republican auxiliary. Not only did the Vare machine pay the rent for the Democratic headquarters, but when it came time for making up the slate for that city's minority-party magistrates, the Democrats waited until a messenger came with a list of William Vare's choices. When J. David Stern, publisher of the *Philadelphia Record*, asked the Democratic leader John O'Donnell to oppose Vare during the 1932 campaign, O'Donnell allegedly replied: "But how could I do that, Dave, when Vare's my best friend and patron? He gave me my job and he has been supporting the Democratic party for years." The relationship of the Pittsburgh Democratic organization to the city's Republican party was similar, but not quite so subservient.[15]

During the reign of Christopher Magee, Pittsburgh Democrats held nearly a quarter of the places on the city payroll. Indebted to Magee for their livelihood, they cooperated with the boss during his disputes with recalcitrant Republicans; sometimes cooperative Democrats won controlled Republican votes, thus allowing them to topple dangerous GOP candidates. When Magee desired to serve in the State Senate, both parties united in his nomination and elected him unanimously.[16]

The dearth of Democrats in Pittsburgh wreaked havoc on the party's formal organization. In 1929 only fifty-two hundred out of the city's one hundred and seventy-five thousand registered voters were listed as Democrats. From the time in 1912 when Joe Guffey gave an assistant $2,500 to pay watchers at the polls and the assistant returned with $1,500, unable to find enough people to hire with the money, to the coming of the New Deal, little had changed. As David L. Lawrence has noted: "Prior to 1932, just a few old faithfuls stuck by the party. It was a long gap between Wilson and FDR. Before 1932 Democrats always played for the minority places."[17]

Many New Deal committeemen have reminisced that when they first began in politics, perhaps only five or six Democrats were registered in

---

15. Columbia University Oral History Project, "The Reminiscences of J. David Stern," (New York, 1954), pp. 44–45, 50–51; Joseph F. Guffey, *Seventy Years on the Red Fire Wagon* (privately publ., 1952), p. 18.

16. Steffens, *The Shame of the Cities*, pp. 107–08.

17. *Press*, Sept. 18, 1933; Guffey, *Red Fire Wagon*, pp. 36–37; interview with Lawrence, Apr. 14, 1964.

their districts, they had to get Republicans to sit as Democratic election judges, a mere dozen of the ward chairmen would show up for meetings with Lawrence at Democratic headquarters, and the party "existed on crumbs from the Republicans." For one committeeman the change in party structure, once the Democrats began winning, was so great that he left politics. Born a Democrat, in politics since 1909, he served as Sixteenth Ward chairman from 1926 to 1934. "I left in 1934 because after FDR got in, the party became too big. By 1934 everyone was running after me for a job, so I just left," remarked the party worker for whom winning brought too many problems.[18]

Winning in Pittsburgh began for the Democrats in 1932; Pennsylvania had been instrumental in gaining the presidential nomination for Franklin Delano Roosevelt. As early as September of 1930, Joe Guffey wrote to FDR, then New York's governor, promising him the sizeable number of sixty-nine and a half of Pennsylvania's delegates at the Chicago convention, which was still two years ahead. After fighting off a stop-Roosevelt movement, the New Yorker's supporters won the majority of delegates in the Keystone State's 1932 spring primary. Although Guffey could not produce the number promised originally, the fifty-five votes Pennsylvania cast for FDR at the nominating convention represented more than any other state had given him, even on the fourth and final ballot. Appearing in Pittsburgh on October 19, FDR made his famous "balance-the-budget" speech, which plagued him when the New Deal began its free-wheeling spending policies. A few weeks later Pittsburgh, along with the rest of Allegheny County, voted for a Democratic president for the first time since 1856—in the face of a Roosevelt defeat in Pennsylvania and the local Republican machine's attempt to tamper with the ballots.[19]

In retrospect, the party workers and their leader admitted that anyone running against Hoover could not have lost, and that the activity of the Democratic organization, which was just gathering momentum, was a negligible factor in the Roosevelt victory. Lawrence commented that the victory was not totally unexpected because the Democratic triumph in

18. Interviews with committeemen, 6W4, 6W6, 8W8, 11W6, 11W14, 13W3, 14W18, 15W8, 20W15, 21W15, 21W7, 27W2, 29W6, quote from 16W12. (To maintain anonymity of committeemen, they are listed by ward and district—hence, 6W4 is read 6th Ward, 4th District.)

19. Letter, Guffey to FDR, Sept. 13, 1930, Archive XVc169, Guffey Papers, W & J; Guffey, *Red Fire Wagon*, p. 75.

the 1930 congressional election stood as a sign of the times. "Anyway," he remarked, "the economic conditions of the country, especially Pittsburgh, shook the people. The people were looking for relief. FDR's coattails and the economic conditions were the main impetus to building the organization."[20]

Economic conditions had indeed reached a miserable level for many Pittsburghers. In December of 1930 welfare agencies undertook the good deed of arranging for the unemployed to sell apples without the formality of obtaining a city license. Purchased by the unemployed for $2.00 a box of 88 to 100, the apples were sold on street corners for five cents apiece, grossing the vendor $4.40 to $5.00. Men lived in squalid packing boxes on the outskirts of the city; and when the police burned them out, a shantytown sprung up in the city's strip district. Named as its honorary mayor, a Catholic priest, Father James R. Cox, presided over his impoverished flock and ultimately led a "march of the jobless" on Washington, D.C., in January 1932. When the fifteenth census was taken in April 1930, over twenty thousand Pittsburghers were reported out of work and fifty-nine hundred laid off; nine months later the special unemployment census of January 1931 found almost sixty thousand unemployed and over nineteen thousand laid off. By 1933 15.7 percent of all Pittsburgh whites and 43.4 percent of its Negroes could be found on the relief rolls. These percentages topped fourteen other northern and southern cities, all having fifty thousand or more Negroes in 1930.[21]

In 1932 the Democratic organization made a special effort to win over the rock-ribbed Republican and economically depressed Negro voters. Keeping in mind that in the two Negro wards of the city, the Third and the Fifth, registration was approximately 80 and 88 percent Republican, respectively, Joe Guffey jumped at Robert Vann's offer to bring the Negro vote into the Democratic fold. Vann, a Negro attorney and editor and publisher of the widely circulated Negro newspaper, *The Pittsburgh Courier*, appeared bitter toward Republican leadership. Four years earlier, after serving as director of publicity for the Colored Voters Division

20. Interview with David Lawrence, Apr. 14, 1964.
21. *Pittsburgh Sun-Telegraph*, Dec. 1, 1930; *Press*, May 10, 1931; ibid., Sept. 27, 1931; *PG*, Jan. 6, 1932; Special Census of Unemployment; General Report, 1931 (U.S. Bureau of the Census); *Press*, Mar. 21, 1931; *Negro Year Book, 1937–1938*, p. 21. These cities were New York, Chicago, Philadelphia, Baltimore, Washington, New Orleans, Detroit, Birmingham, Memphis, St. Louis, Atlanta, Cleveland, Houston, and Richmond.

of the Republican National Committee, he had been refused an assistant attorney generalship for which he had been mentioned. Under Roosevelt he achieved this position, after campaigning vigorously for the New York governor and telling Negro audiences: "My friends, go home and turn Lincoln's picture to the wall. The debt has been paid in full."[22]

Young Negroes, less bound by the tradition of previous generations who might have remembered slavery, spread the gospel of the Democracy. One committeeman visited churches Sunday after Sunday and told Negro congregations that the "Republicans gave you freedom but nothing else." Jobs were badly needed, and the organization's efforts paid dividends in the Third Ward, which Roosevelt carried. The Fifth Ward remained Republican, but FDR's 46.6 percent was 8.2 percentage points greater than Smith's vote in 1928. The foundation for future Negro Democratic voting had been laid.[23]

The Democratic organization did not have to undertake such vigorous activity in all parts of the city. As the unemployment figures indicate, highly industrialized Pittsburgh felt the brunt of the depression to such a degree that Roosevelt and the Democrats benefitted, without much effort on the part of the organization's rank and file. A New Deal committeeman in the Thirteenth Ward recalled: "FDR was the inspiration for the whole thing. They voted for him, even at the local level. It wasn't the machine." An Eleventh-Ward counterpart agreed when he noted, "As effective as I was, if I was there to get people to vote Republican, they would have thrown me out."[24]

Not only did the anti-GOP bitterness emanate from the voter, but it was rampant among the party worker. Many shifted from the Republican to the Democratic organization for reasons not unlike those of their constituents. One such committeeman spoke for thousands of Pittsburghers as he remembered: "In 1930 I changed from the Republicans to the Democrats. I guess I was like a cat. I had my eyes open. You had

22. Guffey, *Red Fire Wagon,* pp. 70–71; Arthur M. Schlesinger, Jr., *The Politics of Upheaval,* vol. III, *The Age of Roosevelt* (Boston, 1960), pp. 430, 436; Ruth L. Simmons, "The Negro in Recent Pittsburgh Politics" (unpubl. M.A. diss., University of Pittsburgh, 1945), pp. 7, 10–11; interview with Emma Guffey Miller, Apr. 27, 1964.
23. Interview with committeeman, 5W1; voting returns percentaged from *Pennsylvania Manual,* 1929 and 1933 eds. (published yearly by commonwealth for its legislature).
24. Interviews with committeemen, 13W3, 11W14.

to be hardy and grab a straw. I was a depositor in four banks and all went
under. I was in bad shape. I felt we couldn't let the Republicans get away
with it." A World War I veteran, active as a precinct official in the
Twentieth Ward, mirrored the dislikes of other survivors of the American
Expeditionary Forces. Referring to the rout of the Bonus Army, he complained, "I disliked Hoover and MacArthur for Anacostia Flats." The
Democratic organization picked up new rank-and-filers, and Roosevelt
garnered his vote from an amalgam of dissidents.[25]

Apparently, however, the city's break from its Republican presidential
voting tradition had been building slowly throughout the 1920s, and the
election of 1932 cannot be looked upon as episodic. In support of the
generally accepted thesis that "the Republican hold on the cities was
broken not by Roosevelt but by Alfred E. Smith"—that "before the
Roosevelt Revolution there was an Al Smith Revolution"—Pittsburgh
gave the pride of New York's Lower East Side 48 percent of its vote. Its
foreign born and their children of voting age in particular, turned out
to cast their ballots for the first Catholic candidate for president. However, an analysis of the voting returns indicates that even before the
"Smith Revolution" there was a "La Follette Revolution" in Pittsburgh.[26]

25. Interviews with committeemen, 15W8, 20W15.
26. The nation's 12 largest cities, of which Pittsburgh was one, gave the Republicans a net party plurality of 1,308,000 in 1924. With the Smith candidacy, a
shift to a Democratic plurality of 210,000 resulted. To this day the Democrats have
not relinquished their big-city plurality. The "Smith Revolution" thesis was popu-
larized by Samuel Lubell, *The Future of American Politics*, 3rd ed. rev. (New York,
1965), pp. 148–55, in which figures cited are published. The thesis was perhaps given
seminal thought in Samuel J. Eldersveld, "Influence of Metropolitan Party Pluralities on Presidential Elections," *American Political Science Review*, XLIII (Dec.
1949), 1189–206. For a discussion of the 1924 La Follette vote, see Richard Hofstadter, *The Age of Reform* (New York, 1960), p. 284. Ruth C. Silva in *Rum, Religion, And Votes: 1928 Re-Examined* (University Park, Pa., 1962), pp. 9–12,
examines the relationship between the La Follette and the Smith vote. Although at
one point she notes, "Therefore, it appears that voting for La Follette was a
transition from the Republican to the Democratic Party for a significant number of
voters," Silva qualifies by continuing, "Smith's apparently greater [than Hoover's]
success in attracting La Follette voters should not be magnified." Admitting that
"there was a tendency for Smith to make his gains in states where La Follette had
been relatively strong," Silva points to the probability "that Smith's gains resulted
largely from the attraction of new voters to the electorate and not merely from
winning the support of La Follette voters." La Follette's role in the establishment
of the New Deal coalition in California is discussed by John Shover in "Was 1928
a Critical Election in California?" *Pacific Northwest Quarterly*, LVIII (Oct. 1967),
196–204. He remarks, "A New Deal alignment, harbinger of the New Deal coalition, appeared in the vote for Wilson in California in 1916, was temporarily shat-

After Theodore Roosevelt, who was running on three tickets, beat the Republican organization in 1912, political normalcy returned when in 1916 Hughes won 57 percent of the total Pittsburgh vote; and normalcy personified reigned when in 1920 Harding captured a phenomenal 71.4 percent. However, the impact of Calvin Coolidge's landslide was diminished in the Smoky City when John W. Davis, the Democratic candidate, obtained only 8 percent of the vote, but Progressive Robert M. La Follette, running on a local Socialist-Labor ticket, reaped 36 percent, 20 percent more than his national average. La Follette's supporters, attacked during the campaign by the Republican county chairman as a "bunch of Reds," brightened when the Wisconsin politician told a Pittsburgh gathering on the Halloween before election day: "It is unnecessary to demonstrate to a Pittsburgh audience that private monopoly does in fact control government and industry. You live here in the shadow of one of the greatest, if not the very greatest, monopoly in the world—the U. S. Steel Corporation." For good measure he attacked Secretary of the Treasury Andrew Mellon as being "the real President of the United States. . . . Calvin Coolidge is merely the man who occupies the White House," he declared.[27]

Comparisons of the La Follette vote with those of prior presidential elections dating back to 1912 show that the La Follette vote bears the closest relationship to the Debs vote of 1912, indicating a firm connection between the support for the Progressive candidate in 1924 and the Socialist standard-bearer of a dozen years earlier. (See table 1.) Ironically, however, the support in 1912 for Theodore Roosevelt, also running as a Progressive candidate, appears much different from La Follette's. In fact, as seen in tables 2 and 3, the Bull Moose Progressives of 1912 in Pittsburgh were based in the native white, upper economic elements of the community, whereas the Progressives in 1924 found support among the foreign, lower economic classes of the city.

The correlations between the La Follette vote of 1924 and those of

---

tered in 1920, only to emerge in the Socialist [La Follette] vote of 1924 and the Smith vote in 1928" (p. 203). Additional information for the same state is provided in Michael Rogin, "Progressivism and the California Electorate," *Journal of American History,* LV (Sept. 1968), 297–314.

27. Election returns were taken from *Pennsylvania Manual,* 1913, 1917, 1921, and 1925 eds., and were percentaged by the author. *PG,* Nov. 1, 1924; Belle Case and Fola La Follette, *Robert M. La Follette,* vol. II (New York, 1953), pp. 1144–45.

TABLE 1
Coefficients of Correlation Between Presidential Votes in Wards

	Debs '12	TR '12	Smith '28	FDR '32
La Follette '24	.75	−.34	.64	.84
Davis '24	—	—	−.40	−.37
La Follette-Davis '24	—	—	.69	.90
Smith '28	—	—	—	.72

NOTE: The correlations for the 1924, 1928, and 1932 votes are based on twenty-eight wards; the correlations for the 1924 and 1912 votes are based on Wards 1–27.
The formula used for the correlations throughout this study is the Spearman rank order formula. Rankings and formula are included in Appendix A.

the presidential elections of 1928 and 1932 show that La Follette's impact on Pittsburgh was greater than described by the Republican-oriented newspapers. (See table 1.) His vote takes on special significance in the light of the complete Roosevelt breakthrough eight years later. If La Follette's vote is compared with Smith's, by ranking their votes by ward, a relatively high correlation is found. However, the correlation of the 1924 Progressive vote with the 1932 Democratic vote shows an even greater similarity and indicates that both La Follette and Roosevelt drew their support from much the same wards. On the other hand, a comparison of the 1928 Smith vote with the 1932 Roosevelt vote shows less

TABLE 2
Coefficients of Correlation Between Presidential Votes and Ethnic Variables in Wards

	TR '12	Debs '12	La F. '24	Smith '28	FDR '32
Foreign stock[a]	−.62	.31	.55	.87	.67
Native stock[b]	.58	−.23	−.27	−.70	−.40

SOURCES: For 1912 foreign and native stocks were computed from 13th Census of Population, 1910 (U.S. Bureau of the Census); for 1924, 1928, and 1932 they were computed from 15th Census of Population, 1930 (U.S. Bureau of the Census).
NOTE: The correlations for the 1924, 1928, and 1932 votes are based on Wards 1–28; the correlations for the 1912 votes are based on Wards 1–27. See Appendix B.
a. Foreign born and native white of foreign or mixed parentage.
b. Native white of native parentage.

cohesiveness, indicating somewhat different support. Davis's 1924 Democratic backing was poles apart from both Smith's and Roosevelt's; but when added to La Follette's on the premise that it, too, was a vote against the Republican organization, the correlation between the 1924 vote combination and both Smith's and Roosevelt's votes increases in each case.

TABLE 3

Coefficients of Correlation Between Presidential Votes and Economic Variables in Wards

	TR '12	Debs '12	La F. '24	Smith '28	FDR '32
Most tenements occupied '12	−.30	.01	—	—	—
Median rental '30	—	—	−.60	−.64	−.57

SOURCES: "Most tenements occupied '12" is taken from *City of Pittsburgh, Annual Report of the Mayor, 1912.* "Median rental '30" is taken from *Social Facts Books About Pittsburgh and Allegheny County,* vol. I, *Pittsburgh Wards* (Pittsburgh, 1945).

NOTE: The 1912 correlations are based on twenty-seven wards; others are based on Wards 1–28. Comparable information for 1912 and 1930 is unavailable. See Appendix B.

Where Smith's and FDR's strength differed the most and FDR's and La Follette's support had the most similarity can best be seen by isolating each candidate's wards of greatest strength. (See table 4.)

TABLE 4

Wards Showing Greatest Support

La Follette '24	Smith '28	Roosevelt '32
16	1	17
24	2	24
17	16	16

Whereas La Follette's and Roosevelt's heaviest support came from the same wards, although in reversed order, Smith drew his best support from two entirely different wards. One of these, the tightly controlled Republican Second Ward, gave FDR his least support. The First and Second Wards, which supplied Smith with his highest ward votes, 77 and 75 percent respectively, also housed the highest proportion of foreign-born population of any wards in the city in 1930. One quarter of the population of both wards was foreign born, and of these two thirds were eligible to vote in the First Ward and about 60 percent in the Second. Italians constituted the largest ethnic group in both wards.[28]

However, La Follette drew much support from the Sixteenth and Seven-

28. Population statistics, based on 1930, were taken from Bureau of Social Research, Federation of Social Agencies of Pittsburgh and Allegheny County, *Social Facts About Pittsburgh and Allegheny County,* vol. I, *Pittsburgh Wards* (Pittsburgh, 1945). Voting statistics were percentaged from returns in *Pennsylvania Manual,* 1925, 1929, 1933 eds.

teenth Wards, two of the three highest foreign-stock wards. (Foreign stock includes both foreign born and native white of foreign or mixed parentage.) His victory in the Twenty-fourth Ward may reflect that German-Austrian ward's approval of his opposition to the United States' entrance into World War I. La Follette reached the immigrants and their children, although to a lesser extent than Smith. The correlation of each candidate's vote by ward with a ranking of the ward's proportion of foreign stock shows that the affinity of the FDR vote for the foreign community stood between that of Smith and La Follette. (See table 2.) La Follette captured the foreign vote, and the Democratic hold on the vote reached its zenith with Smith. FDR's foreign support was weaker than the 1928 candidate's, but showed a gain over La Follette's 1924 backing. Concomitantly, all three candidates had a negative relationship with the native white, of at least second-generation residency, with Smith faring most poorly.[29]

La Follette set the tone for Smith and Roosevelt in wards made up of the lower-economic working class as well. When one correlates each candidate's vote in all twenty-eight wards ranked from highest to lowest by their 1930 median rental, one not only finds no positive difference, but, in fact, a close relationship between the candidates. Each did badly in the high-rental, upper-economic-class areas. (See table 3.)

Although not realized at the time, the "La Follette Revolution" signaled a sorry turn of the tide for Pittsburgh's Republican machine. Viewed over an eight-year period, which included three presidential elections, as well as the 1931 county commissioner race well run by Lawrence, FDR's

29. For figures on foreign stock, the number of native white of foreign or mixed parents in each ward was added to the number of foreign born and subtracted from the native white total in each ward. This process provided figures for the population of native parentage only, as well as for foreign stock, that is, foreign born plus first generation. Table 23, "Population by Sex, Color, Age, etc., for Cities Over 50,000 or More by Ward, 1930," 15th Census of Population, 1930, Pennsylvania, Composition and Characteristics (U.S. Bureau of the Census), p. 751; Lubell, *American Politics*, pp. 140–41, notes the link of the 1924 La Follette vote and his opposition to United States entrance into World War I. This view has not gone unchallenged. For a discussion of the isolationist thesis and further references see R. M. Abrams and L. W. Levine, *The Shaping of Twentieth-Century America* (Boston, 1965), p. 502; Harold F. Alderfer and Robert M. Sigmond, "Presidential Elections by Pennsylvania Counties, 1920–1940," *Pennsylvania State College Studies*, no. 10, *College Bulletin XXXV* (June 9, 1941), 30, shows that there was a very high correlation between La Follette's vote and the foreign-born white population for all of Pennsylvania's counties in 1924. On the county level for foreign-born whites, the La Follette coefficient was higher than Smith's in 1928.

victory does not appear as sharp a break from past Pittsburgh voting tradition as it may have seemed to the average Pittsburgher of 1932. For the rank-and-file party worker, the Roosevelt victory, although joyous, must have seemed less immediate than its desired logical extension—a victory in the closer-to-home municipal election of 1933. In the interim the country passed through the famous "first hundred days" of the New Deal, and many echoed the remarks of a Democratic committeeman who became politically active in 1933. Commenting on his entrance into or-organization politics at that time, he noted, "I was unemployed—but I also had admiration for FDR and the government doing something to get us out of the depression."[30] The Democrats were on the move.

The Demography of Machine Building

The social environment in which Pittsburgh's growing Democratic party made its move was not unlike the pluralistic culture common to other urban centers. Whereas native stock composed 40.6 percent of Pittsburgh's 1930 population, the majority of the city, 51.1 percent, was tied to the foreign community with Negroes and other nonwhites comprising the remainder of the population. As evidenced in table 5, of the ten largest cities in the United States at the beginning of the depression decade, Pittsburgh appeared typical for the demographic information listed. Its proportions of foreign stock and nonwhites were closest to the ten-city mean for these ethnic elements, whereas its proportion of native white was third behind Philadelphia's and Detroit's in its lack of deviation from the mean.

Within the Steel City the proportion of foreign stock in the population slid from 62.2 percent in 1910 to 56.7 percent in 1920 and to 51 percent by 1930; inversely, the percentage of native stock increased during these years, but to a lesser extent. Among the three wards with the highest proportion of foreign stock in their population, the Sixteenth and Seventeenth were represented during all three census years. The Second Ward, among these three in 1910 and 1920, dropped to fourth place in 1930, being replaced by the Sixth. Thus, by the depression decade the three most foreign wards were mill areas or "river wards." The Sixteenth and Seventeenth Wards touched upon the shores of the Monongahela, whereas the Sixth lay on the banks of the Allegheny. All three served as resi-

30. Interview with committeeman, 4W9.

TABLE 5
Ethnic Composition of Ten Largest Cities in United States, 1930

	Native White		Foreign Stock		Nonwhite	
	Percentage	Deviation from Mean	Percentage	Deviation from Mean	Percentage	Deviation from Mean
New York	21.7%	−15.5%	73.3%	+19.9%	5.0%	−4.4%
Chicago	27.9	− 9.3	64.4	+11.0	7.7	−1.7
Philadelphia	38.0	+ 0.8	50.6	− 2.8	11.4	+2.0
Detroit	34.3	− 2.9	57.6	+ 4.2	8.2	−1.5
Los Angeles	49.9	+12.7	36.8	− 16.6	13.3	+3.6
Cleveland	27.0	−10.2	64.9	+11.5	8.1	−1.3
St. Louis	53.4	+16.2	35.1	− 18.3	11.6	+2.2
Baltimore	53.1	+15.9	29.1	− 24.3	17.7	+8.3
Boston	25.6	−11.6	71.5	+18.1	2.9	−6.5
Pittsburgh	40.6	+ 3.4	51.1	− 2.3	8.3	−1.1
Mean	37.2	—	53.4	—	9.4	—

SOURCE: Statistics were compiled from U.S. Department of Commerce, Bureau of the Census, *Statistical Abstract of the United States, 1934* (Washington, 1934), pp. 20–25.

NOTE: Foreign stock was calculated by adding figures for native white of foreign or mixed parentage with those for foreign born. Means were computed by author.

dential areas for a fairly substantial proportion of Poles, and the Sixteenth and Seventeenth housed relatively large numbers of foreign-born Germans and Lithuanians. By 1930, and throughout the entire decade, these wards were the lowest rental areas in the city. In 1934 the Seventeenth and the Sixth ranked among the five wards with the greatest unemployment in the city. By 1940 all three were among the top 40 percent of wards with individuals on the WPA payroll; the Sixth and the Seventeenth Wards were also among the four wards housing the greatest proportion of laborers. The 1932 Roosevelt vote initiated these three wards' role as Democratic bastions throughout the New Deal years. (See table 6 and maps 1–6.)[31]

31. Most information regarding demographic analysis of Pittsburgh wards discussed between pages 40–52 has been collected from the raw data in *Social Facts*, vol. I, *Pittsburgh Wards*. Proportions of foreign stock and native white, 1910–1930, have been calculated from table V, 13th Census of Population, 1910, vol. 3 (U.S. Bureau of the Census), p. 609; table 13, 14th Census of Population, 1920, vol. 3 (U.S. Bureau of the Census), p. 900; table 23, 15th Census of Population, 1930 (U.S. Bureau of the Census), p. 751; unemployment figures for 1934 are from J. P. Watson, *Economic Background of the Relief Problem* (Pittsburgh, 1937), p. 46; voting returns were averaged from various post-election-day newspapers and editions of *Pennsylvania Manual*.

No one ethnic group dominated the foreign-born population of any single ward in the city in 1930; the Poles had the greatest proportion with their 12.1 percent in the Sixth Ward. The Italians, Austrian-Germans, Russians, Czechs, Yugoslavs, Irish, Hungarians, and Lithuanians, all had strongholds in specific wards. Table 7 gives the wards with the highest percentage of each of these ethnic groups. Eight wards in 1930 contained Negro populations greater than the city average of 8.3 percent. Map 2 defines these wards. Negro Pittsburghers made up the majority of the Fifth Ward's population and 40 percent of the Third Ward.

TABLE 6
Demographic Variables in Wards with Largest Proportion of Foreign Stock and in City

	Ward 6	Ward 16	Ward 17	Pittsburgh
	Percentage	Percentage	Percentage	Percentage
Foreign stock '30[a]	65.4%	65.0%	70.0%	51.1%
Foreign-born Polish '30	12.1	5.6	9.9	2.3
Foreign-born Germans '30	1.7	4.7	3.1	2.6
Foreign-born Lithuanians '30	0.6	1.4	1.5	0.5
Unemployment '34	40.8	31.4	42.0	31.9
Individuals on WPA '40	6.4	5.9	9.1	6.2
Laborers '40	15.8	16.4	16.8	8.9
Mean Democratic vote, '32–'41 elections	69.4	72.0	70.6	57.6
	Dollars	Dollars	Dollars	Dollars
Median rental '30	$21.23	$21.66	$19.97	$37.06
Median rental '40	16.21	17.10	16.30	24.62

a. Foreign born and native white of foreign or mixed parentage.

Between 1930 and 1940 the proportion of foreign born within most ethnic groups declined; however, the group that made up the greatest proportion of foreign born in each ward in 1930 continued to do so in 1940 with the exceptions of the Irish and the Russians. (See table 7.) During the 1930s the center of the Irish foreign-born population shifted slightly westward, from the Tenth and Seventh Wards to the Fourth. In the Third Ward the Russian foreign-born population dropped from 8.1 percent in 1930 to 4.1 percent in 1940, whereas the Negro population swelled from 40.1 percent to 51.1 percent. As the Negro population increased from 8,873 to 11,060, it supplanted the area's Russian Jews, who spread to other neighborhoods, especially the Eleventh, Fourteenth, and

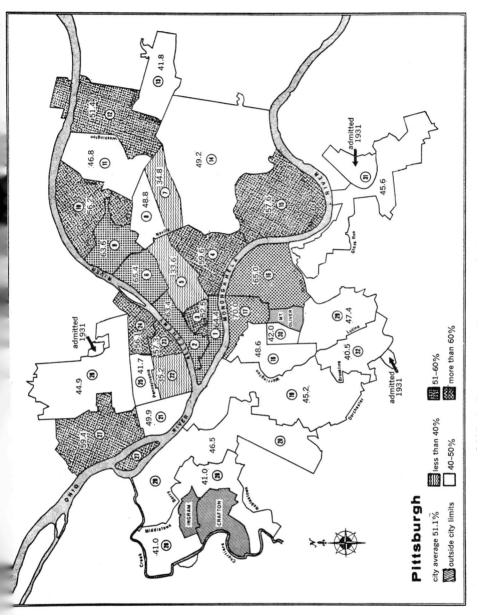

Pittsburgh

city average 51.1%

■ outside city limits

▨ less than 40%

□ 40–50%

▦ 51–60%

▩ more than 60%

MAP 1. *Proportion of Foreign Stock, by Wards, 1930*

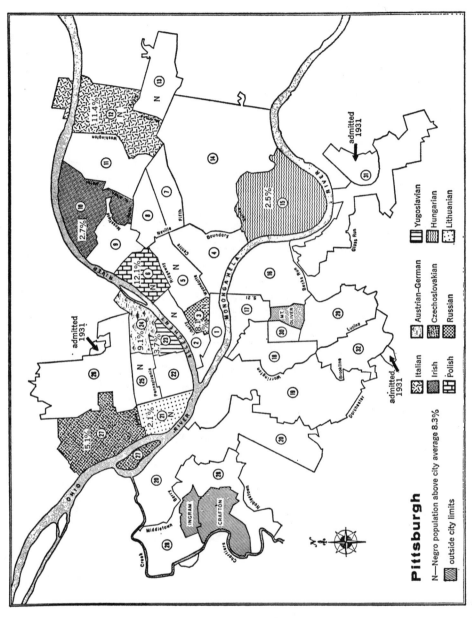

Pittsburgh

N—Negro population above city average 8.3%

outside city limits

Italian
Irish
Polish

Austrian-German
Czechoslovakian
Russian

Yugoslavian
Hungarian
Lithuanian

MAP 1. (b) Ethnic Proportion at Foreign Born and Negro Population Above City Average, 1930

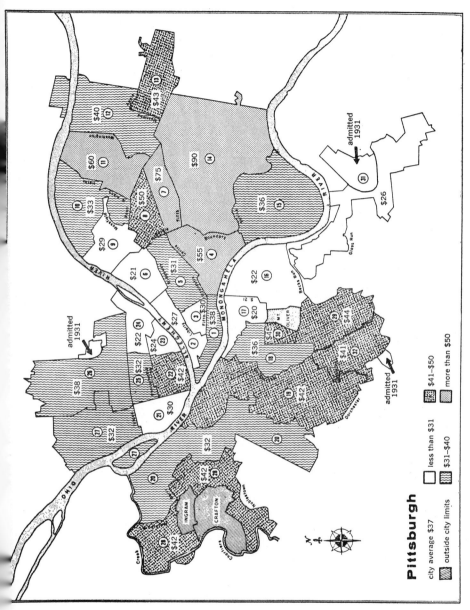

Pittsburgh

city average $37   ☐ less than $31

▨ outside city limits   ☐ $31–$40

▨ $41–$50

▦ more than $50

MAP 3. *Median Rentals, by Wards, 1930*

45

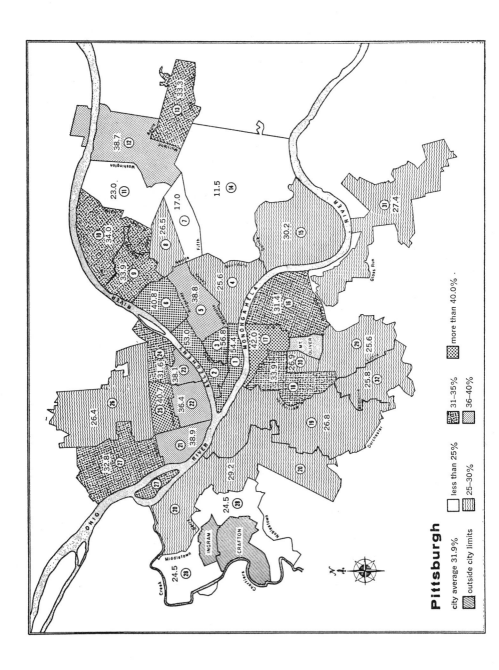

Pittsburgh

city average 31.9%

☐ less than 25% ▨ 31–35% ▨ more than 40.0% .

▨ outside city limits ▨ 25–30% ▨ 36–40%

46

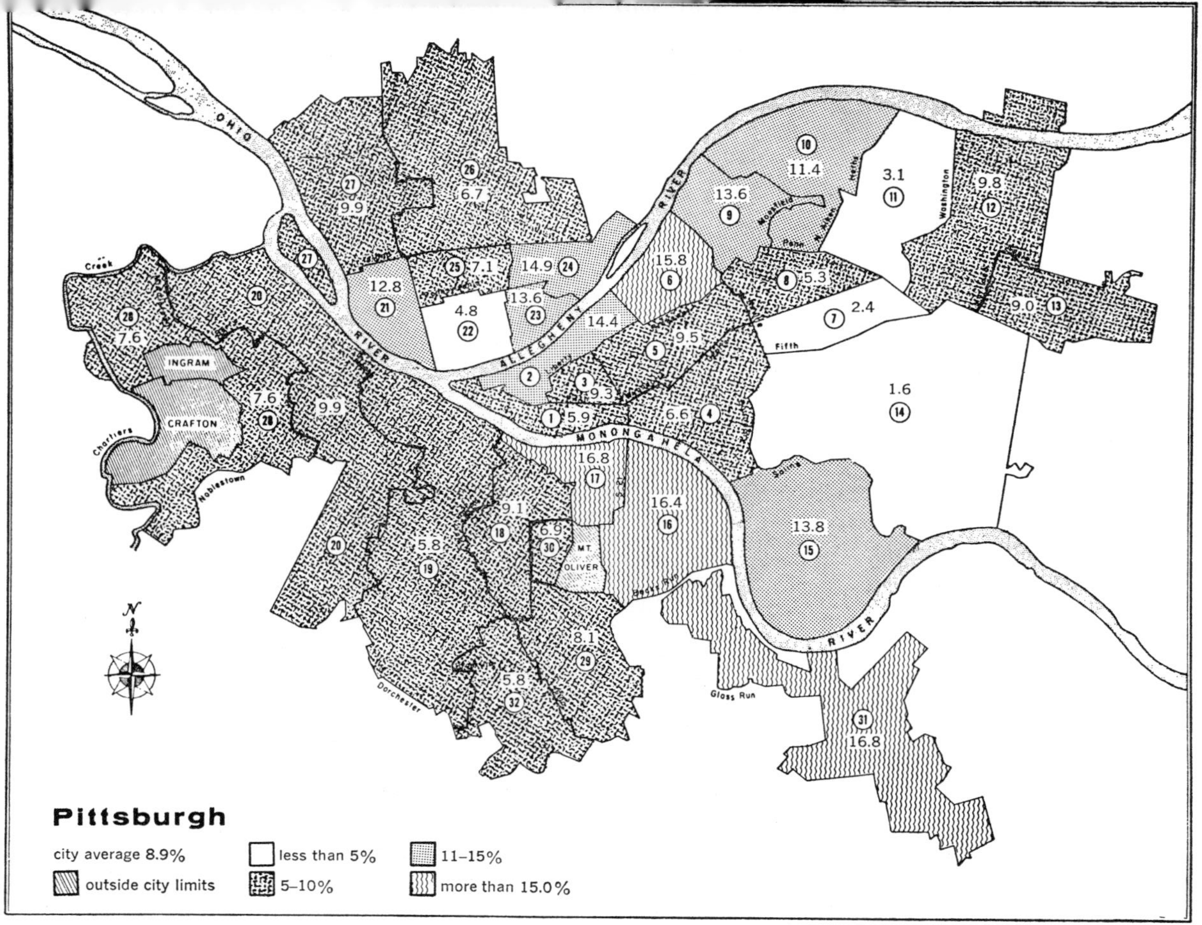

MAP 5. *Proportion of Working Force Consisting of Laborers, by Wards, 1940*

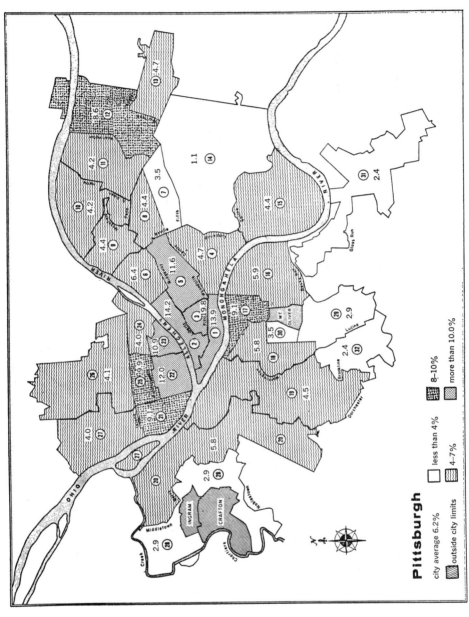

Pittsburgh

city average 6.2%

☐ less than 4%

4-7%

8-10%

more than 10.0%

outside city limits

MAP 6. *Individuals on WPA Payroll, per One Hundred Occupied Dwellings, by Wards, 1940*

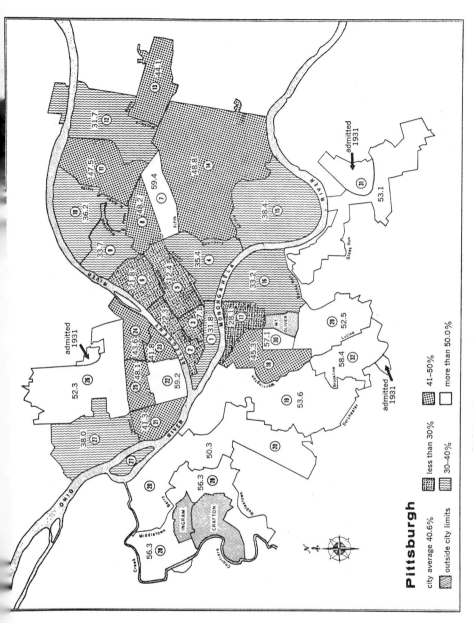

Pittsburgh

city average 40.6%

[hatched] outside city limits

[dotted] less than 30%

[light dotted] 30–40%

[fine dotted] 41–50%

[blank] more than 50.0%

MAP 7. *Proportion of Native White, by Wards, 1930*

49

Sixteenth Wards. Generally, however, no great reshuffling of the ethnic population occurred throughout the city during the depression decade.

TABLE 7
Proportion of Foreign-born Ethnic Groups and of Negroes in Wards with Highest Population of Such Groups and in City

	1930			1940		
	Ward	%	Pittsburgh	Ward	%	Pittsburgh
Polish	6	12.1%	2.3%	6	9.3%	1.6%
Italian	12	11.4	2.7	12	10.1	2.4
Austrian-German	24	9.1	2.7	24	7.0	2.4
Russian	3	8.1	1.4	11	4.9	1.2
Czechoslovakian	27	5.1	1.0	27	2.9	0.6
Yugoslavian	23	3.7	0.6	23	2.7	0.4
Irish (Eire)	10	2.7	1.1	4	1.9	0.8
Hungarian	15	2.5	0.3	15	2.4	0.4
Lithuanian	21	2.1	0.5	21	1.5	0.4
Negro	5	53.8	8.3	5	70.1	9.3

The proportion of native stock in Pittsburgh's population increased from 33 percent in 1910 to 36.8 percent in 1920 and to 40.6 percent in the year after the Great Crash. Both the Seventh and the Twenty-second Wards were represented among the three wards having the highest proportion of native stock during each of these census years, but the third ward of the group varied. In 1910 the Thirteenth Ward had the second highest proportion of native stock, but it was displaced among the top three native-white wards by the Fourteenth in 1920, which, in turn, was displaced by the Thirty-second Ward in 1930. During the two decades leading to the depression, Pittsburgh's concentration of native-white population moved south and west, although it held on to its bastions in the Seventh and Twenty-second Wards. (See map 7.) In the 1920s and the earliest years of the 1930s, the city added the territory that became the Twenty-eighth through the Thirty-second Wards. These southside, suburban wards continually harassed the Pittsburgh Democratic organization during its formative years, for each of the five voted below the Democratic city average for all general elections between 1932 and 1941.

Although the five newest wards in the city were situated on the southside, the three most native wards were geographically dispersed at the beginning of the depression decade, and only one could be found on the city's southside. The Seventh Ward, with the highest proportion of native-white population, lay insulated in the heart of what was the original center of Pittsburgh. Throughout the decade it was the second highest rental area in the city; it had the second lowest unemployment rate for all wards in 1934 and the seventh lowest proportion of individuals on WPA in 1940. Over 15 percent of its working population held professional jobs in 1940, the highest proportion for any ward in the city, whereas only 2.4 percent served as laborers, the second lowest proportion of all wards in Pittsburgh. Only twice during the years between 1930 and 1941 did the voters of the Seventh Ward cast a majority of their ballots in a general election for Democratic candidates. They swung to the Democratic standard-bearer in the 1933 mayoralty race and to FDR in 1936. In the latter election all Pittsburgh wards joined in the Roosevelt landslide, with the president garnering 70.6 percent of the city's vote; the Seventh Ward, however, handed Roosevelt a meager 51.4 percent majority. Throughout the decade, it would be the Steel City's most Republican district. (See table 8 and maps 3–7.)

Situated on the northside of the city, the Twenty-second Ward guards the banks of the Allegheny River as it merges with the Monongahela to form the Ohio River. It was part of the seven-ward complex (Twenty-first to Twenty-seventh Wards) that composed the old city of Allegheny, incorporated into Pittsburgh in 1907. Unlike the Seventh Ward, in which the high-rental status remained constant throughout the decade, the median rental of the Twenty-second Ward skidded from the eleventh highest in 1930 to the eighth lowest for all city wards in 1940. It had the eleventh highest unemployment rate in 1934 and the fourth highest proportion of individuals on WPA by the end of the decade. In 1940 comparatively few laborers lived in the ward, whereas a high proportion of professional workers resided within its bounds. This percentage can probably be attributed to the desire of many staff members of Allegheny County Hospital to reside close to their place of work. Doctors and nurses took up short-term permanent residences near the hospital.[32] Unlike the Seventh Ward, the Twenty-second voted above the Democratic city average in the general elections of the depression decade. (See table 8 and maps 3–7.)

In contrast, the Thirty-second Ward, the third most native ward in

32. Interview with committeeman, 22W6. He noted that these professionals were difficult to control as voters and that they infrequently voted in local elections.

Pittsburgh of 1930, like the Seventh, voted below the Democratic city average. Median rentals in this ward rose from the twelfth highest in the city at the beginning of the decade to the fourth highest by its end. Not only did it have the sixth lowest unemployment rate in 1934, but it placed the third smallest proportion of individuals on the WPA payroll in 1940. Like the other two native-stock wards, comparatively few unskilled laborers resided in the Thirty-second Ward; however, a relatively high proportion of skilled workers, craftsmen, and foremen did populate the area. (See table 8 and maps 3–7.)

Of the three wards with the highest native-white population, the depression hit the Twenty-second the hardest. There the emerging Democratic organization won its greatest support from among the most native wards. In this instance, the economic variables seems to have played a greater role in determining voting behavior than did the ethnic composition of the ward.

TABLE 8
Demographic Variables in Wards with Largest Native-White Population and in City

	Ward 7	Ward 22	Ward 32	Pittsburgh
	Percentage	Percentage	Percentage	Percentage
Native white '30	59.4%	59.2%	58.4%	40.6%
Unemployment '34	17.0	36.4	25.8	31.9
Individuals on WPA '40	3.5	12.0	2.4	6.2
Laborers '40	2.4	4.8	5.8	8.9
Mean Democratic vote, '32–'41 elections	42.5	58.2	56.6	57.6
	Dollars	Dollars	Dollars	Dollars
Median rental '30	$74.83	$41.56	$41.08	$37.06
Median rental '40	45.42	21.66	36.20	24.62

The Pittsburgh Democratic party consolidated its strength during the depression decade within this social and economic environment. After the triumph of Roosevelt in 1932, the organization prepared for its first local test—the mayoralty election of 1933. The election played tricks on the Democratic politicians, fooling them into a false sense of security. At first they believed that Roosevelt's social and economic coalition was responsible for their victory, but they soon learned differently. It remained their task for the rest of the decade to win this support and to elect regular organization candidates.

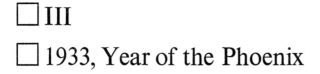

☐ III
☐ 1933, Year of the Phoenix

As the 1933 election returns became final a morgue ambulance pulled up in front of Republican headquarters, allowing some Democrats to ask, "What you got in there, the Republican Party?"
Pittsburgh Sun-Telegraph, *November 8, 1933*

☐ The Democratic magic of Roosevelt's first year in office permeated Pittsburgh politics during 1933. By the time of the fall municipal primary campaign, there were many more names listed in the Democratic contest for the five available city council seats than for the Republican nominations—an unusual situation for Pittsburgh. Paradoxically, rather than the usual dearth of Democratic election workers, by the first day of primary registration it was the Republicans who needed registrars for approximately seventy-five of the city's election districts. The previously ever-present problem of David Lawrence's Democratic organization had befallen the Republicans. "A Disgusted Republican" wrote to the editor of *The Pittsburgh Press*: "A Democratic President is doing things for the country that the Republicans didn't try. Perhaps a Democratic Mayor will give Pittsburgh a New Deal."[1]

Former Republican stalwarts, sensing the atmosphere of political

1. *Pittsburgh Sun-Telegraph* (hereafter cited as *ST*), Aug. 18, 1933; *Pittsburgh Post-Gazette* (hereafter cited as *PG*), Sept. 5, 1933; *Pittsburgh Press* (hereafter cited as *Press*), Aug. 31, 1933, editorial page.

change, moved with the tide. One, John M. Huston, surprised everyone by bolting to the Democrats and becoming a council candidate. He modestly announced, "As there seems to be no hope for better government from the Republican party in this city, many of my closest friends, inspired by the record *our Democratic* President has made in Washington, . . . have urged me . . . to run on the Democratic ticket of the city of Pittsburgh" (emphasis added). Those who remained in the ranks of the GOP became jittery, and the name Republican disappeared from all advertising during that party's primary campaign. When the final registration figures were made public prior to the contest, the number of registered Democrats had increased to thirty-one thousand over their 1929 number and sixteen thousand above the 1932 figure, and organization Boss David Lawrence gloried. He reasoned that if Roosevelt could get eighty-six thousand votes on the basis of twenty thousand registered Democrats, the party's mayoralty candidate should also be able to at least quadruple his vote over the Democratic registration. "The revolt against the Republican machine has got beyond the control of the GOP bosses and workers," claimed the Democrat's state chairman, Warren Van Dyke.[2]

In spite of this surging Democratic tide, the possibility that the Republican nominee for mayor might win still seemed realistic—so realistic as to be the cause of a hotly contested primary race. When Charles Kline had resigned from office under duress, John S. Herron, president of the city council, had succeeded him. However, actual Republican organization power had descended to Kline's former lieutenant, State Senator James J. Coyne. Coyne, a hulking man, easily fit the stereotype of "the Boss," which he was quickly dubbed; and Herron, who had declared war on municipal corruption when he assumed the mayoralty, suffered from the Coyne image after having received the organization's backing for the 1933 Republican primary.

The antiorganization GOP faction, fearing a repeat of 1929, when two independent candidates split their vote allowing Kline to triumph in that year's primary, desired to unite on a single man. Its one real hope for harmony was Judge Frank P. Patterson. A group of business, professional, and financial leaders proposed to Patterson that he run and unify

2. *ST*, Aug. 10, 1933; *Press*, Aug. 27, 1933, editorial page; ibid., Sept. 18, 1933; *ST*, Sept. 15, 1933.

the antiadministration forces. Patterson agreed but first wanted word of agreement from the other two leading candidates, Register of Wills Joseph N. Mackrell and Councilman P. J. McArdle. Word did not come quickly, although Mackrell, with much reluctance, eventually requested that Patterson run. When it became known that well-fixed businessmen such as Ernest T. Weir, Howard Heinz, Leslie Johnston, and William P. Witherow were urging Patterson to run, McArdle complained that he knew no reason why self-appointed groups should pick the candidates.[3]

Nevertheless, McArdle welcomed the support of these same "self-appointed groups" after Patterson withdrew from the race. Most of them backed him as a result of their affiliation with the Citizens League, an organization formed largely from the Citizens Committee of 1931, which had spearheaded the supplies department probe that led to Kline's conviction. The Citizens League, along with the League of Women Voters, also active in the 1931 investigations, provided McArdle with his major support. The determination not to run of the erstwhile Patterson supporter William P. Witherow and of James F. Malone, a former councilman who had been in the party's mayoralty fight four years earlier, cleared the way for a three-cornered Republican race among Herron, McArdle, and Mackrell. The third corner, however, irritated McArdle's backers, and the campaign chairman of the Citizens League hinted that Coyne had put Mackrell up to running in order to split the anti-machine vote.[4]

Only two candidates squared off in the Democratic contest, but for the first time in years Pittsburgh showed interest in the donkey as well as the elephant during the primary campaign. Before the Lawrence organization slated its candidate for mayor, John M. Henry, an old-line Wilsonian Democrat and bitter foe of the county leader, declared for office. Henry had been a member of the Allegheny County Bar since 1909, an assistant United States district attorney for western Pennsylvania in 1917, and had been appointed to Pittsburgh's registration commission by Governor Pinchot, who then had fired him at the request of Lawrence and Joe Guffey. Substitution for Henry on the commission had been part of a patronage deal offered the Democratic organization by Pinchot in return

3. *New York Times* (hereafter cited as *NYT*), Apr. 9, 1933, sec. 4, p. 6; ibid., Aug. 13, 1933, sec. 4, p. 1, *ST*, Sept. 17, 1933.
4. *PG*, Sept. 18, 1933; *Press*, Sept. 2, 1933.

for its assistance given to his program in the state legislature. Pinchot had displayed great enthusiasm for Democratic help when he wrote the president: "I want you to know how very deeply I appreciate the cooperation of the Pennsylvania Democrats, and in particular that of Mr. Guffey, Mr. Lawrence, and Mr. Van Dyke. . . ." Henry suffered as a result of the governor's gratitude, and the dismissal prompted his candidacy in the fall primary.[5]

In the light of Lawrence's splendid showing in the 1931 commissioner's contest, he himself would have been the most logical candidate for the organization to have slated. Primarily because of that showing, however, Lawrence was no longer available. Since the corruption of Boss Coyne and his machine loomed as the major issue, the county chairman's liaison with Coyne in the 1931 election ruined Lawrence's chances for the nomination. The organization needed a candidate who could unite the Democrats and draw the independent vote alienated by Coyne. At a slating meeting one evening, Lawrence's judgment prevailed and William Nissley McNair received the nod of his party. "We needed the independents. He was Protestant, I was Catholic; he was a single taxer and that had appeal in those days of depression," recalled Lawrence. According to many contemporary observers, McNair's apparent lack of willpower and the expectancy that he would be a political puppet may have attracted the Democratic leader to his choice, even more than McNair's other attributes. The irony of this choice will be seen in the light of later events.[6]

McNair, single taxer and perennial candidate, had a background deeply rooted in Pennsylvania history. His ancestors had purchased land from William Penn, and his family was prominent in the state since Revolutionary days. One of his forebears, Alexander McNair, wandered west to become the first governor of Missouri, winning an election against the father of Champ Clark. McNair himself, born in Middletown, Pennsylvania, just south of the state capital, attended Sedler's Academy, Gettys-

5. Clipping, Guffey Papers, Washington and Jefferson College (hereafter cited as W & J), Washington, Pa.; *ST*, Aug. 25, 1933; letter, Pinchot to Roosevelt, May 15, 1933, President's Personal Files 289 (hereafter cited as PPF), Franklin D. Roosevelt Library (hereafter cited as FDRL), Hyde Park, N.Y.

6. Interview with David Lawrence, Apr. 14, 1964; clipping from *PG*, Feb. 18, 1936, McNair Scrapbooks, Pennsylvania Division, Carnegie Library (hereafter cited as PD, CL), Pittsburgh, Pa.

burg College, and the University of Michigan Law School. From Michigan he returned east and joined a Pittsburgh law firm, later branching out on his own. His immediate family had been active in politics, and before long McNair ran and lost in an election for district attorney of Allegheny County. Always a Democrat, he had little chance in the Republican bastion. Nevertheless, he ran for common pleas court judge, spent his 1914 honeymoon campaigning for the office of state secretary of internal affairs, opposed William A. Magee for mayor in 1921, and polled over a million votes running against David A. Reed for United States senator in 1928.[7]

Although not in the limelight, thus not suffering the taint of the candidate, in 1931 McNair had served as Lawrence's campaign chairman. Henry, grasping for an issue, claimed that McNair was as much a friend of Coyne as were Lawrence and Herron. Henry hammered away at two main issues—this alleged linkage of the Democratic and Republican parties and the fact that the Guffey-Lawrence organization seemed as much a machine as the Republican organization. "In 1929, the Democratic machine cooperated with the system of padded [tax] assessments and registrations. . . . In 1931 we saw the machines fighting shoulder to shoulder. . . . No one seriously thinks that my opponent could ever seriously be permitted to be Mayor. If you elect him, you install in the city of Pittsburgh the Guffey-Lawrence machine," the antiorganization candidate declared.[8]

At another time, Henry challenged his listeners to show him that the Guffey-Lawrence combination had anything to offer "except a repetition under the label Democrat of the sad chapter written by the Republican machine," and noted that "a Republican boss or a Democratic boss is equally useful to privilege." A few days later, in order to elaborate on this point, Henry charged that McNair's campaign treasurer acted as tax consultant to the "privileged" Mellon interests, and that M. L. ("Mike") Benedum, millionaire oilman who served as a financial angel for FDR in 1932, actually bossed the Democratic bosses. "If you vote for Guffey's man, who is also Benedum's man, you have voted to continue the rule of utilities and the oil, coal, and steel barons. You have voted to continue the rule of the same crowd of money changers that Franklin Roosevelt

7. Clipping from *Press*, Nov. 9, 1933, McNair Scrapbooks, PD, CL.
8. *NYT*, Aug. 13, 1933, sec. 4, p. 1; *PG*, Sept. 1, 1933.

drove out of Washington. That is not the New Deal. It's the same old deal dressed up in a new deck," he gibed.[9]

According to Henry, the machine, too, stood as the very essence of municipal evil. He claimed that as an agent of wealth, it was concerned with taking away labor's right to representation in Harrisburg, so that the legislature could place the bulk of taxation on the working man rather than on the man of wealth; it caused overlapping and duplication of local government agencies and, concomitantly, higher taxes to pay for them, because it aimed to keep as many party drones as possible on the payroll for long as possible; it encouraged election fraud. In line with his lashing out at machine politics, Republican—and Democratic—Henry suggested a method for determining whether a candidate was a machine man. First, he asked, how much money is being spent to elect the candiate? Secondly, does the candidate dare to criticize his masters? Henry spent little and criticized much; McNair issued full-page newspaper advertisements and allied with Guffey and Lawrence. Henry told his audiences to draw their own conclusions.[10]

Aside from these attacks, Henry concerned himself with a number of other issues. Calling for the repeal of the state poll tax, he claimed it disfranchised a great number of people in time of dire depression. He propounded a tax reduction through "efficient expenditure of tax money" and called for new housing laws and eradication of slums by coordinating city planning, housing, sanitation, and recreational agencies. He also questioned whether McNair, a dry, would enforce liquor regulation after repeal and remarked, "I don't want persecution in the name of temperance."[11]

One mistake marred Henry's active, but unsuccessful, campaign. He exhibited a check signed by the Negro butler of M. L. Benedum, payable to a second Negro and marked "for special assessment purposes." Using this check as evidence, Henry charged Benedum with financing a "huge slush fund" among Hill-district residents. Immediately, Negro leader Robert Vann asserted that Republican organization men worked hand in hand with Henry to obtain this evidence by misrepresenting themselves

9. *Press,* Aug. 26, 1933; ibid., Aug. 29, 1933; ibid., Aug. 31, 1933.
10. *ST*, Sept. 2, 1933, p. 5; *PG*, Sept. 2, 1933, p. 2, Sept. 8, 1933, p. 1; *Press,* Sept. 14, 1933, p. 13, Sept. 15, 1933, p. 25.
11. *ST*, Sept. 13, 1933, p. 10; *Press,* Sept. 9, 1933, p. 3; newspaper clipping, Aug. 27, 1933, Guffey Papers, W & J.

as Democrats, and that the check paid for three days work in distributing handbills. The handbills urged Negroes to become assessed lest they lose their vote in the primary and general elections. "If Mr. Henry can link a six dollar check with a 'slush fund' and accuse the McNair forces of distributing money with a lavish hand, then his conception of the Negro is indeed cheap. Henry forgot that he lost 25,000 Negro votes by taking the check and then accusing Negroes of selling their votes," Vann declared angrily.[12]

It would have indeed been miraculous for Henry to have lost twenty-five thousand Negro votes. Less than twenty-eight hundred Democrats were registered in the two most Negro wards, with the Republicans out-registering the Democrats by more than four to one in the Third Ward and by almost three to one in the Fifth Ward. Despite these odds, Vann's Negro Democratic organization did all it could to win as many Negro voters over to the McNair forces as possible. FDR's New Deal helped. As the primary campaign got under way, Guffey and Lawrence, upon the recommendation of Vann, announced the appointment of five local Negroes to the Pittsburgh office of the Home Owners Loan Corporation. Played off against an article and a table printed in the organization's City-County Colored Democratic Committee's propaganda sheet, *The New Deal Newspaper*, this news aimed to make at least some Negroes think twice. Table 9 is a reproduction of the table that appeared in this newspaper.[13]

The article points out that these obviously approximate figures illustrate the complete disregard that the Republican party had for the Negro. The writer, speaking in the first person, asked: "Negro Voters, are you going to vote for a party that is so flagrantly hostile to us? Awaken, Negroes! Awaken! Again I ask you to see that you are assessed. Get your tax receipt and teach them that we are fools no longer." The Republican high command refused to grant advertising to Vann's *Pittsburgh Courier* because of its Democratic leanings, and the paper made its position regarding the primary election clear when it printed a two-panelled edi-

12. *ST*, Aug. 25, 1933; *Press*, Aug. 25, 1933; *Pittsburgh Courier* (hereafter cited as *Courier*), Sept. 9, 1933.

13. Registration for 1933 from *Press*, Sept. 18, 1933. *New Deal Newspaper* (Pittsburgh), Aug. 20, 1933, Allegheny County Democratic Committee Headquarters Files (hereafter cited as ACDCH), 1933. This newspaper was the official organ of the City-County Colored Democratic Committee.

TABLE 9
How Negroes Are Treated Politically

	Popular Vote	*Percentage*	*Jobs Received*
Italians	14,000	9%	600
Jews	15,000	10	720
Gentiles	66,000	45	2,800
Others	30,000	16	180
Negroes	26,000	16	180
Total	151,000	100	5,100

NOTE: Reprinted from *The New Deal Newspaper,* Aug. 20, 1933.

torial cartoon. The first panel showed closed steel mills, and the second portrayed FDR and McNair walking side by side and carrying a flag emblazoned with the letters "NRA." Dollar signs billowed from the mills' smokestacks, apparently in full use once Roosevelt and McNair took office.[14]

The increasing difficulty in finding Republican party workers began to appear in the Negro areas as well as in the rest of the city. In the Third Ward, one of the best registrars, originally appointed as a Republican, flabbergasted the registration commissioners when she opened McNair headquarters in her district. In the short run, McNair, after doing so well in the Negro wards during the primary, lost them in the general election; in the long run, the Democratic building campaign among Negroes paid off in terms of capturing votes and winning over rank-and-file workers. In the Third Ward more than half the committeemen elected as Republicans in 1934 served in that position as Democrats by 1938, indicating that control of the ward remained in the hands of the same individuals; only their party label had changed. A wholesale movement from the Republican to the Democratic party had occurred.[15]

At one preprimary rally, Dave Lawrence, repeating Vann's comment of a year earlier, told a Negro audience that the Republican party "collected its reward from the colored people for the Emancipation Proclamation" every year since Abraham Lincoln freed the slaves and that it

14. *New Deal Newspaper,* Aug. 20, 1933, ACDCH, 1933; *Courier,* Sept. 9, 1933.
15. *ST,* Sept. 25, 1933. Lists used in the comparison of 1934 Republican committeemen with 1938 Democratic ones were obtained from spring primary election-return books located at Allegheny County Board of Elections, Pittsburgh, Pa. This information is elaborated upon in Chapter VII, where committee lists and various editions of the *City Directory of Pittsburgh* are compared, to obtain occupational information regarding Pittsburgh's party workers.

was time for the Negro to join the Democratic party. McNair picked up the ball when he promised a Negro audience in the Fifth Ward "a square deal for all the people." Generally, however, his campaign centered around the organizational attachment to Franklin Delano Roosevelt and the New Deal.[16]

Full-page advertisements asked that votes be cast for the Roosevelt Democracy; next to every photograph of McNair was one of FDR. A Democratic candidate for city council informed a meeting of the Henry George Club that "every vote cast in the Republican primary is a vote against Roosevelt, a vote against the New Deal, and a vote for the return to power of such reactionary interests and political industrialists as Andrew Mellon." Organization speakers pounded away, night after night, to audience after audience, that Henry played a role in the stop-Roosevelt movement prior to the 1932 convention and that he only "got on the bandwagon after F.D.R.'s nomination."[17]

McNair, himself, kept mentioning Roosevelt. At a major campaign rally he declared, "I am as confident of becoming the next Mayor of Pittsburgh as I am that F.D.R. will pull this country out of the depression before many months have elapsed." Throughout the campaign he attacked Coyne, Mellon, the big utility monopolies, and the high trolley fares, and urged a trackless transportation system for the city. He, too, called for slum eradication and more-efficient running of municipal departments, especially the police, by appointing department heads on the basis of ability rather than politics. However, at one point, equating inefficiency with Republicanism, he noted, "If I am elected I'll clean every Republican out of City Hall. I've seen enough of their work to know how inefficient they are."[18]

McNair's assaults on the utilities were contrary to Henry's claims that M. L. Benedum's backing tied McNair's hands in dealing with the utility companies; the vehement attacks on Mellon and Coyne signified an attempt on the part of the organization to torpedo Henry's charge of an unholy alliance between the Republicans and Lawrence's regular Democrats. In reality, Mellon, as well as the other Republican state power, Joseph P. Grundy, supported Coyne's candidate, Herron, with an eye to

16. *PG*, Sept. 6, 1933; *Courier*, Sept. 16, 1933.
17. *Press*, Aug. 25, 1933; ibid., Aug. 31, 1933; *ST*, Aug. 25, 1933; *PG*, Sept. 4, 1933.
18. *ST*, Sept. 12, 1933; *Press*, Sept. 15, 1933; *PG*, Sept. 15, 1933.

1934. They hoped for Coyne's return of the favor during the next year's gubernatorial and senatorial races, when he could then throw the support of the Pittsburgh machine to their candidate's aid.[19]

Herron premised his campaign on his experience in office, and one of his slogans remonstrated, "Vote for the man you trained." Whereas a McArdle advertisement replied, "Did *you* train Herron or did Coyne?" the newspaper *Unione*, which made no mention at all of the Democrats during the primary campaign, pointed out that it was neither "Coyne nor Mellon, but Herron who demands the vote." Herron believed himself "equipped to give the people of Pittsburgh a sound, conservative, economical and progressive administration." Seeing the need for a "business administration based on some common sense," Herron supported a campaign to "Spend in September, and Buy American—Spend a Dollar and Make a Job" that was run by one of the local newspapers. He rose above partisanship, perhaps because he had little choice in the political climate of the day, by praising the New Deal's National Recovery Administration. He proclaimed: "By aiding the merchants at this time, the stimulation thus given business will go a long way in the restoration of confidence to make possible the recovery which we are all advocating and so earnestly hoping for at the earliest possible time." He advocated economy in government, citing the salary cuts that he and the city council had taken as examples of his faith in that principle's being carried into practice.[20]

All three Republican candidates expended their efforts in opposite directions. The two antiorganization Republican candidates spent their energies attacking each other rather than Herron. McArdle aimed his campaign primarily at the independent voters of Pittsburgh and hoped for a spontaneous upsurge of support at the polls. His political organization appeared extremely loose. Mackrell's campaign seemed to be a mixture of organization and appeal to the independents; he received the endorsement of the United American War Veterans, a group disgruntled with the lack of a soldier's bonus and the first veterans' organization in the district to be organized as a pressure group. Herron and his supporters followed the orthodox organization lines, with ward chairmen and district workers busy day and night. They used all means at their disposal, especially control over the payroll, municipal relief expenditures, and the

19. *ST*, Aug. 27, 1933; *PG*, Sept. 6, 1933; *Press*, Aug. 30, 1933.
20. *ST*, Sept. 13, 1933; *Unione* (Pittsburgh), Sept. 8, 1933; *ST*, Sept. 14, 1933; ibid., Sept. 8, 1933; *Press*, Sept. 15, 1933.

voting machinery, to build, as Mrs. R. Templeton Smith, a Citizens League member, commented, "an organization that would perpetuate the role of the bosses."[21]

The first indication of macing appeared in a blatant fashion. Samuel J. Reno, Republican chairman of the Nineteeenth Ward, summoned that ward's approximately two hundred and fifty city pay-rollers, all party workers, to an evening meeting at the City-County Building. There, in spite of the law prohibiting such a procedure, he told the throng to aid the unfortunates of the ward who could not purchase poll tax receipts by making the purchases for them. Appealing to the party workers' self-interest, he declared: "You know as well as I do that a change in the Administration of this city will mean that the entire organization will pass out for the first time since 1909—and *that our jobs will go with it*. Here we are the organization that comprises about $800,000 of the city's annual payroll and it's up to us to get the voters in our ward to support our candidates" (emphasis added). The meeting then adjourned into district gatherings, and the district leaders, on the spot, figured out how much would be expected of each man. The assessment averaged between five and ten dollars.[22]

At least seven other wards also felt the pinch. In addition, the macing cost deputy coroners twenty dollars apiece to support their boss, and some who were employed by William A. Magee when he was mayor were taxed for his race for councilman. Those still on the city payroll stood in double jeopardy. The assessment deluge, especially after the publicity given to it by Reno's speech, drew immediate fire from Herron as well as the antiorganization candidates. Mackrell called it an "un-American attempt of the city Administration to take part of their [city employees'] already small salaries." Henry, the Democrat, charged that it occurred only "because the people who are the very soul of democracy have permitted a dictatorship of party machine to be fastened upon them." The beneficiary of the payroll's enforced largess, Herron, disclaimed his part in the affair, called for city employees not to take part, and, referring to Reno, bitterly announced: "I hope that the men who are helping me will not do some silly things like going out of their way to hold political meetings in public buildings. We have a headquarters here." However, Herron

21. *ST*, Sept. 17, 1933; *Press*, Sept. 7, 1933; *ST*, Sept. 12, 1933.
22. *Press*, Aug. 29, 1933; *ST*, Aug. 29, 1933.

was not reluctant to use the patronage whip if necessary. When P. J. ("Paddy") Sullivan, a former congressman and Sixth-Ward power, announced support for McArdle, Herron decided to replace as police magistrate Sullivan's son-in-law, William R. McNamara, with one of his own followers.[23]

The political use of relief, which grew so prevalent in Pittsburgh under the Democrats during the later depression years, appeared early in the 1933 Republican primary campaign. In the middle of August, when a *Pittsburgh Sun-Telegraph* reporter found on the city relief payroll a vacationing college boy whose father was steadily employed and whose sister was a schoolteacher, the newspaper editorialized, "Not the Republican chairman, but the recognized welfare agencies should furnish the names of the persons who need relief jobs." At the end of that month, McArdle charged that of the funds voted for work relief in a referendum during the spring of 1932, more than a year earlier, the organization did not permit the spending of the first money until the beginning of the 1933 primary campaign. He also pointed to the building of large and costly work forces (more than twelve hundred men) that duplicated the otherwise routine work of the city's Bureau of Highways and Sewers, and condemned the reduction in hours of experienced workers to provide jobs for political appointees.[24]

A candidate for city council, Robert N. Waddell, who was to be the Republican candidate for mayor four years later, asserted that "ward chairmen in every instance have recommended the employment of the men and women hired, and these appointments number well over 1,000," adding that one of the first appointments as a result of the appropriation was "the ward chairman of the 24th ward, a man reputed to be worth $100,000 to $200,000." A few days later Elmer Holland, head of the Sixteenth Ward Improvement Association, claimed that the city neglected needed improvements in his forgotten South Side ward. He wrote to Mayor Herron: "We do not intend to be a party to your spoils and patronage system. Every member of our organization knows what honest labor is and we do not attack honest labor, but we do object to your using relief money that should be spent in fixing our streets to buy votes."[25]

23. *PG*, Sept. 4, 1933; *ST*, Sept. 30, 1933; *Press*, Aug. 30, 1933; ibid., Aug. 31, 1933.
24. *ST*, Aug. 18, 1933; ibid., Aug. 31, 1933; *Press*, Aug. 31, 1933.
25. *PG*, Sept. 1, 1933; ibid., Sept. 6, 1933; *Press*, Sept. 18, 1933.

Earlier, Herron had denied all such charges and declared that the city council had authorized no relief-work expenditures without the advice of the community's welfare agencies. On the same day of Herron's denial, FDR spoke to officials of the 1933 Mobilization for Human Needs Conference and offhandedly remarked, "There are some cities spending for political purposes instead of purposes of human needs." Some feared that because of the mixing of politics and relief in Pittsburgh, the city would lose out on getting its share of the relief money appropriated by the New Deal legislature. "Already more than a third of the $3,300,000,000 sum has been distributed by the Federal government and it is significant that the city has not received a single penny of the vast sum to date. That is something Mayor Herron might explain . . . ," fretted *The Pittsburgh Press*.[26]

Not only did the Republican organization use relief as a carrot, but it also employed it as a stick. Both McNair and Robert Vann charged that in the economically depressed Negro Fifth Ward, voters who tried to register Democratic were threatened with being cut from the relief rolls. Erasures in the registration books appeared to bear out the claim that police herded fifty voters of the Fifth Ward, Seventeenth District, who registered as Democrats, back to the board and forced them to change their registration or lose their relief aid. McNair attacked such acts by noting: "That's not only commercializing charity. It's prostituting charity!" He also claimed that homeowners delinquent in taxes had been told their homes might be taken unless they changed their registration to Republican and that relatives of Republican apostates were threatened with loss of city jobs, even though covered by civil service.[27]

The third prong of the Republican organization's three-prong campaign to provide its candidate with the 1933 mayoralty nomination, concerned vote and registration frauds. Lincoln Steffens tells how, as early as 1896 in Pittsburgh, the machine counted the reform ticket out in that year's municipal election; the vote frauds perpetrated during the 1931 commissioner's election were common. In 1932 cases of fraud arose in Pittsburgh's Thirtieth and Thirty-second Congressional Districts, with many Republicans, including Coyne, being indicted and a large number

26. *Press*, Sept. 8, 1933; ibid., Sept. 9, 1933, editorial page.
27. Ibid., Sept. 11, 1933; ibid., Sept. 12, 1933; ibid., Sept. 13, 1933; *PG*, Sept. 13, 1933.

finding themselves residents of the federal penitentiary. Democratic Boss Dave Lawrence has noted: "The 1932 Fraud cases, when we got the U.S. Attorney-General to intervene, hurt the Republicans. This was another reason why McNair won—people were fed up with the vote frauds." A New Deal committeeman's comment gives credence to Lawrence's remark. He said: "When McNair ran for mayor, I changed [from a Republican committeeman to a Democratic one]. I didn't like Herron; I was against the Coyne people. I wanted those votes counted!"[28]

The Republican organization also wanted its vote counted, but only in its way. In the Seventeenth Ward a nephew of the local alderman supplied the poll-tax collector with a fifty-cent piece each time a shabbily dressed registrant came forth. Registration rolls of the Twenty-second Ward listed a "James Anderson, Federal Street"; he was subsequently found to be the bronze statue in front of the local library. A Lawrenceville minister allegedly told residents of the Strip district's Second and Sixth Wards what name to use when obtaining a tax receipt. In the organization First Ward the rolls showed three votes from an empty hotel, three from a vacant lot, two from a house that had collapsed, thirteen from a disorderly house, and eleven from an empty building. The Fifth Ward's poll-tax list ran four times larger than in 1932. With approximately sixty-five hundred families living in the area, over twenty thousand voters had been assessed. This proportion caused suspicion in at least one person, who pointed out that in the Fourteenth Ward, having a population of forty thousand, only 11,672 registered for the 1932 presidential election. As a remedy, candidate for councilman William A. Magee urged abolition of the tax qualification and a new state constitution that would provide nonresident overseers and even nonresident members of election boards.[29]

As primary-election day approached, Republican organizational forces attempted to block the usage of voting machines, considered to be more trustworthy than the traditional paper ballots. Foiled in their attempt to

28. Lincoln Steffens, *The Shame of the Cities* (New York, 1957), p. 12; *NYT*, Apr. 30, 1933, sec. 4, p. 6; ibid., June 29, 1933, p. 10; ibid., Apr. 14, 1934, p. 10; *Press*, Nov. 5, 1933; ibid., speech of Lawrence to party workers, Nov. 2, 1936, 1936 Files ACDCH; interview with Lawrence, Apr. 14, 1964; interview with committeeman, 4W2. (To maintain anonymity of committeemen, they are listed by ward and district—hence, 4W2 is read 4th Ward, 2nd District.)

29. *Press*, Aug. 25, 1933; *NYT*, Sept. 17, 1933, sec. 4, p. 6; *ST*, Aug. 25, 1933; *PG*, Sept. 12, 1933; ibid., Sept. 18, 1933.

get the machines examined, a process that could not have been completed until after the primary and therefore would have necessitated resorting to the potentially stuffable ballot box, the regulars found other means of sabotage. On primary-election day, marked as the first for the general use of voting machines in Pittsburgh, the machines broke down in many districts and paper ballots had to be substituted. Although it was generally believed that inexperience, rather than tampering, was responsible, irregularities marked many districts. Mechanics found few instances of genuine breakdown; calls to the election department appeared organized; in one district machines were not even unlocked when the mechanics arrived. Subsequent investigation found in one area Democratic paper ballots hidden in a rubbish pile at the polling place, and in the Sixteenth Ward a party worker was blackjacked when the Republicans stole the ballot box. As a result, an investigating commission advised that the voting machines be used only in the first ten city wards and the three third-class cities of the county, if they were to be effective during the November general election. The Pittsburgh Republican machine lashed out at many targets to preserve its hegemony, and honest elections suffered.[30]

Herron won the Republican nomination, receiving 54 percent of the vote and carrying all but two wards, the Eighteenth and the Twenty-seventh, in which he trailed Mackrell. McArdle, the Citizens League candidate, ran last in the citywide race. Four of the five organization candidates for city council succeeded, but William A. Magee, running as an independent, squeezed on to the Republican ticket. Herron captured a spectacular 92 percent of the machine-controlled Second Ward, where McNair's campaign manager, Cornelius D. Scully, complained that at least one quarter of those who cast a ballot did so illegally. However, the organization candidate received a majority in only eighteen of the city's thirty-two wards. Many of those opposed to Herron in the primary—and 46 percent of the Republicans voting were—would not support him in November. The machine had triumphed, but not overwhelmingly; the Republican party had lost.[31]

A crack in machine solidarity also appeared across the state in Philadelphia. Two independent candidates for the row offices of city treasurer

30. *Press*, Sept. 15, 1933; ibid., Sept. 19, 1933; ibid., Sept. 20, 1933; ibid., Oct. 6, 1933, editorial page; interview with committeeman, 16W5; *Press*, Oct. 21, 1933.
31. Voting statistics were taken from *PG*, Sept. 21, 1933, and were percentaged by author.

and city controller entered the Republican and Democratic primaries and polled a total vote in the two primaries exceeding the combined votes of their opponents. They made a strong showing in the Republican primary against the Vare machine and won the Democratic nomination, ousting the candidates of Vare's Democratic stooge John O'Donnell. A Philadelphia paper exulted: "On Tuesday, for the first time in a generation, the city's voters cut loose from the Vare machine. They licked the plunderbund. They gave their majority support to independent, non-machine candidates." In Pittsburgh, however, the Democratic contest was still the *other* race. The *Pittsburgh Post-Gazette*, in an editorial endorsing McArdle, as an afterthought noted, "The Democrats, too, have a chance for the first time in many years."[32]

The *Post-Gazette* editorial was, if anything, an understatement. McNair carried every ward in the city gaining 88 percent, or 23,365 of the 26,325 total votes cast in the Democratic primary. All five organization candidates for council won nomination. Since thirty thousand registered Republicans stayed home, and approximately sixty thousand Republicans voted for the two antiorganization candidates, some pundits, adding these figures to the thirty-six thousand registered Democrats, foresaw a victory for McNair in the general election. *The Pittsburgh Press* editorialized that McNair, like Roosevelt a year earlier, stood as a focal point for "those who are sick of the old order, who want a New Deal for Pittsburgh as well as the nation." The bolt to the Democrats had begun.[33]

Shortly after the primary, talk grew of running McNair on a third-party ticket in order to ease the political pain for Republicans reluctant to vote Democratic. Then rumors stirred that a McNair headquarters, separated from the regular Democratic one, would be set up in the old Mackrell headquarters in the Hotel Roosevelt. It would be staffed by followers of Mackrell and would exert influence only on the mayoralty campaign. Such a device, however, hardly seemed necessary in the light of the course the campaign took. To exemplify, Herron, a few days after his victory, revealed letters that he had received from two Republicans defeated for council nomination. They congratulated him, one asserting that "all Republicans should earnestly support you in the general elec-

32. *Press*, Sept. 22, 1933; ibid., Sept. 21, 1933; unmarked clipping, Guffey Papers, W & J; *PG*, Sept. 18, 1933.
33. Voting statistics were taken from *PG*, Sept. 21, 1933, and were percentaged by author. *ST*, Oct. 13, 1933; *Press*, Sept. 22, 1933.

tion," the second noting that his victory was decisive enough to "satisfy the most skeptical of your popularity with the people." However, by the end of October both politicians had declared their support for the Democratic ticket.[34]

The McNair forces made a concerted effort to attract the independents and the dissident Republicans to their candidate. Edward Leech, the vehemently anti-Coyne editor of *The Pittsburgh Press*, suggested to the Democratic leader, Dave Lawrence—who agreed—that the party drop one of its council candidates and replace him with William Magee. The ex-Mayor had a large independent following, and Leech reasoned that with Magee on the Democratic, as well as the Republican, ticket, McNair would definitely receive independent support. In addition, the editor pledged his paper to a pro-McNair propaganda campaign. Almost daily throughout the campaign *The Pittsburgh Press* published stories telling of one or another important independent who had shifted to McNair. Hearst's *Pittsburgh Sun-Telegraph* also played up the endorsements, but leaned toward Herron. However, the *Pittsburgh Post-Gazette* stressed independent shifts to Herron and, in comparison with its competitors, tempered its play of the campaign.[35]

Although the Citizens League failed to endorse McNair, it showed no sentiment toward Herron, and its members individually supported the Democrat. Leslie M. Johnston, the group's president, personally endorsed all the Democratic candidates. He charged that under Republican rule the affairs of Pittsburgh had been "criminally mismanaged" and added that the only way to change the condition "is to vote out of power in November the men responsible for this." Day after day, following the strategy of a planned campaign, one after another prominent Republican announced his bolt to McNair. James F. Malone, former president of city council, threw his support to the Democratic candidate; William P. Witherow, executive member of the Citizens League, declared for McNair; Mrs. R. Templeton Smith joined the anti-Coyne ranks; all the members of the Citizens League who served as ward chairmen came over to McNair—after having been promised a slice of the patronage pie. Even half of Herron's opposition in the primary, Joseph N. Mackrell, swung

34. *Press*, Sept. 23, 1933; *ST*, Oct. 13, 1933; *PG*, Nov. 1, 1933.
35. Interview with Lawrence, Apr. 14, 1964; *Press*, Oct. 8, 1933; ibid., Oct. 10, 1933.

to the Democrats. One ward leader, after noting that *The Pittsburgh Press* printed a new endorsement each day, remarked, "Well, that is pretty good campaigning."[36]

Although *The Pittsburgh Press* printed a full-page advertisement listing the names of all shifters, the name of the Citizens League's primary candidate was missing. McArdle's reluctance to endorse McNair raised much regret among his former supporters; they desired solidarity, but McArdle remained with the Republicans. One Republican candidate for council branded those who left the party as "political guerrillas." Of Mackrell's and Malone's bolting, Herron told a huge rally: "Well do you know how much the party misses them? Just about as much as we'd miss two small boys who got up and left this audience." As for the support that Mrs. Smith's League of Women Voters gave McNair, Herron proclaimed, "They are going to have an awful time controlling both parties, so the Republican organization won't be the only one harassed."[37]

Despite massive defections, several important Republicans remained at Herron's side. The *Pittsburgh Post-Gazette* seemed to approve their loyalty by declaring that Lawrence's calls for independent backing, and its receipt, merely aided him in building his own organization, and that Pittsburgh's activity for McNair was not a sincere fusion movement similar to New York City's nonpartisan program then beginning under the aegis of Fiorello H. La Guardia. McNair was running on a Democratic, not a Fusion, ticket, the paper complained.[38]

Many repeated the charges hurled by Henry during the primary contest. "If the Democrats win, don't you think Mr. Guffey and Mr. Lawrence will simply try to replace the Coyne-Mellon combination with their own machine . . . ?" asked a letter writer who signed himself Real Independent. Democratic champions denied this accusation and pointed out that their party's threat was potential and theoretical, whereas the existence of the Republican machine stood tangibly before everyone's eyes. They stressed that in any event a two-party tradition should be fostered, and if a Democratic machine did arise, the public could vote it out. Regardless of this dialogue between the opposing sides, the defections

---

36. *ST*, Oct. 14, 1933; ibid., Oct. 15, 1933; *Press*, Oct. 15, 1933; ibid., Oct. 22, 1933; ibid., Oct. 24, 1933; *PG*, Oct. 28, 1933; ibid., Oct. 21, 1933; *Press*, Oct. 20, 1933; ibid., Oct. 29, 1933, editorial page.
   37. *ST*, Oct. 25, 1933; *PG*, Nov. 3, 1933.
   38. *Press*, Oct. 19, 1933; *PG*, Oct. 19, 1933; ibid., Oct. 24, 1933; ibid., Oct. 27, 1933; ibid., Nov. 3, 1933; ibid., Nov. 4, 1933.

from Herron discouraged many Republicans. Although the organization Republicans eventually received for their candidate the endorsement of U.S. Senator David A. Reed, they resented his refusal to speak in Pittsburgh, his home district. Reed, seeing so many independent Republicans for McNair and looking to his own campaign for reelection the next year, stayed aloof from Pittsburgh although he spoke in other areas in the state.[39]

In line with previous successful strategy, the city council appropriated a second $300,000 for work relief, and men laid off after the primary again appeared on the payroll. However lackluster and defensive, the Herron campaign, like the tone of his primary fight, said little beyond making a plea that the incumbent mayor and council be continued in office. He cited his and council's experience in municipal affairs and pointed out that a big premium paid for an issue of municipal bonds illustrated the good health of the city's financial credit. Refuting both points, the Democrats noted that experience had become synonymous with stagnation and that Pittsburgh had to borrow $250,000 to meet its payroll. In addition, they pointed out that the city ended the previous year with a $1.5 million deficit that could be expected to increase.[40]

Criticism of the NRA by one Republican damaged the party's campaign efforts. During a speech to Twenty-seventh-Ward Republican workers at the party's headquarters in the Hotel Henry, William H. Coleman, Republican county leader, lashed out at Roosevelt and the NRA. Coleman arraigned the president for "destroying cotton, wheat and hogs while people are starving" and added: "The N.R.A. is wrong and never will succeed. The first ones to destroy it will be the Democrats themselves." The attack came as a surprise because of a speech delivered by Herron earlier at the same headquarters denying charges that the Republican candidates were hostile to the Roosevelt administration. The next day the mayor declared, "The N.R.A. deserves the support of every man and woman in Pittsburgh interested in Recovery" and referred to his being honorary chairman of the local NRA committee and of local Republican support for the NRA parade held in Pittsburgh. He also could have alluded to his support for Amendment Number 8, a $25 million state relief bond issue, to be voted on at the election and made necessary by the ex-

39. *Press,* Sept. 27, 1933, editorial page; ibid., Oct. 3, 1933, editorial page; ibid., Oct. 22, 1933, editorial page; ibid., Nov. 1, 1933.
40. *Press,* Oct. 25, 1933; ibid., Oct. 29, 1933, editorial page; *PG,* Oct. 25, 1933.

haustion of Pennsylvania relief funds, as well as his advocacy of pensions for the blind.[41]

However, the damage had been done. Democratic County Leader David Lawrence declared that on November 7 voters would cast their ballots for "N.R.A. and other important issues," the pro-McNair *Pittsburgh Press* printed a front-page editorial, asking in large type, "Which Do You Want—N.R.A. or the Coyne-Mellon System?" Robert Vann claimed, "That remark made by Coleman . . . drove more Republicans into the [Democratic] camp than any remark that has been made in this part of the state in a quarter of a century." In private Republican leaders agreed; they believed Coleman's attack to be the greatest blunder of the campaign. Several years later, after presiding over Republican defeats in 1932, 1933, and 1934, Coleman an unreconstructed anti-New Dealer, told an audience: "I am one of those Republicans who opposed the New Deal philosophy in Washington. I so expressed myself in October, 1933 and my good friend John S. Herron, then a candidate for mayor of Pittsburgh, and many of his supporters believed that my speech contributed much to his defeat. I could not help it. I was afraid of the destruction of my country. . . ."[42]

The Democrats, too, faced intraparty squabbles. Outbreaks over potential patronage broke out between old-time ward officials and newly formed Democratic clubs. Although the dormant ward organizations of pre-1932 perked up with the FDR victory, a younger group of Democrats decided that perhaps the best method to revive the party would be the establishment of political clubs outside the control of the central organization. In some districts they met with such success that the old-time leaders feared for their political lives. However, the Roosevelt name served as a unifying force, and eventually all factions were drawn into the central organization, with the older members occasionally being displaced.[43]

As a *New York Times* correspondent commented, "The proverbial

41. *Press*, Oct. 25, 1933; ibid., Oct. 26, 1933; ibid., Oct. 22, 1933; ibid., Oct. 26, 1933; *PG*, Oct. 23, 1933.
42. *Press*, Oct. 25, 1933; ibid., Oct. 26, 1933; *Courier*, Oct. 28, 1933; speeches of William S. Coleman, undated speech mss. and undated clipping from *PG*, Archives of Industrial Society 64:18, University of Pittsburgh, Pittsburgh, Pa.
43. *PG*, Oct. 28, 1933. Interviews with committeemen 15W8 and 19W21 indicate such clubs were active in the 15th and 19th Wards; as cited in Chapter 2, 16W12 was an old-timer displaced by the change in party structure.

visitor from Mars might indeed get the notion that it is Mr. Roosevelt himself who is running for Mayor of Pittsburgh." Unswerving from their strategy in the primary, the Democrats attached themselves to FDR, and the president didn't seem to mind. Two weeks after McNair's primary victory, James A. Farley, en route from Columbus, Ohio, to New York City, stopped off in Pittsburgh for twenty minutes. When McNair, Lawrence and his wife, and other Democrats met the national chairman at the railroad station, Farley emphasized that a Pittsburgh win and a large Democratic turnout in Philadelphia during the 1933 elections would greatly influence the possibility of a party victory for governor and senator in 1934. He remarked: "Washington, naturally, is much interested in Mr. McNair's campaign. We hope Pittsburgh does as well for him as it did for President Roosevelt and we are informed that there is an excellent chance for his election." Herron did not appreciate Washington's interference and bitterly warned Republicans, "If Farley were to take charge of City Hall we know what would happen to Republican workers."[44]

Although Republicans repeatedly labeled their opponents as Pittsburgh Democrats seeking office, not Roosevelt candidates, many others agreed with James Malone that McNair was the "personification of the New Deal in the Administration of the affairs of the city of Pittsburgh." The Republicans, looking to FDR's lack of support for that year's Democratic mayoralty candidate in New York City, where he said he would back no local candidate, claimed that this dictum applied to Pittsburgh, as well. However, the Pittsburgh Democrats premised their campaign in this linkage between Roosevelt and the local candidate; it worked so well that it became the strategy for the 1934 gubernatorial and senatorial election throughout the state.[45]

Aside from the overriding issue of Roosevelt and the New Deal, McNair, as he did in the primary, lashed out at Coyne and Mellon, the utilities, a local garbage disposal monopoly, the Republican organization's protection of the underworld; and he came as close as possible to calling for an unqualified single tax, without employing the specific term.

44. *NYT*, Nov. 5, 1933, sec. 4, p. 7; *Press*, Oct. 1, 1933; ibid., Oct. 19, 1933.
45. *Press*, Oct. 24, 1933; ibid., Oct. 25, 1933; ibid., Oct. 28, 1933; *ST*, Oct. 28, 1933; Edward J. Flynn, *You're the Boss: The Practice of American Politics* (New York, 1962), pp. 151–153; Edwin B. Bonner, "The New Deal Comes to Pennsylvania: The Gubernatorial Election of 1934," *Pennsylvania History*, XXVII (June 1960), 51, 58, 66.

On the last issue he espoused a graded-tax law to be extended to a point where the levy on land would reach five times that on buildings. (The existing system of assessment taxed buildings half as much as land.) McNair's critics suspiciously whispered that M. L. Benedum, the candidate's major financial backer, owned a skyscraper and would certainly benefit if such a system would become law.[46]

Exonerating Herron, but indicting Coyne, McNair declared: "Coyne represents everything evil in the community. Who levies tribute on houses of ill fame? The toll levied on them fills the coffers of the Republican machine to buy your votes, so Coyne can remain in power. Jack Herron has nothing to do with this. He may be a good man, but behind him is the sinister face of Coyne." Herron apparently did not disagree to any great extent. While speaking at the University of Pittsburgh, he was asked by a shiny-faced student, "Is State Senator James J. Coyne boss of the Republican Party?" The mayor answered: "It all depends on what you call a boss. He is very prominent." Coyne, himself, summed up his political philosophy when he asserted at a Republican rally, "All a nice man ever gets is a big wedding and a quiet funeral."[47]

Of all the issues during the campaign, "Coyneism" stands as the most misleading. Coyne, even in his heydey, was a boss of only a portion of his party; he had the last word on all Allegheny County affairs in the state legislature, where he killed welfare legislation and new election laws. His recognition, however, had come through designation by a single man and not because he could dominate any election contest at will. After the eclipse of Mayor Kline, State Republican Chairman Edward Martin complied with the disgraced mayor's request for him to recognize Coyne in state affairs. However, Coyne, impatient of advice, prone to ballooning petty differences, never really built a mass base for himself, thus never having a clear title to the rank of boss. The propaganda attacks of the Democratic candidates, the dissident Republican independents, and *The Pittsburgh Press*, nevertheless, combined to portray his as evil incarnate.[48]

To avoid being linked to the politics he claimed that Coyne practiced, and to allay the fears of Republicans whom he hoped to win to his side,

46. *PG*, Oct. 19, 1933; *ST*, Nov. 5, 1933; *PG*, Nov. 6, 1933; ibid., Oct. 26, 1933.
47. *PG*, Oct. 28, 1933; *ST*, Nov. 2, 1933; *Press*, Nov. 4, 1933.
48. *Press*, Sept. 24, 1933, editorial page; *ST*, Nov. 12, 1933.

McNair, at the beginning of the campaign, retracted his threat made during the primary battle to "clean every Republican out of City Hall." He broadened the statement to include "every political parasite"—including Democratic drones—and promised to take the police and fire departments out of politics. The city workers, told that they would lose their jobs if their districts swung to McNair, could rest easily; the candidate would brook no "Coyneism"; he would break with years of Pittsburgh tradition.[49]

Early in his campaign McNair shattered precedent when, for the first time in Pittsburgh history, a candidate addressed an Italian-American audience in its mother tongue. The north side meeting, which packed Carnegie Music Hall with standing room only, was the first ever sponsored by and devoted to Italian-American citizens exclusively, and reflected the rise of Italians to prominence in Pittsburgh's polyglot population. In 1910 Italians composed 10 percent of the total foreign born in the city; by 1940 they represented 19 percent of this group and ranked first among all foreign born, a position they had already occupied by 1930. The crowd's enthusiasm reached crescendo heights when the candidate mentioned the names of Columbus, Marconi, and Balboa (a Spaniard); Mussolini's name was greeted with great ovations when mentioned by other speakers. In understandable Italian, McNair opened with a flowery reference to the great heritage of Italy, "the garden of Europe." Then he spoke of the system of placing a high tax on "economic rents" to relieve the tax burden on small homeowners, and said that this idea originated with an Italian, Filanger—and Ben Franklin.[50]

During the primary campaign, the Italian newspaper *Unione* had made no mention of the Democrats at all. After the primary it praised the Herron victory, editorializing that the "battle may be bitter if Italians don't close ranks and gather around Herron. The victory will be ours if the community understands that having a man like Herron will be to our interest. . . . He knows he owes his victory to the Italians—and he will not forget it. Vote for our Herron." However, in its issue immediately before the election, instead of pressuring for Herron, the paper published open letters by both McNair and Herron supporters. The latter pledged

49. *PG*, Sept. 15, 1933; ibid., Oct. 19, 1933; *Press*, Oct. 20, 1933.
50. *Press*, Oct. 24, 1933, p. 2; "Vital Facts—Countries of Origin of Leading Foreign Born Groups in Pittsburgh," *The Federator*, XIX (June 1944), 19–20; *ST*, Oct. 27, 1933; *Press*, Oct. 27, 1933.

support for FDR and claimed Herron had followed him step by step; the former stressed that McNair "mirrors all your aspirations because he knows and understands you and your language." It continued that Italians often suffer because of the language barrier—"You make your voice louder than others if it is understood." McNair, in closing his talk to the Italians, had followed the same vein when he called on them to mount a guard on election day, adding, "The moment they start cheating, let's start to fight."[51]

The abandonment of the use of voting machines for the election necessitated such a fight. Ultimately, the Election Board ruled out the use of a device designed to prevent voting more than once for a candidate listed on two tickets, when it was found not to operate properly. With GOP candidates listed on both the Republican and Citizens party ticket, a voter would have been able to cast a ballot for his choice on both lines. As a result, four paper ballots went into use on election day, complicating the electoral process and opening it once again to fraud. The first ballot listed the candidates for city and county office; the second carried the twelve constitutional amendments; the third concerned the restriction on Sunday sports; the fourth was the referendum on repeal of prohibition. On the last two issues in a local-option election, Pittsburgh voters rolled up a better than six to one majority for legalizing Sunday baseball and football. In a like manner Pittsburghers voted almost seven to one for repeal, whereas repeal passed in the county by approximately five and a half to one and in the state by four to one. Although repeal and Sunday sports were the focus of controversy in neighboring Wilkinsburg, they were not issues in the Pittsburgh municipal election; neither candidate alluded to the issues in his speeches.[52]

At the final Democratic rally of the campaign, Lawrence announced

51. *Unione*, Sept. 1, 1933; ibid., Sept. 8, 1933; ibid., Sept. 15, 1933; ibid., Sept. 22, 1933; ibid., Nov. 3, 1933.
52. *Press*, Oct. 27, 1933; ibid., Oct. 26, 1933; ibid., Oct. 29, 1933; ibid., Nov. 9, 1933; *ST*, Nov. 2, 1933. The Pittsburgh newspapers printed only the votes concerning Sunday sports and repeal for boroughs and townships, not for city wards. The actual return books for these referendums were located at the Allegheny County Board of Elections, but they were blank. Two groups that lobbied for Sunday sports and repeal, the Western Pennsylvania Brewers Association and the Pittsburgh Steelers football team, did not possess records of the voting data. Thus, the vote for Mayor McNair could not be correlated to the vote on sports and repeal of prohibition, in order to see if there was any relationship between his support and the support for and against the referendum issues.

to an audience of faithfuls, "I am positive we are going to elect the next Mayor of Pittsburgh, although the Republican machine has been planning to make a super effort to steal the election." In anticipation of such a possibility, the Democratic organization took multiple precautions: it organized an army of overseers and watchers to work at the polls; it printed an eight-page pamphlet instructing the election workers as to their rights and their duties, as well as detailing all possibilities of fraud; it demanded, and received, State Police surveillance on election day; it assigned a corps of lawyers to the Democratic headquarers, so that no time would be lost in going to court; it requested that judges of the common pleas court be available all night, so that petitions could be presented to them for impounding ballot boxes if need be; it raised a fund to supply the fifty dollars required to impound each ballot box. To muster the Democratic vote, Joe Guffey sent a postcard to every registered Democrat, asking him to obtain a pledge of support for the minority party from two Republican voters and providing space for the signatures of the potential apostates.[53]

Although the Democrats attempted to cover all possible election-day contingencies, reports of fraud again marred the balloting. In spite of the Democrats' outfitting an army of poll watchers, the GOP, through a combination with its auxiliary Citizens party, mustered twice as many. Chain voting, that is, the handing out of marked ballots plus a small bribe to voters, was reported in the First and Twenty-seventh Wards; voters received unlawful assistance on the north side and in many Oakland districts; a Republican gang, led by Coyne's brother, intimidated a Fourteenth-Ward overseer into signing blank ballots. Nevertheless, such Republican activities could not stem the Democratic tide in Pittsburgh.[54]

Events proved prophetic McNair's final statement, made on the eve of the election. He had optimistically declared, "We will win tomorrow in the same decisive manner that Franklin D. Roosevelt won last year." FDR had won 58 percent of the city's vote; McNair garnered 57 percent. He carried three quarters of the city's wards, beating Herron in the mayor's home ward, the Thirteenth. Besides, his victory in the Fifteenth Ward broke a stronghold for Coyne. The victory swept into office the entire

53. *PG*, Nov. 3, 1933; ibid., Nov. 1, 1933; *Press*, Nov. 5, 1933; ibid., Nov. 2, 1933; ibid., Nov. 1, 1933.
54. *Press*, Nov. 8, 1933; ibid., Nov. 7, 1933; ibid., Nov. 8, 1933.

Democratic slate for city council. In fact, the Democrats won every city office, one seat in the legislature, the sheriff's office, and a newly created juvenile court judgeship. The Republicans held on to only three common pleas and two county judgeships, and the coroner's office. The one-sided victory delighted Roosevelt, and a White House aide wired Guffey and Lawrence, "Congratulations to the Gold Dust twins—Col. Joe and Captain Davey."[55]

In the light of the strong attachment of the Democrats to FDR during the campaign, it is not surprising to find most contemporary observers agreeing with Joe Guffey that the election was an approval of "the gospel of government laid down by Roosevelt." The editors of the *Pittsburgh Sun-Telegraph* believed that the election results "showed that the Democratic tidal wave of 1932 hadn't spent its force." A columnist for the rival *Pittsburgh Post-Gazette* noted that "both independent and organization wards were turning in votes that savored strongly of the Roosevelt vote last year. . . ." In retrospect, McNair, himself, remarked, "They were voting for Roosevelt—they didn't care anything about me."[56]

However, subsequent analysis does not support the contemporary rhetoric. Far from an extension of Roosevelt's vote, McNair's support rested with a different group of voters from those who cast their ballots for FDR in 1932. Comparing both candidates' vote by highest to lowest support in the city's thirty-two wards, no high association is found.[57] (See table 10.) Whereas McNair lost every one of the Republican organization's tightly controlled first six wards of the city, Roosevelt had lost only the Second and the Fifth. The Republican machine, which had abandoned its campaign against the certain winner Roosevelt, fought McNair tooth and nail; there were no surprises in the so-called controlled wards.[58]

Despite the efforts of Robert Vann and his Negro Democratic organization, the Negro Third and Fifth Wards were listed among those carried by Herron. To counter widespread rumors of Republican vote buying— as high as ten dollars a vote—Vann's *Pittsburgh Courier* had told its readers to "take the money, put it in your pocket and then go to the polls

55. *PG*, Nov. 7, 1933; ibid., Nov. 9, 1933; *Press*, Nov. 8, 1933; *ST*, Nov. 9, 1933; telegram, Lela Stiles to Joseph Guffey, Nov. 8, 1933, PPF 451, FDRL.

56. *ST*, Oct. 23, 1933; ibid., Nov. 8, 1933; *PG*, Nov. 8, 1933; ibid., Feb. 20, 1935.

57. Correlation examples are listed in Appendix C.

58. Voting statistics were taken from *Press*, Nov. 9, 1933 (percentaged by author), and from *Pennsylvania Manual*, 1933 ed. (published yearly by commonwealth for its legislature); *ST*, Nov. 5, 1933.

TABLE 10

Coefficients of Correlation Between Roosevelt and McNair Votes, and Between Both Votes and Ethnic and Economic Data

	FDR '32	McNair '33
McNair '33	.16	—
Native stock '30	−.36	.54
Foreign stock '30	.63	−.27
Foreign born '30	.60	−.48
Foreign-born Italian '30	−.06	−.48
Unemployed '34	.35	−.56

NOTE: Table is based on Wards 1–32. See Appendix C.

and vote the straight Democratic ticket for the protection of yourself, your home, your children." Unfortunately for the Democrats, whether they accepted the money or not, too many of his readers failed to heed the editor's call to join their ranks. Nevertheless, Paul Ford Jones, chairman of the City-County Colored Democratic Committee, took a more optimistic view when he addressed his coworkers; said Jones, "Despite the intimidation of the Police Department, racketeer's money and whisky, our Democratic organization not only succeeded in keeping down the Republican majority, but actually carried some of the districts conceded [to] the G.O.P. in the campaign." Two weeks after the election, Negro Democrats organized a permanent party organization in the city's Third Ward.[59]

As seen in table 10, McNair appealed not to the lower-economic-class Negroes and other ethnic groups, but to the upper-income, native-white population. The silk stockings definitely had cast their lot with McNair. Whereas his support was significantly weak in areas of high unemployment, FDR's backing of a year earlier had been much stronger. Although Roosevelt had received little support from the city's native-white community, McNair obtained strong backing in wards with high native population. Concomitantly, the reverse held for the foreign community's support for the candidates. The foreign-born Italians, for whom McNair made such a big pitch during his campaign, gave him even less backing than Roosevelt had received from that ethnic group. This fact, however, did not prevent *Unione* from mistakenly viewing McNair's victory "as an Italian victory like La Guardia's in New York City." It continued, "Italians are no longer voting and acting like sheep," apparently

59. *Courier*, Nov. 4, 1933; ibid., Nov. 11, 1933; ibid., Nov. 18, 1933.

implying that they were voting more independently than ever before. In the Pittsburgh election of 1933, however, they made little break with their previous Republican tradition.[60]

These conclusions are born out by isolating the wards where McNair made his greatest gains over Roosevelt's vote the year before.[61] Among these, the Seventh, the Twenty-eighth and the Fourteenth stand out as the ones that show the greatest gain. They also were among those wards with the highest native-stock population, as well as among those with the lowest proportion of unemployed in 1934. (See table 11.) They gave La Follette his least support; nor did Smith carry them in 1928; however, they were the only ones to go Democratic during the mayoralty election of 1929, indicating their high-economic, low-ethnic base, as well as their independence from Republican-machine control.[62]

TABLE 11
Wards Showing Greatest McNair Gains Over Roosevelt Vote of 1932, with Demographic Comparisons

Greatest Gains	Rank Native Stock '30[a]	Rank Unemployed '34[a]
Ward 7	1	31
Ward 28	5	29
Ward 14	11	32

a. Rank is based on thirty-two wards.

On the other hand, among the wards where McNair suffered his greatest losses in comparison with Roosevelt's 1932 vote, the Sixth, the First and the Third show the most pronounced losses. Among the oldest in the city, they were lower-economic, working-class, ethnic wards. Hard hit

60. Voting statistics were taken from *Press*, Nov. 9, 1933, and *Pennsylvania Manual*, 1933 ed. and were percentaged by author; 1930 population statistics are from Bureau of Social Research, Federation of Social Agencies of Pittsburgh and Allegheny County, *Social Facts About Pittsburgh and Allegheny County*, vol. I, *Pittsburgh Wards* (Pittsburgh, 1945); 1934 unemployment statistics are from J. P. Watson, *Economic Background of the Relief Problem* (Pittsburgh, 1937), p. 46. Watson cites unpublished statistics of Emmett H. Welch, director of research and statistics, Pennsylvania State Emergency Relief Board. *Unione*, Nov. 10, 1933.
61. These wards and those where McNair suffered his greatest losses in comparison to the 1932 Roosevelt vote are listed in Appendix D.
62. Voting statistics were taken from *Pennsylvania Manual*, 1925, 1929, 1933 eds.; *Press*, Nov. 9, 1933; and ibid., Nov. 6, 1929; 1930 population statistics are from *Social Facts*, vol. 1, *Pittsburgh Wards*; 1934 unemployment statistics are from Watson, *Relief Problems*, p. 46.

by unemployment in 1934, they suffered most from the depression. (See table 12.) However, in these areas concentrated activity by the Republican organization, contrasted to the lack of it during the 1932 campaign, probably accounts more for the discrepancy between the presidential and the mayoralty votes than do the demographic characteristics. These were among the least independent wards in the city.[63]

TABLE 12
Wards Showing Greatest McNair Losses from Roosevelt Vote of 1932, with Demographic Comparisons

Greatest Losses	Rank Native Stock '30[a]	Rank Unemployed '34[a]
Ward 6	30	5
Ward 1	26	2
Ward 3	32	1

a. Rank is based on thirty-two wards.

The McNair vote lay outside the growing Democratic strength generated by La Follette and culminating with Roosevelt; it represented a local, independent strength—a vote of a Pittsburgh citizenry disillusioned with the jaded Republican machine. The local discontent filtered down also to the voting for city council when Pittsburgh cast its ballots for the Democratic candidates for councilman, regardless of their political coloration, in the same manner as they did for McNair. Isolating the vote for two candidates for councilman of opposing ideologies, Thomas J. Gallagher and Walter R. Demmler, one finds an extremely high correlation between each candidate's support and McNair's mayoralty vote, indicating straight-ticket voting during the election; concomitantly, a weak relationship with Roosevelt's 1932 presidential support appears. Gallagher, an Irish-Catholic labor leader who went out to work at the age of twelve and claimed firsthand knowledge of "what it meant to be exploited," began his political career in 1924 as chairman of the La Follette campaign committee in the Sixteenth and Seventeenth Wards. He subsequently supported a wide variety of labor and social legislation while a member of the state legislature. Yet, in 1933 Gallagher received a vote for council as closely related to McNair's as did Demmler, a German-Lutheran businessman who, like the mayor, advocated a single

63. *ST*, Nov. 5, 1933. See fn. 62.

tax and who would be the only council member to defend McNair in many of his future tumultous battles with that body.[64]

The import of the local character of the balloting and the effect of straight-ticket voting is further made evident when one considers the labor records of Gallagher and McNair. The same areas that voted for the pro-labor Gallagher supported McNair, who had a record unfavorable to labor. McNair's attitude was highlighted later, in his administration, when in July 1934, during the general strike being waged in San Francisco, the Pittsburgh mayor called on his constituents to forfeit union membership rather than be led in civil war. By February 1935 the Pittsburgh Central Labor Council was demanding the mayor's ouster for various reasons including the fact that he "aided and abetted strikebreakers hired to break the ranks of organized workers. . . ." The vote also illustrates, as might be expected because of Gallagher's political and labor background, that his vote, in relation to McNair's and Demmler's, shows the strongest correlation with Roosevelt's. The relationship, however, is not high.[65] (See table 13.)

The pragmatic Democratic organization, in its wooing of independent support, unconsciously retarded its own consolidation. These voters were more committed to McNair than to his party. The new mayor's mass base was his, not the organization's—and the organization, to its regret, would learn that fact all too soon. Although McNair ran as a Roosevelt Democrat, his support did not lie within the Roosevelt coalition. The Democratic organization helped elect not a New Dealer, but an old-line progressive. William Nissley McNair would have felt more at home with the turn-of-the-century progressive mayors such as Hazen S. Pingree of Detroit, Samuel M. ("Golden Rule") Jones of Toledo, New York's Seth Low, Jersey City's Mark M. Fagan, and Cleveland's Thomas Lofton Johnson, than with his New Deal contemporaries.

Like Fagan and Johnson, McNair espoused Henry George's single tax, and like Johnson, to whom he often compared himself, McNair was a Jeffersonian Democrat. No New Dealer, he once remarked, "I believe the least government is the best government." Just as Johnson had gained

64. Voting returns for Gallagher and Demmler were taken from *Press*, Nov. 9, 1933, and were percentaged by author. Interview with Gallagher, July 27, 1965; clippings from Gallagher File, PD, CL; clipping from *Press*, Apr. 17, 1937, Demmler File, PD, CL.

65. *Press*, July 18, 1937; ibid., Feb. 24, 1935; *NYT*, July 19, 1934, p. 1.

TABLE 13
Coefficients of Correlation Between Votes for Candidates

	FDR '32	McNair '33	Demmler '33
Gallagher '33	.36	.94	.95
Demmler '33	.27	.95	—
McNair '33	.16	—	—

NOTE: Table is based on Wards 1–32. See Appendix E.

fame because of his plan of municipal ownership of public transportation, or the "three-cent fare," McNair, a quarter of a century later, called for the "five-cent fare." He expressed a belief in going directly to the people, paralleling Johnson's eight-year campaign for the political education of the citizens of Cleveland. When the Democratic organization finally caught up with McNair and drove him from office, after regretting their support of the recalcitrant mayor, McNair proclaimed that he knew he was doomed from the start because of the experience of "another man— Mayor Tom Johnson of Cleveland. He had the same ideas that I have, the same philosophy of government. He believed in economic rent. They got him. They shortened his life."[66]

"They" would take less than two years to get McNair, but during that time he would make the life of the Democratic organization miserable. Thus, as one machine crumbled to dust in the fall of 1933, another, like the phoenix, rose from the ruins. Before it could take full flight, however, it would have to rid itself of a burdensome weight—the mayor it helped elect. Upon his victory McNair promised the public a "New Deal at City Hall" and pledged to show the nation that Pittsburgh stood squarely behind President Roosevelt's program of national recovery. He would do nothing of the kind.[67]

66. Clipping from *ST*, Oct. 7, 1936, McNair Scrapbooks, PD, CL; George E. Mowry, *The Era of Theodore Roosevelt, 1900–1912* (New York, 1958), pp. 62–64. For a perceptive study of the relationship between progressives and New Dealers, see Otis L. Graham, Jr., *Encore for Reform: The Old Progressives and the New Deal* (New York, 1967).
67. *Press*, Nov. 8, 1933.

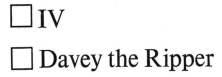

☐ IV
☐ Davey the Ripper

Davey Lawrence thought I was going to be a puppet. Poor Davey, he certainly was fooled.

William McNair to Howard Browning,
Pittsburgh Sun-Telegraph, *June 16, 1936*

☐ Paradoxically, the turbulent McNair years started on a note of harmony for the mayor-elect, the regular Democratic organization, and the president of the United States. Immediately after his victory McNair was ushered to the White House by Joe Guffey and Dave Lawrence, where FDR, after being told that his guest was one of the original Roosevelt men in Allegheny County, jubilantly clasped his hand and instructed the triumphant candidate, "Now give the people of Pittsburgh a good Administration." Back home McNair lauded the president as "a man of the people," declaring, "There's nothing false about him." Nevertheless, within a year's time the mayor would cable Al Smith volunteering to join the Liberty League and commenting, "I can criticize Roosevelt, if necessary." He found it necessary.[1]

This turnabout included a change in relations with the local organiza-

---

1. *Pittsburgh Post-Gazette* (hereafter cited as *PG*), Nov. 11, 1933; ibid., Nov. 18, 1933; clipping from *Pittsburgh Sun-Telegraph* (hereafter cited as *ST*), Sept. 5, 1934, McNair Scrapbooks, Pennsylvania Division, Carnegie Library (hereafter cited as PD, CL), Pittsburgh, Pa.

tion, as well as with Washington. From the very beginning McNair's antics as mayor alienated the party regulars. He announced that he would put his desk in the lobby of the City-County Building so that the public would have free access to their chief executive. Apparently without thought as to how the practical politicians might feel, he declared to a group of ministers that if they were to recommend a candidate for director of public safety, a position abounding in patronage, he would give him favorable consideration. Few took him seriously. Stories of his eccentricities began to spread, leading Robert Vann to theorize that they got into print for the express purpose of building newspaper circulation. "Of course, McNair is going to have a private office and not going to sit in the lobby. Nobody believes that preachers are going to select the Director of Public Safety," noted the editor.[2]

On inaugural day the first Democratic mayor since 1906 told a multitude of job seekers attending the not-too-solemn occasion, "Come up and talk it over." Contrary to Vann's belief, McNair fulfilled his promise to meet with the public in the lobby of the City-County Building, and the public stormed downtown to take him up on his offer, practically tearing off a door leading to the city council chamber. Eventually, forced to move up to the mayor's office because of the lobby's lack of heat, McNair maintained an open-door policy. On a visit to Pittsburgh, Walter Davenport, of Collier's magazine, witnessed McNair as he fielded questions from inquiring constituents about room rentals, dressmakers, and other extraneous matters. He concluded, "I don't recall off hand, ever meeting an important placeholder so oblivious to what the rest of the crowd was thinking."[3]

If "the rest of the crowd" meant the regular Democratic organization, the Collier's correspondent could not have been more correct. The high jinks during his first weeks in office portended the stormy, comic and sometimes sad days ahead. During his aborted term in office, McNair's crusades against high transit fares, the utilities, and the numbers racket came to little; his prolific use of the veto and his noncooperation with local and federal relief authorities delayed Pittsburgh's joining the national recovery program; his week-long hosting of a local vaudeville show,

---

2. New York Times (hereafter cited as NYT), Nov. 15, 1933, p. 1; ibid., Nov. 26, 1933, sec. 4, p. 7; Pittsburgh Courier (hereafter cited as Courier), Nov. 25, 1933.

3. NYT, Jan. 2, 1934; ibid., Jan. 7, 1934, sec. 4, p. 1; Walter Davenport, "Mayor's Day In," Collier's, XCIII (Apr. 21, 1934), 12–13.

along with appearances on radio as guest of Rudy Vallee and Major Bowe's amateur show, increased his reputation as a buffoon as well as a ham. His close associations with Father Peter V. Tkach, a Russian Orthodox priest, whom he appointed traffic commissioner, a post many claimed did not exist; with A. Solly Mazer, facetiously labeled by the press as a "boardwalk inspector" for the municipal government; with Hunky Joe Lewandowski, a former numbers racketeer; and with Bozo Lavery, notorious for his criminal record yet appointed a detective by McNair, all enhanced the mayor's image as a colorful and rather curious character. In addition, McNair was twice arrested and once jailed while in office.[4]

Others considered him more than colorful and curious. When John C. Weaver sent to a friend the prepared text of a speech introducing McNair to a meeting of the League for Social Justice, he received a comment reflecting the thoughts of many Pittsburghers. The friend, a correspondent, was referring to the statement, "But suppose you were certain you had such a plan [the Single Tax], a plan which offered a way out of social strife, by harmonizing diverse ideas? What would you do? You would probably go crazy," when he scribbled, "This is open to an unhappy implication." The Democratic organization, however, cared less about the three-ring circus McNair brought to City Hall than about his being a political maverick. At the time of the mayoralty primary, Dr. Marion McKay, the president of the Civic Club of Allegheny County and also a member of the Citizens League, endorsed McNair by claiming, "Knowing him as I have for many years, I have no fear that he will be controlled by any individual, group or organization." McKay was in the most part correct, and the organization fretted over its lack of control rather than any "unhappy implications" concerning McNair.[5]

Control of the mayor, and in turn of his cabinet, would have conferred on the organization a dictatorship over the city's patronage. With Pittsburgh's 1934 budget geared at $21,252,549, and much of this earmarked for wages and salaries, an independent mayor signified the loss of a golden opportunity for the job-hungry Democrats. The Departments of Public Safety and Public Works stood out as the two prime patronage plums,

4. Clipping from *PG*, Oct. 7, 1936, McNair Scrapbooks; PD, CL.
5. Weaver's introduction of McNair at meeting of League for Social Justice, July 28, 1934, John C. Weaver Social History Collection, Archives of Industrial Society 64:19, Box 13, University of Pittsburgh, Pittsburgh, Pa.; *ST*, Sept. 10, 1933.

with the Bureaus of Police and Fire, under the control of the director of public safety and traditionally deeply enmeshed in politics, accounting for a payroll of over $4 million. During the Republican hegemony the public safety director had reigned as a figurehead of respectability, rarely taking part in decision-making. Even the police and fire chiefs, especially the former, had bypassed the director, reporting directly to the mayor.[6]

The designs of the Democratic organization on the Department of Public Safety ran into a roadblock established by the organization's financial friend, M. L. Benedum, and the ministers of whom McNair had asked for suggestions. The committee of clergymen supported a former prohibition administrator, John D. Pennington; Benedum, in opposition to the desires of Lawrence and Guffey, who advocated a hard-and-tried Democrat for the position, pushed for the appointment of Republican James F. Malone, who had bolted to McNair during the election campaign. The intraparty dispute grew so heated that Benedum wrote to the White House for aid. Reasoning that the independent Republicans should be given representation in the new city administration, in order to win them over completely to the Democratic fold, the oil millionaire informed the president: "Joe, David and I have had a friendly difference as to the method of procedure (of holding the independent vote). They claim it is a Democratic victory and to the victor belongs the spoils. I agree with them to the extent of approaching the danger line but the conditions in Pittsburgh and vicinity are unusual as there was in the past just a corporal's guard of Democrats. Unless we can hold the Republicans who have joined us and add more we are in a dangerous position. I feel that by giving the converts an unusual recognition . . . we can hold all of these and add more."[7]

As a result of the Democratic deadlock over the appointment, McNair asked Herron's safety director, Harmar Denny, to remain in office. Then, in the following order he offered the position to his rival in the primary, John M. Henry, only to renege when Henry accepted; called for Denny's

6. Ordinance no. 366, city of Pittsburgh, *Municipal Record* (hereafter cited as *Mun. Rec.*), 1933, vol. 67, pp. 238–268; *ST*, Nov. 19, 1933.
7. Undated letter, Bendum to Stephen McIntyre, President's Personal Files 2458, Franklin D. Roosevelt Library (hereafter cited as FDRL), Hyde Park, N.Y.; clipping, Guffey Papers, Washington and Jefferson College (hereafter cited as W & J), Washington, Pa.

resignation in a wrangle over ousting a fire chief; finally presented Malone's name to the city council; and when council refused to accept Benedum's candidate, pulled the name of Ralph E. Smith out of a hat, while
commenting: "I haven't talked to him about this yet. I don't know whether
he will take the job or not." Smith took it, eventually to be removed because, as McNair put it, "he started to make appointments for the
organization."[8]

McNair, however, did not pass over one prominent independent Republican, Leslie M. Johnston, president of the Citizens League. Johnston,
who had endorsed McNair during the campaign and was backed by
Benedum, received an important cabinet post when approved by city
council as director of public works. In this position he eventually rose
to become the most important figure of the McNair administration. The
organization was represented in the new cabinet by two men: by City
Treasurer James P. Kirk, Lawrence's insurance business associate and
treasurer of the Democratic County Committee, and by City Solicitor
C. D. Scully, Democratic Campaign Committee chairman during Mc-
Nair's contest with Herron. The mayor, himself, chose Kirk, whereas
Lawrence urged him to appoint Scully. Kirk remained at his post through-
out McNair's tenure in office, and although he did not influence the
mayor's policy, he was instrumental in bringing about his downfall.
Scully served as the first in a parade of city solicitors and, like Safety
Director Smith, fell from office because of his organizational ties.
Throughout his administration, McNair hired and fired at machine-
gun pace.[9]

In the dispute that was arising between the regular organization and
Benedum, Negro leader Robert Vann sided with the wealthy oilman, because Benedum had given his word that Negroes would get proper recognition. Moreover, rumor had it that David Lawrence had blocked the
appointment of a Negro as city assessor, a post valued at $4,500 a year.
Some Negroes, however, feared McNair's possible appointment of James
F. Malone, of the partially Negro Fifth Ward, as safety director, because
they believed he might reward those who had supported him in his Republican primary race for mayor in 1929—namely, the white ward

8. Clipping from *Pittsburgh Press* (hereafter cited as *Press*), Feb. 5, 1934, McNair
Scrapbooks, PD, CL; *ST*, Oct. 8, 1936, ibid.
9. Clipping, Guffey Papers, W & J; interview with David L. Lawrence, Apr. 14,
1964.

leaders of the Third and Fifth Wards, John Verona and David B. Roberts. They feared such rewards would undo the work accomplished by the Negro leaders in building up a Negro organization in those wards.[10]

During the campaign Lawrence allegedly had promised the appointment of a Negro magistrate at the police station in the heart of the Negro district, and the assigning of a Negro to the city's Public Health Department and to minor jobs in the Departments of Public Safety, Public Works, and Parks, Highways, and Sewers. Although the Democrats could point to the 2,290 jobs, including 150 white-collar positions, that Allegheny County Negroes received as CWA workers, Negro politicians grew impatient with the delay in receiving their share of the higher paying municipal payroll positions. A committee of three, led by Benedum's butler, Joe Gould, met with McNair in early January and sought patronage. Robert Vann, seeing this meeting as an incursion of his leadership, explained that there was a factional fight going on and claimed: "Until the white people have an opportunity to organize the new administration and settle their own differences, it ill becomes any Negroes to start disorganizing and breaking up the work that has been done since 1932, when some of the other Negroes now making the most noise about McNair were making speeches for Hoover." Naturally, the work done since 1932 referred to Vann's own organizing efforts.[11]

At the end of January, with the McNair administration almost a month old and the Negro community still looking for its first job, all Negro factions gathered in the offices of Vann's *Pittsburgh Courier* and established a Patronage Committee chaired by Paul F. Jones. One of the men who had met earlier with McNair made clear that his discussion with the

10. *Courier*, Jan. 6, 1934; ibid., Jan. 13, 1934.
11. *Courier*, Jan. 6, 1934; ibid., Feb. 10, 1934; ibid., Jan. 13, 1934. Vann's statement takes on added interest in the light of political scientist James Q. Wilson's explanation of the origins of Negro machine politics. He points out that the Negro political organization, at least prior to the black militancy of the 1960s, was created and shaped by the political organization of the city. The existence of a Negro machine was dependent upon the existence of a white machine. Machine politics required the centralization of leadership, a sizeable stock of tangible incentives with which to reward contributors, a large group of people who would be attracted by the kind of rewards a political machine can distribute, and usually a ward or district system of selecting party leaders, aldermen, and candidates for public office. The prior existence of a machine operating under such conditions meant that the entry of Negroes into politics would take place under forms and rules already established. He maintains that no Negro boss could spring up where there was not already a white boss. James Q. Wilson, *Negro Politics: The Search for Leadership* (Glencoe, Ill., 1960), pp. 23–24.

mayor implied no challenge to Vann's leadership, whereas Vann reported that Democratic leader Dave Lawrence warmly received a new plea for Negro appointments. It was decided that lists of names would be given to Lawrence, who would then approach the various department heads.[12]

McNair, in accord with a patronage policy that held constant throughout his entire administration, shifted the onus to his department directors when he was told by one Negro at a church meeting: "We have read in the papers that we are to have Negroes for this and that. A whole month has passed and no appointments have been made. Negroes have been getting the mop and slop jobs for years. We expect three major appointments—the magistrate's job, the city assessor's job and the assistant city solicitor's job. We knew little of you when your name came up for election, but we understood that you were an exponent of the New Deal. And we are waiting for that New Deal to materialize." McNair answered that they should have told him they wanted jobs before the election, that it was up to the department heads, and that a Negro delegation would have to stand in line behind an Italian delegation. A few days earlier the spokesman for one Italian delegation informed McNair, "Mr. Mayor, one day you're our hero and the next day you're a bum."[13]

McNair attempted to recoup his losses in the Negro community when, early in March of 1934, he nominated Negro realtor and businessman Charles E. Jackson for a post as police magistrate. However, after the finance committee of the city council tabled the nomination, a story broke that Jackson had been convicted of an embezzlement charge. In making the nomination, McNair had bypassed the Patronage Committee, and many Negroes believed the nomination to be a grandstand move on the part of the mayor, who knew more of Jackson's background than he let on and realized that the nomination would be aborted. The Patronage Committee decided to back Jackson, in spite of his past, but also filed a petition to the effect that some Negro should get the job. Subsequently, 4,000 people signed another petition in support of Jackson—but to no avail. Council defeated the nomination seven to one, making clear that it based its disapproval on the nominee's criminal record, not his race. The position finally went to a white man, one of McNair's cronies Theodore L. Moritz; and the Negro community had to wait for the swearing

12. *Courier*, Feb. 3, 1934.
13. *Courier*, Feb. 3, 1934; clipping from *Press*, Feb. 5, 1934, McNair Scrapbooks, PD, CL.

in, a month later, of Wilbur Douglass as assistant city solicitor to win representation in the municipal government.[14]

Throughout this period, as the McNair administration passed through its first winter into its first spring, the Democratic organization's influence diminished to such an extent that one observer could remark, "Dave Lawrence rarely shows his face at City Hall any more." On the other hand, one face seen frequently belonged to Mrs. R. Templeton Smith, leading light of the League of Women Voters. Soon after his election McNair chose as his unofficial budget adviser Mrs. Smith, who quickly outgrew her quasi authority and began to exert a Svengali-like influence over the new mayor. Lawrence later complained that Mrs. Smith kept warning McNair to "watch out for Lawrence because he's a crook." Her sister Mrs. J. O. Miller, William P. Witherow, and Public Works Director Leslie M. Johnston, all ranked among those wielding the most influence over McNair; a list of his closest advisers read like the membership directory of the Citizens League.[15]

In an attempt to gain at least some leverage over the recalcitrant chief executive, Guffey and Lawrence appealed to the White House to muzzle their Frankenstein's monster. Democratic National Chairman James Farley phoned McNair just as he was engaged in a press conference. The mayor listened intently and then, turning to the reporters, said: "A great pity, a great pity. Just as we are having a nice cozy chat, Mr. Farley tells me for God's sake shut up for a few days. Sorry gentlemen, drop in tomorrow." Farley, earlier, had endorsed Joe Guffey for the important 1934 Senate race, but McNair emphasized that city employees could be anti-Guffey and anti-Lawrence in the primary if they wished to be and would not be penalized under any conditions. In return, Guffey, speaking to a party rally at Washington, Pennsylvania, launched a veiled attack on the mayor when he declared to the crowd: "Do not lose faith if some Democratic officeholder should fail to measure up to his responsibilities. . . . We will, perhaps, at times elect the wrong man to public office. . . ."[16]

The "wrong man" tried to run for another office. Despite an earlier

14. *Courier*, Mar. 10, 1934; ibid., Mar. 17, 1934; ibid., Mar. 31, 1934; ibid., Apr. 21, 1934; ibid., Apr. 28, 1934; *Mun. Rec.*, 1934, vol. 68, pp. 169, 172.

15. Clipping from *Press*, May 20, 1934, McNair Scrapbooks, PD, CL; interview with Lawrence, Apr. 14, 1964.

16. Walter Davenport, "Mayor's Day In," p. 144; clippings from *Press*, Dec. 29, 1933, ibid., Mar. 9, 1934, Guffey Papers, W & J; clipping from *ST*, Jan. 30, 1934, Guffey Papers, W & J.

determination to curb his insatiable appetite to campaign for public office, and in direct opposition to the wishes of the regular organization, McNair undertook a hopeless race for the gubernatorial nomination in the 1934 Democratic spring primary. Not only did the mayor lose to the regular candidate, George Earle, but he also greatly increased the organization's antagonism toward him. By summer rumors spread that the Democratic machine planned to introduce a ripper bill at the coming session of the state legislature. Such a bill, aimed at "ripping" the mayor from office prior to completion of his full term, had precedent in Pittsburgh politics. During a turn-of-the-century factional dispute between the Magee-Flinn Pittsburgh machine and the Quay state Republican organization, a mayor had been removed from office.[17]

From the time of his election, McNair feared the possibility of some form of a ripper bill. At first he saw the Republicans as its proponent. After his 1933 victory the GOP, which had fought with full force a city-manager plan while still in control of Pittsburgh, experienced a change of heart once the Democrats captured city hall. The mayor-elect countered, "That's an old trick of organized politics to try to institute a city manager plan of government when they are licked and a reform mayor is elected." By March of 1934, however, after his first bouts with the Democratic organization, he told a throng of newsmen: "Davey Lawrence will never let me serve out my term. He'll rip me out of office or throw me in jail."[18]

McNair did all he could to forestall the inevitable and made the ripper, at least in Pittsburgh, an issue in the 1934 gubernatorial campaign. He canvassed the city, speaking at a multitude of antiripper rallies, and informed his listeners of the organization's intention to remove him from office because he "would not go along with it." He noted that a ripper "was contrary to democratic government and a violation of the principles of representative government"; he advised voters to find out how

17. Clipping from *ST*, Jan. 30, 1934, Guffey Papers, W & J; clippings from *Press*, May 24, 1934, editorial page, ibid., Aug. 12, 1934, McNair Scrapbooks, PD, CL. For details of 1901 ripper see the following: Lincoln Steffens, *The Shame of the Cities* (New York, 1957), pp. 138–42; Frank C. Harper, *Pittsburgh: The Forge of the Universe* (New York, 1957), pp. 149–54; commonwealth of Pennsylvania, *Legislative Record*, 1901; C. S. Scully, "The Pittsburgh Ripper," *The Annals*, 19 (Mar. 1902), 299–300; *PG*, Feb. 15, 16, 1935.

18. Clipping from *PG*, Nov. 15, 1933, McNair Scrapbooks, PD, CL; clipping from *ST*, June 16, 1936, ibid.

the legislative candidates stood on such a bill. At one such meeting John Huston, an erstwhile Republican who had become a Democratic-organization councilman, contradicted McNair by declaring that the ripper rumor originated in the mayor's own office as a result of the Mellon interests' desire to divide the Democrats. Then Huston gave vent to the organization's chief plaint by charging: "There is nothing in City Hall but the old Republicans who were here before we were elected. Let McNair go back to Jimmy Coyne and the Republicans. That's where he belongs. He has sold out to the Mellon interests." Huston also challenged McNair to provide the name of the attorney that the mayor claimed had sat down with him a few days earlier and told him that if he went along with the organization, he would avoid one of three alternatives—a ripper bill, impeachment by city council, or indictment by grand jury. Although Mc-Nair refused to reveal his source, it was subsequently learned to be none other than Robert Vann.[19]

Two days following McNair's clash with Huston, one of the mayor's intimates informed an audience that Democratic gubernatorial candidate George Earle had promised to oppose the ripper movement; but when Earle arrived in Pittsburgh the next day for a campaign meeting, he denied making any such statement and declined to make his attitude known. On the other hand, Earle's Republican opponent, William A. Schnader, adopted a definite stand. "I am for home rule in local government and against any notion that the Pennsylvania Legislature by ripper legislation or in any other way should interfere with home rule in Allegheny County," he announced to a Republican gathering that included McNair, who had slipped into the meeting hall a few minutes before the statement was made. Schnader's pronouncement forced Earle to fire off a telegram to a municipal payroll meeting pledging himself against a ripper.[20]

A ripper, however, can work both ways, and at the same meeting an assistant city solicitor introduced a resolution for such a bill directed at the city council, with which McNair constantly warred. It would have torn out the council of nine men elected at large and substituted a bigger council elected by ward or district, not unlike the structure governing Pittsburgh prior to the city charter of 1911. Mr. W. D. Grimes, who

19. *PG*, Oct. 11, 1934; ibid., Oct. 22, 1934.
20. Ibid., Oct. 12, 1934; ibid., Oct. 10, 1934; *Press*, Oct. 16, 1934; *PG*, Oct. 22, 1934.

introduced the resolution, asserted: "This small Council of necessity usurps the power of the executive. They all want to act as Mayor, and they do act as Mayor." The issue was put to a voice vote, and McNair, chairing the meeting, claimed that the ayes had it. Although ultimately the resolution came to nothing, it did reflect the bad feeling existing between the mayor and his council. In his less than two years in office, McNair would veto eighty-three bills; city council would override sixty-nine of these vetoes, agree to six, and table eight bills.[21]

McNair not only flayed the city council, but told the city's pay-rollers: "If this ripper bill goes through in January, I won't be the only one to go. Others will go, too, and I want that considered. . . ." With the election imminent, the pay-rollers, during an unprecedented meeting, voted their support for the Republican nominee for governor. McNair, who called the assembly, unmistakenly made clear his sympathies for Schnader; and his influential director of public works, Leslie M. Johnston, first proposed the motion for the Republican's endorsement. Apparently, Earle's telegram of the previous week made little impression on the McNair camp. At this final payroll meeting both candidates spoke, but the Democrat complained of getting short changed. Thus, as the election returns poured in and Earle, despite McNair's opposition, marched to victory, the chances of Earle's abiding by the pledge not to support the ripper diminished with each new vote tallied in his favor.[22]

With the arrival of the new year, the Democrats occupied Harrisburg; and McNair, inaugurating his second year in office, fired his fourth public safety director. This act brought down on the muddling mayor the wrath of the entire city, let alone the Democratic organization. His embarkment on an economy program, which prompted the furloughing of municipal plumbing inspectors at a time when hundreds of complaints about unsanitary conditions had gone unanswered, further exacerbated the situation. *The Pittsburgh Press*, which during the 1933 campaign had sounded the clarion call for McNair's election, initiated a crusade to crucify him politically. "The city government of Pittsburgh is obviously in the hands of a man either mentally incompetent to run it or else determined to run it into a ditch," the paper editorialized. Throwing the

21. *PG*, Oct. 22, 1934; *Mun. Recs.*, 1934–1936, vols. 68–70. A tally was made of the veto messages in the Index of each year's *Municipal Record*, and then the history of each ordinance was followed to determine whether the vote stood or not.
22. *Press*, Oct. 19, 1934; *PG*, Oct. 31, 1934.

book at McNair, it scored him for a chamber of horrors of executive rule, namely, the firing of veteran employees without notice or explanation; the frequent and unexplained changes of important government officials; the defiance of city ordinances having to do with zoning, sanitation, and building inspection; the terrorization of the city payroll by means of unjustified reprimands, sudden furloughs, and summary discharges; and numerous other violations of office. The paper advocated impeachment.[23]

The Civic Club of Allegheny County, closely scrutinizing the provision in the city charter that permitted any "20 freeholders" to bring charges against the executive, gave serious thought to McNair's impeachment. A Nineteenth-Ward alderman called for a meeting of all the ward's district committeemen in order to prepare a demand for the mayor's dismissal after McNair had removed a police magistrate and replaced him with his personal friend, Albert S. ("Solly") Mazer. The *Pittsburgh Post-Gazette* found this incident "utterly indefensible" and decried "the boorishness and unfairness with which Mayor McNair has suddenly dismissed city employees without giving them any reason for his action." Previously, the rival *Pittsburgh Sun-Telegraph* had urged a city-manager plan for Pittsburgh.[24]

The Democratic organization desired no part of impeachment proceedings or of a city-manager form of government, since a ripper bill appeared the best method of disposing of McNair while still maintaining control of the municipal machinery. Impeachment would have moved Republican president of the city council, Robert Garland, into the mayor's office, so the regular organization forced its Nineteenth-Ward alderman to abandon his plans, and began to study the 1901 legislation in preparation for a similar measure aimed at McNair. Reports of secret meetings abounded, and the name of C. D. Scully arose most often as the machine's choice for successor to McNair. Meanwhile, Democratic leader David Lawrence disclaimed any knowledge of such meetings and denied the drafting of any legislative measure to remove the mayor from office.[25]

McNair, not one to suffer abuse quietly, announced, "When they start

---

23. *NYT*, Jan. 6, 1935; sec. 2, p. 7; ibid., Feb. 17, 1935, sec. 4, p. 6; *Press*, Jan. 25, 1935, editorial page; ibid., Jan. 28, 1935; ibid., Feb. 3, 1935.

24. *ST*, Jan. 29, 1935; *Press*, Feb. 2, 1935; *ST*, Jan. 18, 1935.

25. *Press*, Jan. 28, 1935; ibid., Feb. 2, 1935; ibid., Feb. 3, 1935; *ST*, Jan. 27, 1935; ibid., Feb. 3, 1935; *PG*, Feb. 4, 1935.

to bring impeachment proceedings against me, I'm going to start to bring some action of that kind myself." He decided to carry his fight to the state capital and requested the attorney general to institute a *quo warranto* proceeding aimed to remove from office the city controller and three councilmen—the controller because he allegedly lived outside of Pittsburgh and the councilmen because they allegedly voted for an ordinance in which they personally were interested, in violation of the city charter. The attorney general, viewing the matter as a local one, shifted the issue back to the county district attorney and McNair abandoned his plan.[26]

On his return home from Harrisburg, he attempted to rally church support to his cause and, more pragmatically, conferred with the local legislative delegation, offering municipal patronage to win their favor in case a ripper bill actually came to a vote. Moreover, McNair's aides carried out an organized effort to mobilize the city's payroll against the ripper by assessing workers one dollar apiece to enroll in the "McNair Five to One League." The league's secretary related its express purpose when he declared, "Our idea is to block the ripper bill, and also give support to the Mayor's Five to One tax plan." Some pay-rollers who refused to contribute complained of being confronted with a threat that they would be "put on a list."[27]

Despite Lawrence's denials and in face of McNair's opposition, during the second week of February 1935 a north side legislator, William A. Shaw, introduced the controversial piece of legislation into the Pennsylvania House of Representatives. The bill provided for the abolition of the office of mayor and the substitution, at a lesser salary, of a city commissioner, appointed by the governor to serve until January 1, 1937, when a permanent commissioner would be elected at the general election. Originally the bill had called for the governor's appointment to be effective until January 1, 1938, the end of McNair's term, but Democratic leaders amended the draft to include a shorter appointive term in order to capitalize on holding the election simultaneously with FDR's running for a second time.[28]

Supplementary to the ripper feature, the bill proposed amendments to

26. *Press*, Jan. 28, 1935; ibid., Feb. 4, 1935; ibid., Feb. 13, 1935; ibid., Feb. 5, 1935; *ST*, Feb. 4, 1935.
27. *Press*, Feb. 8, 1935; *ST*, Feb. 10, 1935.
28. Commonwealth of Pennsylvania, *Legislative Journal* (hereafter cited as *Leg. Jour.*), 1935, pp. 417, 446; *Press*, Feb. 11, 1935; *ST*, Feb. 11, 1935.

the city charter that would have provided for the election of the city solicitor and the Civil Service Commission by the city commissioner and the council—a choice previously in the sole domain of the mayor; it would have abolished the power of magistrate vested in the mayor; it advocated giving the city controller authority to employ his own solicitor rather than having to depend on the city's law department for legal advice. Its proponents reasoned that if the controller was to control adequately the chief executive, he should not be forced to rely on an attorney indebted to the mayor for his job. In general, the legislation aimed at a wholesale dilution of the executive's power, although its advocates formally labeled it a bill "relative to better government of cities of the second class," Pittsburgh being the only second-class city in Pennsylvania.[29]

The outlook for passage of the legislation appeared bright in the Democrat-controlled House, but less so in the Republican Senate. There Coyne, despite his 1933 debacle, still maintained the last word over all policy affecting Pittsburgh and Allegheny County. Moreover, he sat on the Senate's Committee on Municipal Government and would oversee the bill; however, six Pittsburghers were represented on the House's thirty-member Committee on Cities, and at least four definitely favored a ripper. At the same time as the introduction of the ripper, to complicate matters further, state Senator Frank J. Harris introduced a city-manager bill, to take effect in 1938. This legislation was drafted by the Civic Club of Allegheny County, which veered away from its original intent of impeachment. Grasping the opportunity provided by the hectic state of municipal affairs and feeling the ripper to be politically motivated, the Civic Club hoped to institute a reform it had long since advocated. Committee pigeonholes had killed such bills in the two previous legislative sessions, the latter of which witnessed David Lawrence's urging Democratic House members to support a city-manager plan. McNair, seizing on the chance to complete his full term, pointed out that he had been on the committee that had sponsored the 1933 legislation and still favored the plan—"at the end of the expiration of my term as Mayor."[30]

Once the House's Committee on Cities had promptly reported out the

29. *Leg. Jour.*, 1935, pp. 417, 446; *Press*, Feb. 11, 1935; *ST*, Feb. 11, 1935.
30. *Press*, Feb. 11, 1935; *Leg. Jour.*, 1935, p. 374; *Press*, Feb. 6, 1935; *PG*, Feb. 9, 1935; ibid., Feb. 12, 1935; ibid., Feb. 14, 1935.

ripper, McNair hinted that State Democratic Chairman Lawrence was "digging his own grave" and threatened to fire all Lawrence's appointees on the city payroll, whose numbers diminished rapidly as a consequence of successive purges. "People are not going to let Davey say, 'Here, I'll name the Mayor of Pittsburgh. I don't care how you voted.' " cried the angry mayor, adding that in any event Coyne would not want to turn the city over to Lawrence. He further threatened to resign as mayor prior to its enactment, if and when he became convinced that the ripper bill would be written into the lawbooks. Such a contingency, he theorized, would enable Council President Garland to become mayor, and the Republican Senate would never consent to ripping one of their party from office.[31]

The Democratic organization met the challenge. Representative John J. O'Keefe, chairman of the Allegheny County delegation, introduced an amendment to the city charter, providing that the city council should choose an immediate successor if the mayor were to resign. This action aimed at preventing the Republican council president from automatically succeeding to the mayoralty. The machine forces also juggled legislative procedure so that the O'Keefe amendment would be voted on prior to the original ripper—making sure of its effectiveness if McNair carried out his threat to resign. Being retroactive, the measure served as double insurance: even if the mayor were to resign immediately and Garland assumed office, the bill would remove Garland once enacted. Lawrence tied up the five city council votes necessary to elect a replacement when he formed a coalition of three Democrats—Kane, Gallagher, and Huston —and two Republicans—McArdle and Anderson. For the latter two, this support portended their shift of party allegiance to the Democrats prior to the 1935 primary.[32]

On the other hand, McNair's friends came to his aid. With slight regard for relevance, Congressman Theodore L. Moritz, the mayor's former secretary, delivered a ten-minute speech on the floor of the United States House of Representatives against the ripper legislation being discussed in the Pennsylvania assembly. Subsequently, he brought his friend the mayor to see the president of the United States. In an interview lasting seven minutes, FDR displayed the well-known Roosevelt charm—and

31. *PG*, Feb. 13, 1935; *Press*, Feb. 12, 1935.
32. *Leg. Jour.*, 1935, p. 441; *Press*, Feb. 13, 1935; ibid., Feb. 14, 1935; *ST*, Feb. 13, 1935; *Press*, Aug. 16, 1935.

guile—and made no commitment with regard to the ripper. McNair reminisced that the interview began with the chief executive's asking, "Well, how are things?" Moritz snapped: "Rotten. They're trying to rip this man out of office." Roosevelt inquired who was doing it, and the congressman answered, "Davey Lawrence." "Did you see Joe Guffey?" FDR asked. They spoke a little longer, and the president said that he desired to maintain harmony in the Democratic party. Impressed by his host's courtesy, McNair, upon leaving, told Moritz: "Say that fellow's all right. He's with us." Moritz snorted: "Wait a minute! Did he say he was against the ripper?" He had not, the mayor admitted. Moritz again asked, "Did he say he was going to see Joe Guffey about it?" And again McNair admitted he had not; in fact, he realized that the president promised nothing and merely sent him out smiling but empty-handed.[33]

Within a few days after his interview, the mayor lashed out at Roosevelt as being the guiding force behind the ripper. Some political observers saw in his statement an attempt to curry favor with the GOP leaders in the hope that the Republican-controlled Senate would quash the ripper. Earlier Senator Coyne had squarely attacked the bill when he remarked: "Why should Harrisburg wash Council's dirty linen? Let them wash it themselves. Let them get a judge and set themselves up as a jury if they want to get rid of McNair. The [impeachment] law lets them do that." The statement led to immediate rumors that a Coyne man, former Congressman M. J. Muldowney, would replace Leslie M. Johnston as director of public works, but Johnston, himself, served as a leading defender of McNair during the ripper controversy. He took to the air waves, describing the legislation as "un-American and a foul blow of selfish politicians, desperate for power," and urged the public to send telegrams to their representatives in the General Assembly. Moreover, he noted that under the McNair administration the city payroll had been freed from political domination.[34]

The payroll activities during the 1934 campaign and the antiripper McNair Five to One League point up the exaggeration involved in Johnston's remark. With an extraordinarily bad sense of timing, almost immediately after Johnston's speech, a petition calling on the state senate to oppose the ripper was circulated among the pay-rollers working in

33. *ST*, Feb. 14, 1935; clipping from *ST*, Oct. 18, 1936, McNair Scrapbooks, PD, CL; *Press*, Feb. 20, 1935.
34. *Press*, Feb. 26, 1935; *ST*, Feb. 15, 1935; *Press*, Feb. 14, 1935.

the Pittsburgh Department of Public Safety; Thomas A. Dunn, director of the department, headed the list of signers. In the days following, while the Democratic majority pushed the O'Keefe amendment ahead by sending the ripper back to committee in the House of Representatives, Pittsburgh's Democratic municipal employees received orders to change their registration to Republican.[35]

Richard L. Smith, Republican head of the Fire Bureau, allegedly issued the command for the change, but after a first-day shift in registration of forty-three city employees, mostly firemen, the swing stopped. Although denying his seriousness, McNair wisecracked to friends, "If a lot of Democrats suddenly changed to Republican it might change Davey Lawrence's mind about the ripper bill." Fire Chief Smith claimed that no orders had been given but noted that "there might have been a suggestion"; Public Safety Director Dunn disavowed giving any orders and claimed that he always registered Democratic and had no intention of changing. Payroll casualties, however, occurred during and long after the controversy, affecting both camps. One Italian precinct worker, who had served as a traffic court clerk, lost his job when he advocated the ripper among his neighbors. Another committeeman, who had served as a plumbing inspector during McNair's tenure and had taken the mayor's side, found himself without a job once McNair left office.[36]

As both sides maneuvered, both sounded the trumpet of victory. Following his usual weekend arrival in Pittsburgh, Secretary of the Commonwealth Lawrence told a meeting at Democratic headquarters that enough votes had been promised in Harrisburg to rip McNair from office; United States Senator Guffey stepped into the fray and began to use his sizeable influence to line up proripper votes. On the other hand, Coyne conferred with McNair several times and predicted the defeat of the legislation in the Republican state senate. At antiripper rallies speakers scored Lawrence again and again, while McNair was the target of diatribes cast by organization forces. McNair declared that he would attend no committee hearing held by the House, but intended to wait until the ripper reached the Senate before testifying.[37]

35. *ST*, Feb. 15, 1935; *Press*, Feb. 19, 1935; *Leg. Jour.*, 1935, p. 490.

36. *PG*, Feb. 20, 1935; *Press*, Feb. 20, 1935; interviews with committeemen, 11W14, 9W7. (To maintain anonymity of committeemen, they are listed by ward and district—hence, 11W14 is read 11th Ward, 14th District.)

37. *ST*, Feb. 24, 1935; ibid., Feb. 25, 1935; *PG*, Feb. 25, 1935; *Press*, Feb. 18, 1935; ibid., Feb. 20, 1935.

The O'Keefe amendment, aimed at City Council President Garland and labeled by one legislator as a small ripper, passed the House by a vote of 123 to 65 just as the Committee on Cities was beginning hearings on the big ripper, aimed at McNair. The hearing opened when Austin L. Staley, a former assistant city solicitor who left his post when the mayor fired Scully, presented a brief containing clippings from Pittsburgh's three newspapers that summarized McNair's convulsive career as mayor. The lawyer branded conditions in Pittsburgh as intolerable. Taking the stand in McNair's defense, Public Safety Director Dunn, an old-line Democrat whom many believed McNair had appointed for the express purpose of defending him against the ripper, charged that Pittsburgh would suffer serious civic injury if the mayor "could be torn from office by the will of a very small minority." Dunn pointed out that no one charged McNair with dishonesty, but rather that the organization feared him because of his political independence. "He is not building up an organization so he can succeed himself," declared the safety director.[38]

Other witnesses expressed a different attitude toward McNair. Patrick Fagan, representing the Central Labor Union of Allegheny County, which had been antagonized by the mayor's antiunion attitudes, remarked: "The man is insane! There is no doubt of that. . . ." Less dogmatic but more baiting, Representative Herman P. Eberharter asked Dunn, "Would you call it an act of honesty if the Mayor calls to his office members of the legislature to offer positions on the city payroll on condition they vote against the ripper bill?" The proripper testimony of Republican Councilman McArdle and the presence at the hearing of his colleague Charles Anderson, in addition to their conferring with David Lawrence prior to the session, gave increased credence to rumors that the two councilmen would receive Democratic support at the next election. "From every angle the purely 'ripper' moves carries the labor of politics," editorialized the *Pittsburgh Post-Gazette*.[39]

McNair agreed; commenting on the hearing, he called the plan "bossism in its worst form." He ranted: "It is right? Davey Lawrence cracks the whip in Harrisburg and McNair walks out as Mayor in Pittsburgh. It is [the public's] right to say who should be Mayor—not Davey Lawrence." He then attempted to stall the ripper further by declaring that

38. *Leg. Jour.*, 1935, pp. 707–08; *ST*, Feb. 26, 1935; clipping from *PG*, Oct. 7, 1937, McNair Scrapbooks, PD, CL; *Press*, Feb. 26, 1935.
39. *Press*, Feb. 27, 1935; *PG*, Feb. 28, 1935; ibid., Mar. 1, 1935; *ST*, Feb. 27, 1935.

before the bill became law he would appoint a deputy mayor, probably Leslie M. Johnston, a move that would not be covered by the O'Keefe legislation. McNair chuckled: "Then, when the new commissioner comes in to take office he'll find the deputy in the chair. What can they do about that?"[40]

Lawrence did little to dispel this increasing image of bossism when he issued a letter to Pittsburgh ward chairmen requesting that they submit to party headquarters lists of persons that they have endorsed for appointment to the newly conquered state payroll. Critics roared their disapproval; one declared: "In the tossing of state patronage to the ward satraps a clear idea is given of what would happen if the organization through its ripper project should get control of the municipal government. Ward chairman rule would promptly be restored." Moreover, Lawrence's earmarking of ward chairmen as patronage dispensers alienated the Pittsburgh Democratic legislative delegation, which yearned for control over the state payroll in their districts.[41]

Nevertheless, in a caucus of Democratic members of the state House of Representatives, Lawrence demanded that they pass the ripper; they did. Indicating that he felt responsible for McNair's election and regretted it, Lawrence allegedly told the caucus, "I put him in and I'll take him out." Less than two hours later the House passed the ripper on second reading and sent it forward for final passage. On March 6 three roll calls marked a heated debate witnessed by Lawrence, who paced up and down through the House chamber overseeing the action like an expectant father.[42]

Opponents of the ripper employed the 1901 law as precedent for their argument. Homer S. Brown, Negro representative from Pittsburgh, read from the four-to-three dissenting opinion of the state supreme court regarding the 1901 law, which stated, "Every member of the court concedes that this legislation is vicious" and that its "vice consists in flagrant violation of the fundamental law." "Well did that learned jurist see into the future," Brown remarked, continuing, "Never in the history of the legislature was there a more vicious measure." Also alluding to the 1901

40. *Press*, Feb. 25, 1935; ibid., Mar. 1, 1935.
41. *PG*, Mar. 2, 1935; *ST*, Mar. 5, 1935.
42. *PG*, Mar. 5, 1935; *Press*, Mar. 5, 1935; *Leg. Jour.*, 1935, p. 783; interview with Assistant City Clerk Louis DiNardo, Feb. 4, 1965; *ST*, Mar. 6, 1935. The interview with DiNardo made clear Lawrence's role as the driving force behind the ripper.

legislation, Al Tronzo, the second antiripper representative from Pitts-burgh, declared: "Ripper legislation weakens the political party sponsor-ing it. Diehl [the turn of the century mayor ripped from office] was an honest man. He, too, wouldn't play politics."[43]

John J. O'Keefe, leader of the ripper advocates, stressed McNair's offenses while in office. He scored the mayor for interfering with the administration of justice and for endangering the health of the city through his dismissal of sanitary inspectors, but never once did he men-tion McNair's party recalcitrance. During the debate one representative from Montour County, distant from Pittsburgh, shouted: "Why are we wasting all this time. This is not our fight. Let Pittsburgh go back home and fight it out in the courts." However, this legislator, as well as 122 others, voted for the bill's passage, as the House sent the ripper on to the Senate by a vote of 123 to 69. If the Senate would follow the House's lead, McNair's fate was sealed since Governor Earle made his position crystal clear when he announced before the hearing, "If there is sub-stantial support for a ripper bill I will sign it should it come to my desk."[44]

Rumors of McNair's resignation swept City Hall once news of the decisive vote reached Pittsburgh. He did not resign, but badly shaken, he summoned organization Councilman John Huston to his office, offer-ing to dismiss a number of department heads and other officials and asking for suggestions of substitutes amenable to the council and the Democratic machine. The organization, however, refused to deal with the mayor; and McNair, in an attempt to pressure it, dismissed a member of the Board of Assessors and three clerks in the traffic court, all organiza-tion men. He then went to Washington to speak again to the president, noting as he embarked, "If Roosevelt wants me to get out as a party menace, so the Democratic organization can have the city payroll and rackets to pay its campaign expenses, then I'll get out." Rebuffed in the capital, Pittsburgh's mayor grimly returned home.[45]

Back in Pittsburgh McNair received a surprising amount of support. One advocate wrote to FDR that the city's government had never been handled in such an economically efficient manner as under the McNair administration and declared, "It is commonly believed that the White

43. *Leg. Jour.*, 1935, pp. 910–15; *PG*, Mar. 7, 1935; *Press*, Mar. 6, 1935.
44. *Leg. Jour.*, 1935, pp. 910–15; *PG*, Mar. 7, 1935; *Press*, Mar. 6, 1935; ibid., Feb. 26, 1935.
45. *Press*, Mar. 7, 1935; ibid., Mar. 8, 1935.

House is lending active support to Lawrence and Guffey in their attempt to oust our outstanding incorruptible Democratic Mayor." Another of Roosevelt's correspondents agreed, remarking that McNair was "like a clean tonic in these gloomy days in Pittsburgh." She claimed that the mayor was giving the "city better government than it has had for years— but not considered better by a group that cannot get at the payroll or other money." The executive board of Mrs. R. Templeton Smith's League of Women Voters resolved unanimously against the ripper and offered to testify to that effect before the state Senate's Committee on Municipal Government. The league's letter to state Senator Max Aron claimed, "We have not enjoyed so good a government in the city of Pittsburgh for many years as we are now enjoying under Mayor McNair's administration." Pittsburgh's Chamber of Commerce adopted a resolution declaring the ripper a "wrongful denial not only of the principle of justice and sound public policy but of the sovereign rights of the people of Pittsburgh." The chamber held that the bill did not deserve legislative action. Moreover, newspaper polls run by the *Pittsburgh Post-Gazette* and the *Pittsburgh Sun-Telegraph* showed overwhelming support for McNair against the ripper, although there was positive sentiment in favor of a city-manager form of government.[46]

As McNair took reprisals against friends and relatives of those Pittsburgh legislators who voted for the ripper, firing some from their municipal payroll jobs, the Democrats attempted to garner the votes of Republican senators. They offered a judgeship to one in exchange for his vote, and Lawrence conferred with several others. Congressman Moritz asserted that Joe Guffey had inquired of him how he liked living in Washington, and had advised him to "go easy on this anti-ripper business" if he wished to continue as a resident of the capital city. The organization also rewarded the faithful; Austin L. Staley, who launched the principal attack on McNair at the Harrisburg hearings, won an appointment as special state attorney general.[47]

Necessity forced the Democrats into such maneuvers. The O'Keefe bill

---

46. Telegram, Hugo Noren to FDR, Mar. 7, 1935, Democratic National Committee File, Pa., Official Files, FDRL; letter, Ann Demmler to FDR, Feb. 26, 1935, Alphabetical File, 1933–36, McNair, FDRL; *Press*, Mar. 8, 1935; *PG*, Mar. 7, 1935; ibid., Mar. 13, 1935; ibid., Mar. 14, 1935; *ST*, Mar. 6, 1935; ibid., Mar. 8, 1935; ibid., Mar. 15, 1935.
47. *PG*, Mar. 9, 1935; ibid., Mar. 13, 1935; *Press*, Mar. 9, 1935.

was pigeonholed in the Senate's Committee on Municipal Government, with little chance of being reported out. Coyne's opposition to the big ripper indicated that a two-to-one vote against the bill would be rallied when it came time for the upper house to vote—if it ever got the opportunity to do so. Chances for its being reported out of committee also appeared slim since only five of seventeen members were Democrats—an additional four Republicans were needed to get the bill to the Senate's floor. Most Republicans, following the lead of their Allegheny County counterparts, opposed the ripper. Thus, when the committee chairman Max Aron announced a hearing for March 20, he evoked much surprise. Most observers expected the bill to remain bottled up in committee following the usual Senate procedure when a piece of legislation appeared doomed. The granting of a hearing indicated strong pressure behind the ripper movement; it paved the way for more vocal fireworks.[48]

A bevy of witnesses, including representatives from the League of Women Voters, Leslie M. Johnston, Thomas A. Dunn, James F. Malone, and Grant Curry (a member of the Pittsburgh Civil Service Commission), defended McNair against the ripper. Johnston stressed McNair's Mennonite background, his education, his three college degrees, his moral courage and his sense of humor; in addition, he revealed to the senators how the organization had approached him for specific jobs when he had assumed office in the Department of Public Works. Moreover, he claimed that regulars dangled before him two private jobs at salaries of $18,000 and $10,000 if he would resign from his position.[49]

On the other side, Dr. C. L. Palmer, representing western Pennsylvania's medical and health associations, testified how McNair's activities toward the Health Department imperiled the well-being of Pittsburgh; reminiscent of Patrick Fagan, he declared that McNair was mentally off-balance. Elmer Graper, University of Pittsburgh professor and chairman of the Police Research Commission, charged that the mayor had interfered with police functions and that "the situation had become intolerable." John Huston's testimony that McNair had offered him virtual dictatorial power over all appointments if he would exert his influence against the ripper highlighted the session. Back in Pittsburgh the mayor reacted to Huston's remark by claiming that the offer was part of a plot

48. *Press*, Mar. 7, 1935; ibid., Mar. 11, 1935; ibid., Mar. 16, 1935.
49. *ST*, Mar. 20, 1935; *Press*, Mar. 20, 1935.

of his own making to ascertain how the councilman stood on the ripper. Finally, as the hearing concluded, Chairman Max Aron chuckled, put the bill away, and said he did not know what would happen next. "We are in no hurry. I don't think that there will be any more hearings unless there is an urgent demand for one. It seems we heard plenty yesterday. The Committee will not take any action for at least two weeks," announced the state senator.[50]

He might very well have said two months. Although Senator Aron scheduled a meeting of the committee for April 1, a day organization Democrats claimed was most appropriate for anything concerning Mayor McNair, Senator Coyne requested and received a delay. No date was set and the committee did not consider the ripper until a surprise meeting held on the evening of June 3. Then, as a result of a nine-to-seven vote, the committee lined up against immediate action on the bill. Moreover, Senator Alonzo S. Batchelor, of Monaca, sponsored a resolution to authorize a probe into alleged lobbying in behalf of the bill—but not against it. Many considered the move to be an antiripper tactic to keep the original bill off the floor; and McNair, who had had a bed moved into his office in expectation of a siege if the ripper passed, began to rest more easily; he returned the bed to the Health Department.[51]

Immediately, a citizens committee, much like that which sparked the Kline supplies investigation in 1931, rallied around Batchelor's not-yet-adopted resolution and offered him the assistance of counsel. On June 17, after much wrangling, the Senate approved the resolution, whereas it defeated a counter move to investigate all lobbying, including that carried on against the ripper bill. The Batchelor resolution, which established a three-man board of inquiry, began:

> Whereas, the real objection to having the said William McNair serve as mayor for the full term for which he had been elected seems to be that his independence in the administration of his official duties, especially his dispensing of political patronage, is not satisfactory to the Democratic organization of the city. . . .

Apparently, McNair had made his point.[52]

50. *ST,* Mar. 21, 1935; *Press,* Mar. 31, 1935; ibid., Mar. 22, 1935.
51. *Leg. Jour.,* 1935, pp. 4418, 4579; *Press,* Apr. 2, 1935; ibid., June 4, 1935; *PG,* Feb. 4, 1935; *ST,* June 3, 1935; ibid., June 4, 1935.
52. *PG,* June 11, 1935; ibid., June 18, 1935; *Press,* June 18, 1935; *Leg. Jour.,* 1935, pp. 4418, 5611–12.

Nevertheless, almost inviting trouble but at the same time exuding a newfound confidence, McNair called for a vote on the ripper. "The vote would put the Senators in their true light and those who voted for it would prove that they don't know what real democracy is," he stated. The Senate's knowledge of "real democracy," however, would not be put to test; for the Committee on Municipal Government, in a postmidnight session, adopted by an eight-to-six vote a motion to postpone indefinitely action on the bill; Coyne's influence loomed large over the result. With two days left for the session—and at least three needed to pass a bill—the ripper died in committee. Immediately, McNair announced his candidacy for county commissioner, declaring, "I'm going to get the Guffey crowd."[53]

Although the ripper died in committee and the city-manager bill met with the same fate, the lobby probe carried over to the fall session of the 1935 legislature. This later hearing represented Republican political maneuvering; the committee of three was not named until the GOP state senator from Chester, William H. Clark, was convicted of malfeasance and extortion on charges brought by the Democratic governor and the attorney general. The GOP claimed that Democratic accusations against Clark had not been made until one day after the Batchelor resolution; Democrats declared that the lobby hearing was a vendetta in revenge for Clark's conviction. At Clark's trial two Republican senators told how David Lawrence had offered them patronage in return for their proripper votes. When the senators gave the same testimony at the lobby probe, Lawrence denied all charges, sticking by his earlier statement that "if there ever existed a sincere desire to inquire into the alleged attempt to bribe Republican old-guard senators into voting for the so-called ripper, the burlesque scheduled to start tomorrow would have been over months ago." The hearing resulted in no action.[54]

At about the same time as the inquiry, Pittsburgh witnessed a heated campaign for county commissioner. Prior to the primary McNair had announced his support for Coyne on the Republican ticket, as well as his own candidacy on the Democratic. Many interpreted the endorsement for Coyne as the result of a growing friendship that had begun with the

53. *ST*, June 18, 1935; *Press*, June 18, 1935; ibid., June 20, 1935; *PG*, June 20, 1935; ibid., June 21, 1935.
54. *PG*, Oct. 10, 1935; ibid., Oct. 16, 1935; ibid., Oct. 22, 1935; ibid., Nov. 28, 1935; *Press*, Oct. 15, 1935; ibid., Oct. 22, 1935; ibid., Oct. 23, 1935; ibid., Oct. 24, 1935.

Senator's vigorous fight to save McNair from the ripper. By the time of the general election, McNair, having been defeated in the primary, swung his support to Coyne; and following the 1934 precedent, a mass payroll meeting endorsed the Republican ticket. Moreover, a letter mailed to each city employee stated, "Let's back the Mayor wholeheartedly in his stand against our common enemy, those who seek to rip him and us from our jobs." Signed by the "Employees Committee," the letter carried a replica of the city seal over the slogan "Rip the Rippers!"[55]

Recognizing the paradox, *The Pittsburgh Press* editorialized, "Strangely enough, the pressure is again being applied in behalf of the same machine against which the voters—including 70,000 registered Republicans —rebelled in the municipal election two years ago." Ironically, the ripper brought McNair and Coyne together; it further illustrated the quicksilver-like substance of Pittsburgh's early depression politics. By 1935 the Democratic organization, still a political infant, had not yet consolidated its gains. Alliances and personalities shifted swiftly: in 1931 McNair managed Lawrence's campaign for commissioner and Coyne lent Republican support to the Democratic candidate; by 1933 Coyne supported Herron for mayor and was vilified for that support during McNair's campaign run by Lawrence; two years later Lawrence, formerly close to Coyne, tried to oust McNair, the man he had helped elect as mayor, and faced the iron opposition of Coyne—McNair's savior.[56]

Blocked in its ripper efforts by Coyne and the Republican-controlled state Senate, David Lawrence's Democratic organization sought elsewhere the goose that laid the golden egg. Until it was able to retrieve the elusive city payroll, other sources had to be explored. With the city department heads politically divided and the pay-rollers still an amalgam of antiorganization Democrats, regular Democrats, and Republicans, McNair's attempts to influence the large army of municipal jobholders drowned in a sea of political uncertainty. The county went Democratic in 1935, despite the admonition to "rip the rippers!" Moreover, the New Deal's work-relief legislation suggested additional patronage opportunities. Here too McNair did all in his power to frustrate the organization. He almost succeeded.

55. *ST*, Sept. 8, 1935; *Press*, Oct. 29, 1935; letter of City Employees Committee, General Election, 1935, Publicity File, files of Allegheny County Democratic Committee Headquarters, Pittsburgh, Pa.
56. *Press*, Oct. 30, 1935, editorial page; *ST*, Feb. 17, 1935.

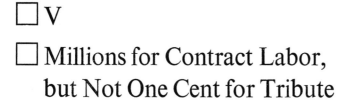

□ V

□ Millions for Contract Labor, but Not One Cent for Tribute

That federal gang tried to rip me out of office, so it's so long to them as far as I'm concerned. And I'm not going to turn over any city money to them to build up a Democratic organization.
　　　　　　　　　　　　William N. McNair, Pittsburgh Sun-Telegraph,
　　　　　　　　　　　　October 5, 1935

□ As in many other communities, it was Pittsburgh's and Allegheny County's private relief agencies that shouldered the economic burden resulting from the early impact of the Great Depression. However, during the depression decade control of organized relief shifted from private to state and national control, from the do-good social worker to the bureaucratic administrator and local politician. In 1922 private funds had supplied more than 54 percent of all direct relief aid in Allegheny County, whereas thirteen years later, in 1935, they provided less than 1 percent; in 1931 private agencies had expended for work relief one million dollars, a figure that was dwarfed more than twenty times by the federal government's spending in 1937. Relief became a subject that permeated the nation's thought and sapped its resources as well as its resourcefulness. For many unfortunates it became a reality of everyday life.[1]

In January of 1931, with more than 20 percent of its gainful workers

1. Ralph Carr Fletcher and Katherine A. Biehl, "Trends in Direct Relief Expenditures in Allegheny County, 1920–1937," *The Federator*, XIII (Mar. 1938), 67–72; Ralph Carr Fletcher and Katherine A. Biehl, "Work Relief and Work Programs in Allegheny County, 1920–1937," *The Federator*, XIII, (May 1938), 121–26.

and almost 10 percent of its total population unemployed, Pittsburgh groped for a solution to its economic problems. The next month, at the invitation of Howard Heinz and R. B. Mellon, seventy-five businessmen gathered to discuss the situation. Out of this meeting grew the Allegheny County Emergency Association and its "Pittsburgh Plan." The plan advocated that corporations and individuals make voluntary contributions to be used for the payment of wages to previously unemployed residents for needed municipal or semipublic improvements that otherwise could not be undertaken because of lack of financial resources. The municipality or institution that would benefit by the work furnished would pay for materials and skilled labor; the association would supply and pay for all other labor. In May of 1932 Pittsburgh's public works director reported city improvements costing more than $2.3 million, almost half of which the Allegheny County Emergency Association had provided. However, the association was short-lived, exhausting its resources long before that date.[2]

The state, too, attempted to soothe the wounds of the early depression years. In the beginning Pennsylvania had left the burden of relief to local relief machinery and voluntary groups; but although the local poor boards raised taxes by over 50 percent from 1928 to 1932, revenue collected for relief purposes declined during this period. Stepping into the breech, the state passed the first Talbot Act of December 1931, which appropriated $10 million for use by the poor boards. However, these boards failed in their job; the money, instead of supplying food, clothing, and other necessities, went for the bureaucratic needs of postage, office expenses, and the like. Under this system persons unfriendly to the concept of relief frequently controlled its distribution. Moreover, instances of issuing food orders to groceries in which board members had a special interest were rife. By the end of the summer of 1932, the Talbot funds were diminished to such an extent that Pennsylvania faced a new relief crisis. To meet the situation, in August of 1932 the legislature appropriated additional relief monies, and the Woodward Act created the State Emergency Relief Board (SERB), which assumed direct control of the administration of Pennsylvania's unemployment relief.[3]

2. Clippings from *Pittsburgh Press* (hereafter cited as *Press*), Mar. 21, 1931, ibid., Feb. 7, 1932, ibid., June 17, 19, 1932, File of Pittsburgh Unemployed, Pennsylvania Division, Carnegie Library (hereafter cited as PD, CL), Pittsburgh, Pa.; Fletcher and Biehl, "Work Relief and Work Programs," p. 121.

3. Commonwealth of Pennsylvania, Bureau of Research and Statistics, *Pennsyl-*

During this period of trial and error, many localities of the city took matters into their own hands, disregarding the formal attempts of the official government. Precinct workers played a large role in these self-help operations, but by no means did the political party always benefit. The activities were intracommunity and generally extrapolitical; frequently clergymen or neighbors determined the needy, and churches often distributed baskets and goods collected by politicians and community organizations. One New Deal committeeman from the Fifteenth Ward recollected: "We called in clergymen of the ward and asked who was needy. This put us above criticism. One minister kept asking for more baskets, and we found out later he had nothing to eat himself."[4]

In the same ward neighborhood leaders established the Fort Black Community Club, which lasted from 1929 to 1936. Not permitted to raise money through Bingo at the local Christian Church, they had decided to sponsor a street dance that ultimately brought in about three hundred dollars. From then on, these successful activists determined to organize on a formal scale. One precinct worker recalled, "We knew people's circumstances better than some of the welfare agents;" he noted that the organization supplied food baskets, ran Bingo games and dances, and paid gas and electric bills for those in need. "The neighbors knew who faked or not," he remarked, while asserting that the club held the community together. Although politics had originally made little difference in the Fort Black Community Club, this committeeman, who had aligned with the GOP when the organization began, ended his term as its last president a staunch Democrat. Eventually, since there were more Democrats than Republicans active in the group, the party of Roosevelt gained political mileage.[5]

Just south of this ward, in the southernmost extremity of the city, residents of the Thirty-first Ward crossed over into Mifflin Borough and opened an old coal mine. Led by the area's Democratic Club, they dug coal and distributed it throughout the community. Truckers received every fourth load as payment for their services, until the city council ap-

---

vania *Public Assistance Statistics: Summary, 1932–1940* (Harrisburg, 1940), pp. 1–2; Richard C. Keller, "Pennsylvania's Little New Deal" (unpubl. Ph.D. diss., Graduate Faculty of Political Science, Columbia University, 1960), pp. 68–69, 77, 89.

4. Interview with committeeman, 15W1. (To maintain anonymity of committeemen, they are listed by ward and district—hence 15W1 is read 15th Ward, 1st District.)

5. Interview with committeeman, 15W8.

propriated $500 for this purpose. When relief workers told Negro residents of the Fifth Ward to sell their radios, one Democratic committeeman put a stop to it. He had fifteen tons of coal dumped into the middle of a local street so that residents could help themselves, and also obtained drums of oil to be used for lighting when the electric company dimmed the homes of those behind in their bill payments. Democrats in the Eleventh Ward, taking advantage of the blue laws prohibiting the public showing of movies on Sunday, obtained use of the empty theaters for private showings and used the proceeds to fill food baskets. In the Nineteenth Ward every resident who desired it received a plot of ground, fifty feet square, for subsistence planting. This land-giving, organized by the West Liberty Community Council, was kept free of politics, although several members of the local Roosevelt Club served on the board of the community council.[6]

A small group of unorganized dwellers of the Twenty-second Ward obtained entrance for many into the neighborhood's Allegheny General Hospital by forging the signature of the district's state legislator on letters requesting admission. When the politician learned of this, keeping in mind the economic hardship of the times, he merely asked, "What bastard can sign my name better than me?" And in another north side neighborhood, immediately after the stockmarket crash, the Republican chairman of the Twenty-seventh Ward organized the Golden Rule Club to furnish the needy with food, fuel, and clothing. Although the Golden Rule Club was listed as nonpartisan, a year after its organization the ward's emerging Democrats organized a political club for relief. In 1932, when the Republican chairman died and his nonpartisan organization folded, the Democrats were handing out about three-hundred bags of flour a month. Working with clergy from the local churches, precinct politicians suggested worthy recipients and a committee investigated each case. The red tape entangling official welfare agencies did not bog down these community self-help organizations.[7]

Despite these relief efforts, the massive problem of unemployment remained. Jobs, as well as foodstuffs and clothing, were needed. As state funds began to diminish late in the summer of 1933, the Roman Catholic Bishop of Pittsburgh told Lorena Hickok, Harry Hopkins's roving trouble-

6. Interviews with committeemen, 31W5, 5W1, 11W14, 19W21.
7. Interviews with committeemen, 22W7, 27W2.

shooter: "Inadequate though it may be the emergency unemployment relief has been and is the most stabilizing force we have. The Pennsylvania Board may run out of funds this fall and may be unable to immediately get more. If this happens the federal government will have to put up the money, or—well, God help us all!" Roosevelt intervened before the Lord's help was necessary. In November of 1933 the Washington-based Civil Works Administration got under way.[8]

During January 1934, its peak month of employment, the CWA put 319,000 Pennsylvanians to work. However, two months later work-relief funds allocated to Allegheny County were exhausted, and the program ended in the Pittsburgh area after an expenditure of $4,300,000 for wages. As the federal cutback lopped off 27,000 men and women from the CWA payroll, the state made plans to hire them on a newly created Relief Works Division. The RWD gave preference to those who had served on the federal project, if they were eligible for relief, and eventually provided Pittsburghers with 14,000 jobs. The fall of 1934 witnessed the rise of still another state agency, the Local Works Division, which carried the burden of emergency employment until the federal government once again came to the aid of the states with its WPA program.[9]

Roosevelt personified the federal government to thousands of Pennsylvanians and other Americans, who looked to his use of national power as the only way out of their economic plight. In the steel town of Homestead, a Federal Emergency Relief Administration investigator found only two pictures hanging in the home of one Croatian immigrant family on relief. The first rendered a vivid presentation of the Last Supper; the second was a newspaper portrait of the president.[10]

Across the Monongahela River in Pittsburgh, however, the city's mayor, William Nissley McNair, thought something less of FDR, his work-relief program, and relief aid in general. Just as the mayor had

8. Hickok Report, Aug. 7–17, 1933, Aug. 12, 1933, Aug.-Oct. 28, 1933 File, Hopkins mss., FDRL.

9. Fletcher and Biehl, "Work Relief and Work Programs," p. 122; Commonwealth of Pennsylvania, Bureau of Research and Statistics, *Public Assistance Statistics*, pp. 1–2; *Press*, Mar. 30, 1934; clipping from *Pittsburgh Post-Gazette* (hereafter cited as *PG*), Aug. 15, 1934, Relief Works Division File, PR, CL.

10. Hickok Report File, Aug. 12, 1933, Hopkins mss., FDRL; reports of Hazel Reavis, Federal Emergency Relief Administration—Works Progress Administration Narrative Field Reports, Nov. 14, 1934, Hopkins mss., FDRL.

appeared to be cooperative with the Democratic organization during the 1933 campaign, he had also posed as a friend of welfare legislation. McNair had attacked Senator Coyne by declaring: "Any man who can walk through the many streets and alleys in his Senatorial District and observe on every hand evidence of unspeakable economic and social injustices—slums, poverty, men and women prematurely aged from long hours of toil for sweatshop wages—and then by his vote and support of his party at Harrisburg permit such conditions to go on, I say that such a man does not belong in public life." However, by the time of the House's hearings on the ripper, McNair was lashing out at social service workers and taking a stand antithetical to his apparently favorable attitude toward relief less than two years before.[11]

When one Democratic precinct politician brought a man desperate for work to McNair, the mayor gave him a letter of recommendation that said, "Do you want to buy a duck?" The mayor, using an expression made popular at the time by comedian Joe Penner, thought he was being funny; to the supplicant and the rest of Pittsburgh, McNair's attitude toward helping those routed by the depression did not seem at all humorous.

Immediately after his election to office, the new mayor asserted that his first task would be to find jobs for the unemployed of Pittsburgh. In November 1933 McNair added what appeared to be a harmless corollary when he agreed with President Roosevelt that cities should not depend too much on the federal government but should try to help themselves. During the early days of FDR's administration, while speaking to a Human Needs Conference in early September 1933, the pragmatic president, perhaps not foreseeing his massive federal work-relief programs, had told his audience that he looked upon government relief work as an emergency measure and that the duty in the end would be restored to "individual citizens, to individual responsibility and to private organizations." Moreover, he had criticized local areas for coming hat in hand to the federal government without carrying their own share of relief aid. At this point the Pittsburgh mayor and the president of the United States still saw eye to eye. However, as Roosevelt and his brain trust began to experiment with new relief programs involving more and more federal intervention, McNair stubbornly adhered to his original ideas.[12]

11. *Press.* Aug. 29, 1933; ibid., Feb. 24, 1935.
12. Interview with committeeman, 15W8; *PG*, Nov. 9, 1933; *Pittsburgh Sun-Telegraph* (hereafter cited as *ST*), Sept. 9, 1933.

In addition, the mayor consistently fought city council's pleas for state or federal aid. When the CWA began cutting its Pittsburgh labor force during late January 1934, the council protested to Eric Biddle, the CWA state administrator, on the grounds that the city's work-relief program would be disorganized, placing a financial burden on the city that it could not afford. Biddle replied that he had to follow nationwide policy and sympathized, *"Since the city authorities of Pittsburgh have been so extremely helpful in development of the Civil Works Program,* I am particularly distressed at the conditions represented by your Council, and I trust that speedy Congressional action will make it possible to carry out the program of your city" (emphasis added).[13]

On the other hand, three months later McNair branded the CWA's local successor, the Relief Works Division, "the brainchild of swivel chair generals who infest Washington so much that a visitor can't get a hotel room." When vetoing council's relief appropriations to supplement federal funds, he complained—as he would so often do—that Pittsburgh was getting shortchanged. "I don't know what's the matter with those fellows in Washington and Harrisburg," declared the irate mayor. "Here we are in Pittsburgh paying hundreds of millions of dollars every year in federal taxes. Only a little bit of it has been given Pennsylvania for the Relief Works Division. By the time Pinchot's henchmen and Commissioner Buck McGovern's boys get their say in, very little is allocated to Pittsburgh." With the coming of the summer of 1934, the council unanimously overrode McNair's veto of an ordinance introduced by Councilman McArdle authorizing a $500,000 bond issue to be used to provide food, clothing, fuel, and shelter, as well as other assistances, for the city's needy. This time, McNair held that relief was no longer a temporary problem and bonds were not the answer. In keeping with his single tax philosophy, he suggested a 10 percent increase on ground rent, claiming that increasing taxes would alleviate the need for a bond issue.[14]

By the end of 1934, McNair and the city council had clashed over other relief issues. Twice the council overrode executive vetoes of consent ordinances, permitting the city to join with the Allegheny County Authority in launching a $24 million PWA building program. The issues involved were local ones: the charging of tolls for the use of the bridges

13. City of Pittsburgh, *Municipal Record* (hereafter cited as *Mun. Rec.*), 1934, vol. 68, pp. 63, 70.
14. Clipping from *PG*, Apr. 12, 1934, Relief Works Division File, PD, CL; *Mun. Rec.*, 1934, vol. 68, pp. 386, 445–47.

constructed under the plan and the building of a toll-collecting plaza at the south end of Pittsburgh's Liberty Tubes. These issues would stall the slow-moving PWA program for many months. McNair, however, saw the situation in a broader perspective. Rankled by a dilution of his power brought about by council's shifting the control of the traffic court business personnel from the mayor to the city controller and the treasurer, McNair envisioned the consent ordinances as "a usurpation of the rights of the Chief Executive of the city." Not only did McNair perceive the issue as a clash between himself and the city council, but he further believed the PWA projects, involving a $19 million federal loan and a $5 million grant, to be "an attempt and an actual plan of invasion of the local government's rights . . . by injecting the authority and power of the Federal Government into local activities. . . ." The battle between mayor and council was joined; the struggle between the mayor and the federal relief policy took root.[15]

Moreover, the mayor, always on the alert against the Democratic organization, feared the use of large relief payrolls for political purposes. When, in October of 1934, his director of public works, Leslie M. Johnston, submitted a work-relief plan for Pittsburgh as part of the Local Works Division (LWD) program being set up by the state with federal funds, the mayor stated definitely that politics would play no part. By so noting, he scotched rumors of the party faithfuls' preempting supervisory positions.[16]

This attitude carried over to the Emergency Relief Appropriation Act of 1935. As Congress debated President Roosevelt's $4,880,000,000 work-relief program, McNair attacked the WPA legislation as "wholesale bribery of the electorate." Assailing Roosevelt for attempting to pave the way to have himself reelected in 1936 by spending tremendous sums of money, McNair declared, "As long as he spends it, who is going against Santa Claus!" Once Congress filled Santa's bag and approved the relief act, McNair and Johnston appeared before the city council on May 6, 1935. They urged the members to delay any appeals for federal funds, claiming that the city could make the same improvements by means of private contract work without government money. The mayor contended

15. *Mun. Rec.*, 1934, vol. 68, pp. 549–53, 612–13, 617–20, 646–49, 652; *PG*, Sept. 17, 18, 1934; ibid., Oct. 17, 1934; ibid., Nov. 6, 1934; *Mun. Rec.*, 1934, vol. 68, p. 648.
16. *PG*, Oct. 9, 1934.

that the federal government not only might curtail at almost any time its contributions but it continuously forced men onto relief by declaring that only workers on the relief rolls could be eligible for WPA work.[17]

In rebuttal, Councilman John Kane declared, "We don't want word to get out that the city does not want federal money." The mayor, however, did not wait to hear from the councilman. He departed as Kane spoke about "people criticizing the President for trying to remedy a condition he had nothing to do with creating." As McNair left the room, he remarked in an aside: "Go on make your speech. We're not interested." Johnston, attempting to soften McNair's remarks, explained that he and the mayor merely wanted to avoid waste in relief projects. When Kane proposed a conference between the council, relief officials, the works director, and the mayor, Johnston added his amen to the suggestion, saying, "That's right, that's right." The meeting ended on a note of near harmony—a note that would sound less and less frequently as the Pittsburgh Works Progress Administration program sputtered in its attempt to get off the ground.[18]

Early in August threats of strikes over the so-called WPA "security wage scales" plagued the WPA state administrator, Edward N. Jones, and its local Pittsburgh district head, John F. Laboon. Organized labor—especially the large building trade unions—in league with organizations of the unemployed, protested vehemently against the wage scales. Citing WPA wage rates of fifty-five dollars a month for unskilled labor, sixty-five dollars for semiskilled, eighty-five dollars for skilled, and ninety-four dollars for professional and technical workers, a representative of the Pittsburgh Building Trades Council protested to Jones that the scale forced upon labor a rate far below the schedule for which labor had fought so long to attain. He added that government was doing what it would not permit private industry to do—namely, setting up arbitrary wage rates without benefit of collective bargaining. Others voiced the fear that low wages on government projects would bring down wages paid in private business. Jones, who had no control of the pay schedules set by Washington, merely consented to report the objections of Harry Hopkins's office in the nation's capital. Laboon, however, pointed out that organized labor represented only 15 percent of the employables on relief.

17. *Press*, Mar. 16, 1935; *PG*, Mar. 16, 1935; *Mun. Rec.*, 1935, vol. 69, p. 265.
18. *Mun. Rec.*, 1935, vol. 69, p. 267; *PG*, May 7, 1935.

"We can put the other 85 percent to work on our W.P.A. projects and organized labor can be cared for on P.W.A. contract work," declared the district administrator.[19]

According to Lorena Hickok, Laboon, who was faced with putting 57,000 individuals to work on WPA projects, stood in a much better position than many of Jones's local administrators. She wrote to Hopkins that "he has been in charge of the work program in Alleghany [sic] county under the relief setup and therefore knows where he's 'at.' " When Miss Hickok had visited with Laboon on July 19, she found him in the process of forwarding to Harrisburg for approval project ideas already started under the previous program. At that time the Pittsburgh administrator expected to put approximately two thousand men to work in ten days to two weeks. Laboon was showing strains of worry; for although he had developed enough projects to put his case load to work for a few months, if city and county appropriations for supplies and materials met with approval, he had no idea where he was going to get enough projects meeting specifications to put men to work for a year. Ironically, however, because of the mayor of Pittsburgh's lack of cooperation, a dearth of men to fill the project positions was to exist for many months.[20]

By the end of the first week in August, McNair, declaring that the federal government was draining Pittsburgh of revenue and putting too little back, told Laboon: "I'm going to holler about it. About six months from now there will be another alphabet setup and your proposition will stop." Laboon countered that if the city did not appropriate funds for its share of the WPA program, he would go ahead with boondoggles. "We'd have to put these 57,000 employables on relief to work sweeping streets, shoveling snow, or perhaps we could find a hill to tear down," asserted the WPA administrator, who, along with his state boss, Edward N. Jones, showed determination to take all eligible employables off the direct relief rolls by November 1. Jones claimed that there was little danger of delay in putting the 57,000 to work.[21]

At the same time McNair queried, "How much of this money is for relief and how much for political purposes?" Other critics also saw political implications in the slow takeoff of Pittsburgh's and Pennsylvania's

19. Hickok Report File, July 24, 1935, Hopkins mss., FDRL; ST, Aug. 9, 1935.
20. Hickok Report File, July 24, 1935, Hopkins mss., FDRL.
21. ST, Aug. 7, 1935; ibid., Aug. 9, 1935; ibid., Aug. 11, 1935.

WPA programs. On August 12 a correspondent for the State News Service pointed out that three weeks previously Jones had announced federal approval of 260 projects, involving $2.5 million dollars and aimed at providing jobs for 15,000 people, but that not a single project had been started. He went on to conjecture that "the future program for Pennsylvania is being delayed until just before elections." However, it was McNair's recalcitrance more than any political motivations on the part of the Democratic organization that stalled the initial activities of WPA in Pittsburgh and Allegheny County.[22]

A day after the State News Service broadcast its accusations, with the WPA allocation for Allegheny County standing at $47 million, Jones wired Harry Hopkins that he had asked the county to contribute $7 million and the city $6 million. He stated: "Yesterday City Council approved ordinance and called a special meeting for tomorrow to authorize immediate contribution of $2 million cash and people's bond issue of $4 million. Confident county will authorize its $7 million quota next week." The city, however, approved the $6 million only after council unanimously overrode two of McNair's vetoes. Undaunted by council's action, the mayor threatened to stymie the entire relief program by refusing to sign the $2 million promissory note issue designed to finance the city's initial contribution to the work program.[23]

McNair delivered his ultimatum at a conference of bankers and real-estate men called to discuss the bond sales; only one of the eighteen executives present openly favored the bond issue. The meeting occurred on the same date, August 23, that the mayor wrote his vetoes of the note and bond issues. Moreover, his attitude must have been shaped by an answer he received from Washington that day, regarding a question he had posed about Pittsburgh's contribution to the WPA. Expressing a fear that funds would be exhausted before the projects were completed, McNair had requested of Hopkins that federal monies for Pittsburgh projects be earmarked specifically so that all work would reach completion. At the same time he had inquired whether the city would be

22. *ST*, Aug. 11, 1935; letter, no. 39, Aug. 12, 1935; mimeographed copy of State News Service release, 1935 File, Files of Allegheny County Democratic Committee Headquarters (hereafter cited as ACDCH), Pittsburgh, Pa.

23. Telegram, Jones to Hopkins, Aug. 13, 1935, WPA Record Group 69, Pa. 610, Box 2376, June-Aug. 1935 Folder, National Archives (hereafter cited as NA), Washington, D.C.; *Mun. Rec.*, 1935, vol. 69, pp. 468–88; *ST*, Aug. 23, 1935.

"permitted to carry out projects which in our opinion are most necessary and useful or will projects have to be selected which we feel are not essential in order to give more employment at this time." The reply he received—that "allocations made for projects under W.P.A. are for specific projects in amounts sufficient to meet estimated cost of completion of each project"—apparently did not satisfactorily answer his first question and completely avoided his second. Thus, McNair followed his natural bent and proceeded to veto the city's efforts to cooperate with WPA.[24]

By the end of the month, the mayor ordered all city activities related to the Works Progress Administration abandoned. He also fired the chief city engineer, Charles M. Reppert, who had earnestly defended the WPA program before the meeting with the bankers and real-estate men and had been drawing up a master plan for city cooperation with the federal work project. Fortunately for the federal government, Philadelphia, where the WPA also started out slowly, was "the only community . . . in Pennsylvania where *both* legislative and administrative branches of government [were] absolutely indifferent to, and non-cooperative with, the W.P.A." (emphasis added), Edward Jones pointed out to Hopkins.[25]

In Pittsburgh the city council, constantly overriding the mayor's vetoes, shouldered the burden of the Steel City's relief responsibility. Anticipating McNair's refusal to sign the bonds authorized by council, Councilman William A. Magee, a former mayor himself, urged that McNair be brought into court and compelled to consent; City Solicitor William D. Grimes informed McNair of the possibility of mandamus proceedings being brought against him. During the debate over the $4 million bond issue, Magee acidly attacked McNair and his public works director, Leslie M. Johnston, for their view that all work projects should be carried on by means of contract employment. Recognizing that the concept of private contract work was meant to introduce into the unemployment relief situation the element of efficiency, Magee held that "we have found by actual experience that when we hire equipment and let contracts, there

24. *ST*, Aug. 23, 1935; telegram, McNair to Harry Hopkins, Aug. 22, 1935, with answer from Lawrence Westbrook to McNair, Aug. 23, 1935, WPA Record Group 69, Pa. 610, Box 2376, June-Aug. 1935 Folder, NA.

25. *ST*, Aug. 28, 1935; ibid., Aug. 29, 1935; report, Jones to Hopkins, Aug. 27, 1935, WPA Record Group 69, Pa. 610, Box 2377, Sept. 1935 Folder, NA.

is a minimum of workers employed and a maximum of machines." He continued by noting that the major aim was "one of providing employment for the greatest possible number of human beings in the national crisis." Jobs, not efficiency, stood as the supreme goal of the federal government's work-relief program. McNair, constantly concerned about waste in government spending, conceived this goal as undesirable.[26]

One councilman, however, shared the mayor's penchant for efficiency and feared that the city would be left holding the financial bag if the federal government were to withdraw its funds before the completion of Pittsburgh's WPA projects. Walter Demmler, pointing to a WPA Sponsoring Certificate that stated, "It is agreed that the W.P.A. is under no obligation to complete any project," introduced a motion, which prevailed, to write to State Administrator Jones and ascertain the definite terms upon which the $25 million he had pledged to Pittsburgh was available. Cagily, Jones replied less specifically than in any previous pronouncement by remarking, "A sufficient sum has been set aside by me to pay for the employment of one person out of every family receiving relief residing in the city of Pittsburgh." With the WPA allocation premised on Pittsburgh's agreeing to furnish funds amounting to $6 million for material and supplies, the city's rescinding its responsibility would have jeopardized the federal appropriation whatever its amount and terms.[27]

Overriding the mayor's vetoes, the city council agreed to raise its share of the work-relief monies by means of the $2 million loan and the $4 million people's bond issue slated for approval by referendum during the 1935 election. Money lenders, however, declined to bid on the $2 million promissory note because of its size and the mayor's constant threats not only to leave the note unsigned but to sabotage the project indefinitely. Council, deciding to split the note into smaller amounts, passed, again over the mayor's veto, an ordinance providing for the sale of ten notes of $50,000 each. Had this plan been successful, a proposal to borrow the remaining $1.5 million in a similar manner would have been advanced. However, the day scheduled for the opening of bids on the ten notes found McNair enjoying the sunshine and salt air of Atlantic City, New

26. *Mun. Rec.*, 1935, vol. 69, p. 464; *ST*, Aug. 13, 1935; ibid., Aug. 23, 1935.
27. *Mun. Rec.*, 1935, vol .69, pp. 562–63, 674.

Jersey. Without the mayor present the bids could not be opened, and the city had to return to six bidders their sealed offers. Council, to little avail, petitioned the district attorney to take the mayor into court on a mandamus action designed to compel him to be present at the next bid opening. Meanwhile, the Allegheny County Home Owners and Taxpayers League filed a court petition seeking to block the sale of the promissory notes.[28]

McNair also obstructed the $4 million bond issue by failing to serve formal notice of the referendum on the election board at least sixty days prior to the balloting, as required by law. Moreover, he failed to issue a proclamation required to be published in two city papers once weekly during at least the thirty days before the election. Claiming that he had no notification to issue the proclamation, the mayor commented, "Well, we can hold it in April." However, the city held its spring primary election in April, and a municipal bond issue could only be presented at a general election. In any case April would have been too late for Pittsburgh to give effective cooperation to the WPA program.[29]

There still remained 10,000 people, unemployables and their families, who could not be absorbed by the work-relief program and would become charges of the city. McNair suggested that they be billeted in a tent pitched at Mayview, the city poorhouse and mental hospital, rather than have Pittsburgh appropriate funds to provide for their food, shelter, fuel, and clothing. When the city's Supplies Department actually received a requisition for a tent 40 feet by 100 feet, which could house no more than 150 jammed beds, it had no alternative but to purchase it. One councilman commented, "You wouldn't put a dog in it." The mayor's general relief stand became an issue during both the 1935 primary and general elections for county commissioner. During the primary, in which McNair ran for election to the county office, Democratic organization candidate John J. Kane attacked the mayor's "idiotic and inhuman relief plan calculated to starve the needy and the jobless" and charged McNair with getting "aid and comfort of those reactionary Tories, who would like to see the unemployed starve." During the general election Kane's organi-

28. *ST*, Sept. 4, 1935; ibid., Sept. 6, 1935; ibid., Sept. 9, 1935; ibid., Sept. 10, 1935; ibid., Oct. 5, 1935; *Press*, Oct. 17, 1935; *Mun. Rec.*, 1935, vol. 69, pp. 561–62.
29. *Press*, Oct. 17, 1935; ibid., Oct. 18, 1935; *PG*, Oct. 18, 1935.

zation running mate, George Rankin, Jr., pressed the matter still further: Rankin, assailing the mayor's pronouncement to "send them to Mayview," wryly commented: "I say that anyone who talks like that should be sent to Mayview himself. And I don't mean the home for the indigents. I don't mean the poorhouse." By the end of October, McNair folded his tent pitched at Mayview, leaving the taxpayers with a $235 bill, which city council requested the controller not to pay.[30]

The city administration opposed still another relief measure, the providing of shoes and clothing for schoolchildren who had been forced to leave the classroom because of lack of proper wearing apparel. The city council had approved the allocation of $40,000 for such purposes when the Board of Education had reported to it that 175 children had been forced to drop out of school because they had no clothing and that 2,600 others faced the same fate. Despite the fact that the city had this fund, McNair refused to permit Welfare Director Southard Hay to take action. Instead, in late October he suggested that the needy get their shoes from the Pennsylvania State Emergency Relief Board's warehouse in Harrisburg, although in September an official of the SERB had advised Assistant United States Relief Administrator Aubrey Williams that the SERB was unable to provide even a limited allowance for shoes and clothing during the summer and "as a result the lack of shoes and clothing in this state is great."[31]

When a delegation of north side mothers came to McNair requesting him to release the $40,000, he stood firm, appearing as a paradigm of the proponent of limited government. One mother proclaimed: "We don't care where the money comes from, but we want our children to get an education by being able to go to school. It's up to you to see that they get clothing. That's your job, isn't it?" Immediately, the chief executive replied: "Oh, no it isn't. I'm only here to keep order and pay the police and firemen and take away your garbage and sewerage and to provide water for you." Previously, almost two years to the day, during his campaign

30. *ST*, Sept. 8, 1935; ibid., Sept. 14, 1935; *Press*, Oct. 22, 1935; ibid., Nov. 26, 1935; speech of Kane, Sept. 15, 1935, David L. Lawrence Speech Folder, Primary Election, 1935, ACDCH; undated speech by Rankin, Candidate Speech File, General Election, 1935, ACDCH.
31. *Press*, Oct. 14, 1935; ibid., Oct. 24, 1935; Emmett H. Welch, director of research statistics, to Williams, Sept. 6, 1935, WPA Record Group 69, Pa. 610, Box 2377, Sept. 1935 Folder, NA.

for mayor, McNair attacked his opponent by rhetorically inquiring, "Is it possible a man can be so vicious as to keep people in starvation? . . ." By 1935 the shoe was on the other foot, but Pittsburgh's needy schoolchildren had to search hard for a pair for them.[32]

Only after six weeks of controversy did the mayor relent and permit his welfare director to order the shoes. Sending Hay a letter from one of the stops on his self-exiled speaking tour of the South—a tour he undertook to escape having to sign WPA bonds—McNair admitted that public opinion had forced his hand. Pressure from the Board of Education and such civic groups as the women's contingent of the local Unemployed Council, which threatened to picket his office as well as his home, forced the mayor to capitulate. Unrelentingly, however, Public Works Director Leslie M. Johnston, who had changed his registration from Democratic to Republican during the ripper hearings, appeared before city council and maintained that the SERB should still be responsible for the shoe purchases. Nevertheless, by November 22 an order was written for 4,408 pairs of shoes, which were paid for out of municipal funds, and the distribution went along smoothly.[33]

The organization of WPA across Pennsylvania also followed a bumpy road. One of Philadelphia's biggest problems was that the city and the county covered the same geographical area; if one sponsor failed to be convinced, there was no other to turn to. On the other hand, in Allegheny County, divided into a myriad number of political subdivisions, "a great deal of finesse" was required "to keep everyone happy at all times" because of the plethora of proposals and counterproposals. To add to Philadelphia's problem, neither its legislative nor its administrative branches of government would cooperate with the WPA program. In Pittsburgh at least the city council was sympathetic. The similarity between the two communities was found in their uncooperative mayors. "Pittsburgh has a very dizzy mayor who does not want to have a great deal to do with the program," a WPA assistant regional engineer reported back to his immediate superior. Moreover, he concluded, the director of public works would have nothing to do with any program "except under his

32. *Press,* Oct. 26, 1935; *PG,* Oct. 28, 1933.
33. *Mun. Rec.,* 1935, vol. 69, pp. 629–32; *PG,* Oct. 31, 1935; *New York Times* (hereafter cited as *NYT*), Oct. 31, 1935; *Press,* Oct. 31, 1935; ibid., Nov. 22, 1935; ibid., June 7, 1935.

own terms which were to work under an out and out lump sum granted him to run the show."[34]

State WPA Administrator Edward Jones placed the blame for Pittsburgh's lack of cooperation squarely on the shoulders of Public Works Director Johnston, "the banker's plant in the McNair Administration." Noting that Johnston maintained an almost hypnotic influence over the mayor, Jones asserted: "If the $25,000,000 allotted to Pittsburgh by the W.P.A. has to be spent on rural roads instead of city wharves and other worthwhile undertakings, the blame will rest on the shoulders of Svengali Johnston. Some day he will have a lot of explaining to do." Indeed, the early WPA projects open to Pittsburgh residents did center outside the city in the county's suburban and rural areas, funnelling funds from payrolls to transportation costs. Hiring trucks at $1.25 an hour during the second week of October, the local WPA office transported Pittsburghers to work on the gravelling and paving of seventy miles of dirt roads outside the city, thereby skirting the mayor's blockade. Other such attempts to create jobs outside of McNair's jurisdiction continued during the following months.[35]

Despite such attempts and FDR's plea on October 14 to United States Comptroller General John Raymond McCarl to expedite projects in Massachusetts, New Jersey, New York, and Pennsylvania "where we have the largest number of unemployed," Allegheny County, as a result of McNair's opposition, stood at the foot of all Pennsylvania counties in placing men and women with the federal work-relief program. As of October 22, only 13 percent of the quota in the Fifteenth District (Allegheny County) had found work with the WPA, although Washington had sent word to start hiring on thirty-three additional projects. By the end of the first week in December, Jones informed Harry Hopkins that because of the attitude of the mayor of Pittsburgh, the program in that district had been held back. Nevertheless, Jones noted that 25,000 were on the rolls of the WPA, but tempered his optimism by adding: "I doubt very much whether the quota of 57,000 will ever be reached. I think

34. Report, Jones to Hopkins, Aug. 27, 1935, WPA Record Group 69, Pa. 610, Box 2377, Sept. 1935 Folder, NA; memo, John McClellan, assistant regional engineer to George D. Babcock, acting field representative, WPA Record Group 69, Pa. 610, Box 2377, NA.

35. ST, Oct. 7, 1935; ibid., Nov. 27, 1935; PG, Oct. 11, 1935; ibid., Oct. 19, 1935; ibid., Oct. 31, 1935.

when we get to 45,000 we will have exhausted the quota." At the same time Harold Ickes's slow moving PWA employed only 215 workers throughout the entire county.[36]

Those fortunate enough to be carried on the WPA rolls were not so fortunate as to get paid immediately. Changes in bookkeeping procedures, decentralization of authority, and the red tape of bureaucracy were responsible for the delay. Between October 1935 and the beginning of 1936, officials reported strikes and threats of strikes to be rife throughout the district. The local WPA administrator, John F. Laboon, ascribed the delay to the bureaucratic procedure of having to send payrolls to Washington via Harrisburg, instead of forwarding them directly to the nation's capital. The government returned the pay by the same circuitous routing. Ultimately, an agreement was reached to continue direct relief until an individual received his WPA salary, and in early December a state representative, Elmer Holland, successfully advised a committee of unpaid workers to establish a disbursing office in Pittsburgh, which expedited wage payments. Nevertheless, on the national scene Roosevelt fretted over complaints about the slowness in paying WPA workers and asked Harry Hopkins to check up on every locality where pay was more than one week in arrears.[37]

Mayor McNair, on the other hand, played the disbursement difficulties to his own advantage and asserted: "I wouldn't speak to Mr. Laboon or any of that crowd. Any man who puts men to work and doesn't pay them isn't a decent, respectable citizen." McNair probably would not have put them to work at all, but a showdown with the Pennsylvania governor forced him to cooperate, at least on the surface, with the Works Progress Administration. At the beginning of the WPA operation, Harry Hopkins had announced that the government would cut off direct relief aid to the states once the works program came into full swing. Although

36. Cablegram, FDR to Comptroller General McCarl, Oct. 14, 1935, Official Files 444c (hereafter cited as OF), WPA File, Sept. 16–Sept. 30, 1935, FDRL; *Press,* Oct. 22, 1935; ibid., Oct. 23, 1935; Jones to Hopkins, Dec. 7, 1935, WPA Record Group 69, Pa. 610, Box 2377, Oct. 1935 Folder, NA; *PG,* Dec. 13, 1935.
37. *Press,* Oct. 29, 1935; ibid., Nov. 8, 1935; ibid., Nov. 13, 1935; ibid., Nov. 19, 1935; ibid., Nov. 27, 1935; ibid., Dec. 1, 1935; Telegram, Holland to Hopkins, Dec. 4, 1935, with answer from Corrington Gill, WPA Record Group 69, Pa. 610, Box 2377, Oct. 1935 Folder, NA; memo, FDR to Hopkins, Dec. 17, 1935, Hopkins mss., Confidential Political File, 1933–1938, Box 67, White House Folder, FDRL.

November 1 stood as the target date for the cessation of the dole, Mayor McNair, late in September, claimed that the federal government was bluffing. As November 1 approached, Hopkins forecast an extension of the deadline date to the beginning of December, and on the advice of one of his Pennsylvania aides made it clear to Governor Earle that the December deadline would be a final one.[38]

Immediately, Earle announced that since the state's direct aid resources would be depleted by January 1, each local community would have to share the burden after the first of the year. He then called a special relief session of the state legislature for that month. The high cost of Pennsylvania's direct relief burden had already forced Earle to beg Washington for an extra million dollars so that there would be "no starvation in Pennsylvania." The governor, while discussing the relief situation in conjunction with his calling for a special session of the legislature, singled out the state's two largest cities and announced: "In Pittsburgh and Philadelphia, if the Mayors won't cooperate it means that a terrific burden of relief will be on those cities because of their refusal. The burden will be tremendous. We might as well call a spade a spade in these matters."[39]

In reply to Earle's warning, McNair reavowed his determination not to lift a finger to aid in the government's plan for providing jobs for those on the relief rolls. Hitting at the political implication in WPA, the mayor commented that Pittsburgh could raise ten million dollars in special taxes and put thousands to work if city council would approve his and Johnston's plan, "but we won't send it [the money] to Eddie Jones in Harrisburg for him to toss around among Earle's political hangers-on in big salaries." In this statement McNair followed a recurrent theme in his attacks against the federal works program. Three weeks earlier, in answering the equity suit to block the sale of municipal notes brought by the fiscally conservative Allegheny County Home Owners and Taxpayers League, McNair, although the defendant, agreed with the league and claimed that any Pittsburgh contribution to the WPA would be "furnished to Edward N. Jones for the purpose of assisting the Federal government

38. *PG*, Dec. 9, 1935; ibid., Oct. 25, 1935; *ST*, Sept. 24, 1935; memo, Thad Holt to Hopkins, Nov. 13, 1935, WPA Record Group 69, Pa. 610, Box 2377, NA.

39. *PG*, Nov. 14, 1935; telegram, George Earle to FDR., Oct. 5, 1935, OF 200L, Oversized Box 109, FDRL; Earle to FDR, Oct. 18, 1935, President's Personal Files 1999, FDRL; *Press*, Nov. 15, 1935.

in hiring political employees." He feared the building of a controlled and powerful political force by the Democratic organization, which he had been battling since his assumption of office.[40]

The governor, however, lashing back at McNair's charges, placed Pittsburgh's relief problem right at the mayor's door, asserting that he was responsible for keeping 40,000 out of work. In a telegram dated November 18, Earle gave the Pittsburgh city administration twelve days in which to make up its mind and "show concrete evidence" of cooperation with the federal works program. If McNair did not accept $2.5 million a month from the federal government through WPA by sponsoring work projects and contributing up to 20 percent of the federal allocations for materials, Pittsburgh itself would have to shoulder the entire $2.5 million burden. At the time, only 17,831 of Allegheny County's 57,000 quota were employed, and most worked on highways outside the city. Nevertheless, McNair called Earle's statement a bluff; insisted that city council legalize Bingo before he would agree to discuss work relief; threatened to leave town in order to avoid any peace conferences; and sent Earle a copy, "with compliments," of his forthcoming *Saturday Evening Post* article, "The Waste of the People's Money," which aired his views on federal relief. At the same time that McNair increased his recalcitrance, the United States Conference of Mayors petitioned Congress to continue federal work relief and direct aid for 1936–1937, and urged all cities to "take proper steps to insure adequate and proper cooperation and contributions from their own states."[41]

A day after Harrisburg's ultimatum, State WPA Administrator Edward N. Jones appeared before a session of the city council to explain the same plan—that if the city would pay the cost of materials, WPA would pour out $2.5 million a month to hire the unemployed for work projects. Jones added that the program would automatically end on July 15, 1936, thereby changing his original pledge of federal aid from $25 million to $17 million. He pointed out that such a program could not be financed by the city alone, which had collected only $21 million in taxes during the fiscal year 1934. McNair, charging that the federal government had taken $80 million in taxes out of the city and the state had requisitioned an addi-

40. *Press,* Nov. 16, 1935; ibid., Oct. 28, 1935.
41. *Mun. Rec.,* 1935, vol. 69, p. 664; *Press,* Nov. 19, 1935; *ST,* Nov. 19, 1935; ibid., Nov. 20, 1935; Democratic National Campaign Committee 1936, *Highlights on Relief,* p. 7, 1936 File, ACDCH.

tional $50 million, shouted: "What community can stand such a drain? If they let us keep that money, we'll take care of the unemployed. They're robbing us." In keeping with his single-tax philosophy, the chief executive demanded that the council increase the city tax rate to twenty-six mills on land to finance the work-relief program. He advocated a tax rebellion, proclaiming, "We had a whiskey rebellion here once; let's start a tax rebellion here right now."[42]

Bypassing the city's law department, the council sought the advice of four outside attorneys, including Cornelius D. Scully, who had been the organization's favorite to replace McNair had the ripper succeeded. It then went into executive session in order to find the quickest method of skirting the stubborn mayor so that work relief could begin. McNair had absented himself from his duties and from Pittsburgh by journeying to New York City for a guest appearance on crooner Rudy Vallee's radio program. In defiance of the absent mayor, council made plans to inaugurate a curtailed work-relief program. Pending a conference with Jones, the council tentatively decided to give work-relief officials power to undertake improvements on city streets, playgrounds, and similar projects that would require little or no materials and supplies; however, the nine councilmen made no attempt to post city funds for purchase of the otherwise required material. McNair reacted by calling the WPA "a political octopus reaching out its tentacles to devour the municipal government."[43]

Ultimately, the patience of state officials with McNair diminished to an apparent point of no return. On November 27 the State Emergency Relief Board endorsed Earle's demand that the mayor cooperate in work-relief plans or lose state aid in distributing direct relief. The bipartisan board's decision was premised on the belief that under the circumstances extending aid to Pittsburgh would, in effect, be placing an additional burden on every other municipality in the state that cooperated by supplying their share of the financing. In an attempt to give added force to the threat to cut off Pittsburgh's relief, Earle and the board had a notice mailed to each relief client in the Pittsburgh area explaining that McNair's lack of cooperation made the situation intolerable and

42. *ST*, Nov. 20, 1935; *Press*, Nov. 20, 1935.
43. *Press*, Nov. 21, 1935; *ST*, Nov. 26, 1935; *The Bulletin Index*, Nov. 28, 1935, McNair Scrapbooks, PD, CL.

that the enclosed check was their last. The note claimed that McNair "had capriciously done everything in his power to block the work program, thus making it impossible for the federal government to proceed with its work projects." As evidence that the state meant business, officials wired County Relief Director George P. Mills, informing him that $400,000 had been allocated to Allegheny County for the payment of cash relief, but it was to be used for such payments only in that portion of Allegheny County outside the city of Pittsburgh.[44]

McNair seized the opportunity of a Thanksgiving Day radio address to label the cutting of relief funds as "political embezzlement," and the Allegheny County Emergency Relief Board (ACERB) appealed to the SERB not to let the differences between the mayor and work-relief officials "plunge 132,000 individuals into a situation where they are actually without food." Shortly afterward, on November 29, the council sent a telegram to Earle asking him to reconsider his order until it had exhausted every avenue of promoting a work program. Moreover, it passed the two ordinances designed to put into effect a curtailed WPA program in the city. The ordinances, introduced by Councilman McArdle on November 25, empowered the WPA to undertake grading, draining, and other minor improvements on city streets, parks, and playgrounds and alleviated the city's need to supply materials.[45]

Before their passage, however, Councilman Demmler, the only city father who showed any sympathy at all to the mayor during the relief crisis, rose and questioned a section of one of the ordinances that read that the WPA would bear the cost for the projects. He then reiterated his earlier statements made in the council on September 6, 11, and October 5, questioning the Works Progress Administration's obligation to complete the work. He also wondered if the city could assess property owners benefitting from those improvements, such as fixing of sidewalks, that resulted from federal work. Less worried about technicalities, Councilman John J. Kane, Pittsburgh's printing pressmen's union leader and a county commissioner-elect, retorted, "I think you will all agree that the most important question before this body is, how can we take care of the unemployed in Pittsburgh." It was Kane who moved that the council

44. *Press,* Nov. 29, 1935; *NYT,* Nov. 29, 1935, p. 36.
45. *Press,* Nov. 29, 1935; *Mun. Rec.,* 1935, vol. 69, pp. 660, 673–79; *ST,* Nov. 29, 1935; *NYT,* Nov. 29, 1935, p. 36.

communicate with Governor Earle and ask him to reconsider his action.[46]

Influenced by city council's promise to do everything in its power to break the impasse between McNair and the WPA, Earle temporarily rescinded his order forbidding the sending of state relief funds to Pittsburgh. In a telegram to Councilman P. J. McArdle, chairman of the council's finance committee, the governor recognized council's cooperation and remarked that "reactionary interests, who do not care whether our citizens starve or eat," created the crisis. McNair, however, flatly announced that he would not permit Welfare Director Southard Hay to spend any available money for stopgap relief until the dispute over the work-relief issue was completely settled. Before a session of council, the mayor charged that its proposed appropriation for work relief was illegal and that all other city expenditures for relief were likewise illegal.[47]

McNair and his public works director presented three conflicting demands to council. McNair opposed a city appropriation for work-relief projects because it would burden the small homeowner; he demanded a 25 percent boost in city taxes to provide direct relief; Leslie M. Johnston presented the third solution, urging council to borrow $2 million for public improvements and attempt to obtain $8 million more from the federal government. Denying the existence of a relief emergency, McNair declared the situation would continue for ten years "if we don't get some brains in Washington." "And other places," retorted Councilman Kane. The mayor claimed that Johnston could put 3,000 people to work within a day, and Councilman Magee shot back, "How are we going to feed the others?" McNair, claiming as little desire to see people starve as Magee, asserted that he had humanity, whereas the councilman did not—to which Magee replied that they were discussing the chief executive's duty in office, not humanity. "What is my duty?" demanded McNair. "To obey the ordinances of Council," answered the former Pittsburgh mayor. "Oh yeah," cracked McNair. "I'd be in jail half the time if I listened to you fellows."[48]

On December 1, the federal government gave Pennsylvania a parting gift of $3 million. Then, true to its word, it put the state entirely on its own with respect to direct relief. In Pittsburgh council awaited an answer

46. *Mun. Rec.*, 1935, vol. 69, pp. 660, 673–79.
47. *Mun. Rec.*, 1935, vol. 69, pp. 684–85; *Press*, Nov. 30, 1935.
48. *Press*, Nov. 30, 1935; *ST*, Nov. 30, 1935.

to a request of the previous day for a meeting with Earle, the chairman of SERB, and Edward Jones. As usual, McNair vetoed even council's curtailed work-relief measures, making Pittsburgh the only municipality in the state that refused to cooperate; for although the Philadelphia City Council opposed WPA, its new mayor-elect, S. Davis Wilson, assured work-relief officials that he would initiate and support their program. Also true to form, the Pittsburgh City Council overrode the veto, while the mayor demanded that the WPA deposit the money in the city treasury and all work be done through private contractors as suggested by his public works director. Meanwhile, Pittsburgh's District WPA Director Laboon announced that although the city had not furnished tools, he felt that he could obtain picks and shovels sufficient for the men to begin work on the limited work relief. Some time earlier the ACERB's work division had purchased some thirty thousand dollars worth of shovels, half of which the city still had, and he hoped to commandeer these.[49]

Pressure began to build and the mayor could not long ward it off. The Joint Committee on WPA, a group formed in July principally to fight for union scale wages on federal projects, viciously attacked the mayor and threatened to establish a picket line to fight McNair's obstructionism. Made up of virtually every organized labor union in the county, its affiliates included the Central Labor Unions of Pittsburgh and McKeesport, as well as liberal groups like the Pennsylvania Security League and the League of Social Justice. The Joint Committee on WPA bluntly warned McNair to end his "starvation blockade," accusing him of using every legal trick and illegal dodge to bring the "haunting spectre of starvation close to 132,000 residents of the city."[50]

On December 4 McNair capitulated. Accusing Earle of wanting to see Pittsburgh's poor starve, the mayor said: "I am made of softer stuff. I can't see people faced with the threat of hunger to prove my point. Therefore I surrender unconditionally. I quit cold. I'll go all the way with this rich man in Harrisburg and the politicians who are running W.P.A. behind the scenes. . . . As fast as Council sends me ordinances, bond issues —anything—I'll sign them." McNair backed up his announcement of surrender by directing City Solicitor William D. Grimes to file an appli-

49. *Mun. Rec.*, 1935, vol. 69, pp. 684, 695–96; *Press,* Dec. 1, 1935; ibid., Dec. 2, 1935.
50. *Press,* Dec. 3, 1935; clipping from *PG,* Dec. 4, 1935, McNair Scrapbooks, PD, CL.

cation at once with Edward Jones for ten engineers to aid the city in an appraisal of the South Pittsburgh Water Company. He charged Earle, a millionaire, with "dirty politics," called him the "pampered son of fortune," and asserted, "I do not trust him." He forecast that the work-relief program would waste both city and federal funds and that it "is shot through from top to bottom with the most vicious type of politics."[51]

Once the air cleared, District Administrator Laboon held a long conference with City Engineer Henry Johnson, Jr., to discuss the situation; Laboon estimated that 3,000 men could be put to work immediately. At the very same time the city controller moved into court to speed up action on the taxpayer's suit to enjoin the city from borrowing $500,000 to pay its initial share of the proposed program; his purpose was to dispose of the case immediately so that the money could be borrowed. Cooperatively, the court of common pleas, deciding against the Allegheny County Home Owners and Taxpayers League, ruled against an injunction. City officials moved quickly. They announced that the first $500,000 in short term notes of the $2 million in bonds authorized by council would be advertised the next day (December 7) and bids would be opened in a week. McNair promised to open the bids and sign the notes, clearing the way for the city to obtain the needed cash by December 17 or 18.[52]

The recalcitrant mayor and his director of public works, however, made the going rough and assured new delays in Pittsburgh's cooperation with the Works Progress Administration. McNair filed exceptions to the court's ruling; and although the judge dismissed his petition, the financial house that was awarded the note issue withdrew its bid as a result of the mayor's delaying action. Since the bonds could not be advertised for another ninety days, McNair was able in this period to file an appeal. Moreover, Johnston insisted on waiving all responsibility for improperly executed projects and damage claims that might have resulted. He further demanded that the city pick its own engineering personnel for WPA assignments and that he be given a major role in supervising all WPA work. Councilman Kane asserted that these actions represented sabotage. When Kane resigned from council to assume his post as county commissioner, he sniped at McNair by announcing, "I want to assure you, the members of Council, that when I assume the office of County Commissioner I will cooperate

51. *Press,* Dec. 4, 1935.
52. Ibid., Dec. 4, 1935; ibid., Dec. 6, 1935.

with the City Council to the best of my ability because there is no other agency in the city from which you can expect cooperation."[53]

Others became impatient with the mayor and his followers. When Johnston, substituting for an ill McNair, spoke to a crowd of 150 WPA workers in a south side school, they heckled his pleas for work relief by contract at the "going wage." A member of the audience yelled, "You built scab bunk houses all over the South Side in 1920." In that year the public works director had served with the A. M. Byers Steel Company, but he denied the antilabor charge. When McNair requested an appointment with FDR for Johnston and himself toward the end of January 1936, "to discuss fundamental policies having to do with work relief which cannot be solved by local or state bodies," the president denied the request.[54]

During that year, McNair, the mayor who had "surrendered unconditionally," maintained his stance and continued a long line of vetoes of ordinances designed to cooperate with the WPA. In June an ordinance authorized and directed the mayor and the director of the Department of Public Works to carry out and complete unemployment relief projects in conjunction with the WPA; McNair, following his unveering course, vetoed it. He still viewed the Works Progress Administration as a "shameless waste of money." However, council disagreed and once again overrode the veto.[55]

City council's advocacy of work relief perhaps can best be explained by the pressures weighing upon it, as well as the obvious requirement of meeting an emergency situation. During 1935, when the mayor fought so hard against the federal program, council received approximately 115 requests from groups or individuals for improvements, such as paving sidewalks and fixing streets, bridges, and playgrounds. Several asked that their requests be included in the WPA master plan. Elected by citywide balloting, council faced citywide pressures: when the Beechview Civic Club asked for the construction of a new engine house, the Fifteenth

53. Ibid., Dec. 15, 1935; ibid., Dec. 19, 1935; *PG*, Dec. 18, 1935; ibid., Dec. 19, 1935; ibid., Dec. 24, 1935; ibid., Dec. 27, 1935; *Mun. Rec.*, 1935, vol. 69, p. 745.

54. *Press*, Dec. 17, 1935; *PG*, Dec. 17, 1935; McNair to FDR, Jan. 17, 1936, with answer from Marvin McIntyre, Jan. 22, 1936, Alphabetical File, 1933–1936, McNair, FDRL.

55. *Mun. Rec.*, 1936, vol. 70, pp. 279, 329–30. For other 1936 vetoes see *Municipal Record* for that year.

Ward Citizens Committee requested the building of a swimming pool, and the Thirty-first Ward Non-Partisan Welfare Association sought a continuing appropriation to furnish coal to needy families, council stood up and took note.[56]

Only when one considers McNair's economic philosophy, his propensity for limited government, his coterie of advisers, and his distrust of the regular Democratic organization can one understand the mayor's reversal in his thinking regarding relief. In 1933 McNair had attacked the Pittsburgh Republican administration because "thirty cities have asked for federal funds to tear down their slums [and] this Mayor and Council won't take a penny from the government. They would rather keep the poor on welfare so they can throw them off if they vote Democratic. They don't want any credit given to President Roosevelt." It did not take him long to trade places with this GOP administration philosophically as well as officially. An advocate of local control masquerading in New Dealer's clothing, a Manchester liberal in the wrong party at the wrong time, McNair could not accept the depression decade's experimentation with economic planning and expanded federal government.[57]

He could accept and even foster relief and public works programs when conducted on the local level; but when the relief system ballooned into a massive federal project with directives originating in Washington and Harrisburg, McNair feared the outside bureaucracy, which he, himself, could not control. The mayor appeared amenable to local projects originating from and directed by the office of Public Works Director Leslie M. Johnston, but he took his vehement stand against projects controlled by David Lawrence and Edward Jones. Although not interested in building his own machine—McNair made this fact clear during his first month in office, and his erratic appointments seem to bear this out—he despaired in knowing that the hostile Democratic organization would control relief and attempt to use it for political purposes.[58]

McNair felt that the control of relief would be much safer in the hands of a man like Johnston, who was more interested in efficiency than in

---

56. *Mun. Rec.,* 1934, 1935, vols. 68, 69. Communications between the public and council were tallied from the index of *Municipal Record.* The "Communications From" section of the index indicates all requests submitted to council.

57. *PG,* Oct. 28, 1933.

58. Clippings from *Press,* Feb. 5, 1934, McNair Scrapbooks, PD, CL. This article contains McNair's comment on the building of a machine.

providing jobs for the needy—and who was his ally. Besides, McNair's base of support rested with the upper class areas of Pittsburgh. The silk stockings had made him their candidate, and, in turn, he looked to them for advice once in office. Surrounding himself with men like Johnston and generally reflecting the civic desires of the upper class, McNair reinforced his own Manchester liberalism with the anti-big government predilections of his chief advisers and political friends.

The mayor's distaste for economic planning was surpassed only by his advocacy of the single tax. "I say you can no more plan the laws of economics than you can plan the laws of gravity," he once wrote. Viewing FDR as a second and more radical William Jennings Bryan, the Pittsburgh mayor continued: "There are certain rules you must obey because they are in the very nature of things. . . . The law of economic rent, for example, is a fundamental. No matter where you go, in whatever period of history, you will find that when a million people assemble and build a city, there will be certain desired sites that will go skyhigh in price because it is there that the most money is made." Unable to free himself from his single-tax theory and his laissez-faire economics, McNair remained inflexible at a time when political pragmatism ruled the day; he abided by his principles but abetted the suffering of Pittsburgh's needy.[59]

Still another factor helps to explain Mayor McNair's actions. As has been indicated, he feared the Democratic organization's control over the WPA payroll. The organization, starved for municipal patronage, had to look elsewhere for the tangible rewards of politics, and the federal works projects seemed a logical arena. The political potential of controlling so many thousands of jobs had been unprecedented in history. In his *Saturday Evening Post* article, "The Waste of the People's Money," published just as his showdown with Governor Earle had reached a head, the mayor charged that "a political octopus is growing around the work relief program. . . . The whole issue is rapidly becoming a political Frankenstein monster which will destroy its creators." Moreover, on the day of his unconditional surrender, he asked why he and Johnston could not get money to spend on their program. Rhetorically, he answered, "They insist on doing it themselves, so that they can build up their political machine here." Bitter in apparent defeat, seemingly beaten in his fight against

59. Clipping from *ST*, Oct. 18, 1936, McNair Scrapbooks, PD, CL.

what he believed to be a Leviathan government and its urban political appendage, Mayor William Nissley McNair was perhaps never more correct.[60]

60. William N. McNair, "The Waste of the People's Money," *Saturday Evening Post*, CCXII (Nov. 30, 1935), pp. 7, 70; clipping from *PG,* Dec. 4, 1935, McNair Scrapbooks, PD, CL.

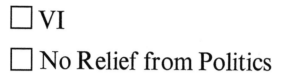

☐ VI

☐ No Relief from Politics

It might be well for some official in Washington to remind W.P.A. Administrator Jones that the initials in his title do not stand for Ward Politics Administration.

Editorial, Pittsburgh Post-Gazette, *December 14, 1935*

☐ It was a jubilant day for David Lawrence when, on October 6, 1936, he wired FDR: "Some more Roosevelt luck. Mayor McNair resigned and Cornelius D. Scully sworn in to fill vacancy by City Council." Pittsburgh, rocked with surprise by its mayor's unexpected resignation, witnessed in awe the triumph of the Democratic organization in its running battle with William Nissley McNair. The mayor stepped aside when his dismissal of organization stalwart James P. Kirk as city treasurer plunged Pittsburgh into financial chaos; council refused to confirm the mayor's new appointee for the office and the city's bills went unpaid. McNair, fearing that he would be taken to court and this time removed from office, decided to resign rather than be "another Charlie Kline."[1]

1. Telegram, Lawrence to Marvin McIntyre, Oct. 6, 1935, Democratic National Committee (hereafter cited as DNC), Pa., File, Official Files 300 (hereafter cited as OF), Franklin D. Roosevelt Library (hereafter cited as FDRL), Hyde Park, N.Y.; clipping from *Pittsburgh Press* (hereafter cited as *Press*), Oct. 6, 1936, McNair Scrapbooks, Pennsylvania Division, Carnegie Library (hereafter cited as PD, CL), Pittsburgh, Pa.; *New York Times* (hereafter cited as *NYT*), Oct. 7, 1936; interview with committeeman, 28W6. (To maintain anonymity of committeemen, they are listed by ward and district—hence, 28W6 is read 28th Ward, 6th District.)

McNair's successor, an organization favorite, gave an immediate indication that he would cooperate with the federal WPA program when, as one of his first acts in office, he dismissed Public Works Director Leslie M. Johnston. Shortly after becoming mayor, Scully thanked Washington for an administrative order saving the jobs of 9,000 Allegheny County WPA workers and emphasized that "preventing hardship to so many of our people was a most humanitarian action." This continued cooperation throughout his tenure in office resulted in the organization's being free to use work-relief patronage as it willed, and it seized the opportunity; it also obtained free rein over the lucrative municipal payroll of approximately 6,000 jobs.[2]

Relief in Pittsburgh, as in the entire state of Pennsylvania, had been riddled with politics since the creation of the Civil Works Administration during the fall and winter of 1933–1934. Even prior to that time, opponents had accused the GOP city administration of holding back the benefits of a 1932 relief bond issue until the approach of the mayoralty primary and general election of 1933. During her August 1933 visit to Pittsburgh, Lorena Hickok reported back to Harry Hopkins: "Our chief trouble in Pennsylvania is due to politics. From township to Harrisburg, the state is honeycombed with politicians all fighting for the privilege of distributing patronage. . . ." Since the GOP controlled the state until 1935, most of these politicians were Republicans.[3]

At the end of November 1933, the city council considered the enabling legislation for Pittsburgh's part in the CWA program. Councilman Robert Garland, during a discussion of who would serve on the projects, remarked: "You can't have ward chairmen on this. The thing is too big for that." By the beginning of 1934, however, disappointed job hopefuls claimed that one needed the approval of his ward chairman prior to getting a CWA post and that the Republicans were building up a "super political machine." The Democratic state leader, Joseph F. Guffey, brought the complaint to the attention of Hopkins. In a statement prior to meeting with the federal administrator, Guffey irritatedly demanded,

2. Clipping from *Press*, Oct. 13, 1936, McNair Scrapbooks, PD, CL; *NYT*, Oct. 11, 1936, sec. 4, p. 7; telegram, Cornelius D. Scully to Aubrey Williams, Dec. 10, 1936, WPA Record Group 69, Pa. 610, Box 2377, National Archives (hereafter cited as NA), Washington, D.C. For evidence of Scully's cooperation with WPA, see *Municipal Record*, 1937–1941, vols. 71–75.

3. Hickok Report, Aug. 7–12, 1933, Aug.–Oct. 28, 1933 File, Hopkins mss., FDRL.

"I want to know why it is necessary for an applicant for a C.W.A. job— a project from which President Roosevelt and Harry Hopkins requested all politicians to be kept out—to see his Republican ward chairman before he can receive consideration." The Pennsylvania Democrat also scored the state's civil works Administrator, Eric M. Biddle. Hopkins, however, defended Biddle, as well as the entire program, and hit back at Guffey for being as much involved in making the state administrator's road a difficult one as the Republican politicians.[4]

From all over the nation, aggrieved Democrats wrote Washington that the Republicans were using the CWA as a tool in building their local political machines. In Pennsylvania the female vice-chairman of the Democratic State Committee wrote Guffey's sister, National Committee-woman Emma Guffey Miller, "We shall never be able to build up a strong Democratic organization in the state as long as jobs such as employment superintendent, C.W.A. and all the other heads of the departments are given to Republicans"; and from the steel capital came the hope "that some way may be found to put this federal relief in the hands of some real Americans in Pittsburgh instead of the hands of the Republican organization." Although the Democratic organization had apparently solicited these complaints (Harry Hopkins told Louis Howe, Roosevelt's secretary, that he had on file copies of letters sent out by the organization inviting the accusations), it was true that Republicans did gain political mileage from the CWA program in those areas where they controlled its local administration.[5]

The CWA was not alone in reflecting Republican partisanship; other agencies during the early New Deal also showed the GOP influence in Pennsylvania. When in June 1933 Pittsburgh's newspapers announced the opening of the Federal Farm Loan Office, with a Republican at the

4. Clipping from *Pittsburgh Post-Gazette* (hereafter cited as *PG*), Nov. 24, 1933, ibid., Jan. 11, 1934, CWA File, PD, CL; clipping from *Press,* Jan. 18, 1934, ibid., undated, Guffey Papers, Washington and Jefferson College (hereafter cited as W & J), Washington, Pa.; clipping from *Press,* Jan. 20, 1935, CWA File, PD, CL.
5. Searle F. Charles, *Minister of Relief: Harry Hopkins and the Depression* (Syracuse, 1963), p. 54; letter, Katherine C. Henderson to Emma Guffey Miller, Dec. 20, 1933, Emma Guffey Miller File, DNC, Women's Divsiion, Pa., File, FDRL; William A. Shaw to Emma Guffey Miller, Dec. 20, 1933, Emma Guffey Miller File, DNC, Women's Division, Pa., File, FDRL; Hopkins to Howe, Feb. 2, 1934, Hopkins mss., Federal Emergency Relief Administration—Works Progress Administration Confidential Political Files, 1933–1938, Box 65, Folder Ma-Mi, FDRL.

helm, Guffey angrily informed Washington, "We can and will make Pennsylvania a Democratic state but I think we are entitled to some help from Secretary Wallace and Henry Morgenthau." He also complained that Republicans still ran things in the Department of Labor's affiliates, the United States Employment Service, and the United States Conciliation Service, which operated in Pennsylvania.[6]

Once the Democrats won over the state in the gubernatorial and senatorial elections of 1934, things began to change; and Guffey could aid some of the patronage-starved "real Americans" in Pittsburgh, as well as the rest of the state. During the ripper-lobby probe, one woman active in Pittsburgh politics testified that her husband had been fired from a Local Works Division (LWD) job because she had held a meeting for Mayor McNair. She maintained that her husband later applied for relief work and had been told to "get a letter from your Democratic ward chairman." Moreover, one observer estimated that in October of 1934, even before the Democratic state victory, Guffey had been instrumental in placing at least five hundred Pennsylvanians in emergency jobs in Washington, practically all exempt from Civil Service, and in filling eight to ten times as many federal jobs in Pennsylvania itself.[7]

Foremost within the state were the rich offerings of 2,500 positions within the Home Owners Loan Corporation. Then, too, the usual positions as United States marshals, attorneys, and internal revenue collectors, plus hundreds of appointments as postmaster, made more grist for the patronage mill. Citizens expressed fear of the growth of a new political leviathan. One Pennsylvanian, writing to Louis Howe, complained: "The Republican State Organization is in a bad way. It is entirely possible that the voter . . . may use the Democratic party to administer another lesson to the Vare-Mellon-Grundy [Republican] machine. But this cannot be done by building up another machine, as Guffey is trying to do, with all the evil characteristics of the machine it is going to replace. Guffeyism has become as odious to decent citizens as Varism." However, Guffey's control was not as monolithic as this writer implied. When a native Pittsburgher, corresponding with Howe, blamed the organization leader for rewarding three Republicans with patronage plums, Guffey

6. Guffey to Marvin McIntyre, June 5, 1933, DNC, Pa., File, OF 300, FDRL; undated memo, Francis Perkins to McIntyre for Guffey, Labor Department, 1934, File, OF 15, FDRL.
7. *PG,* Oct. 23, 1935; clipping from *Press,* Sept. 30, 1934, Guffey File, PD, CL.

informed the president's secretary: "Neither I nor the Pennsylvania State Democratic Organization had anything to do with these appointments. They are simply another example of how appointments are made in Pennsylvania by some of our administrative officials without contacting or making reference to me or the Pennsylvania State Organization."[8]

Guffey did, however, play an important role in choosing the first Pennsylvania WPA administrator, Edward Noel Jones, telling Hopkins in a letter of introduction for the nominee, "He is my candidate." Jones, a Pittsburgher, traveled the road from political press agent for Republicans Magee and Coyne to the same position for Democrats McNair and Earle. Immediately prior to assuming his office in the Keystone State's Works Progress Administration, he served as Earle's secretary of labor, despite organized labor's opposition. At one point he was considered front-runner to succeed McNair if the ripper bill passed. Some observers believed that Jones's close ties to Guffey threatened Earle's power in the state, and most agreed that he was not averse to making political appointments. "Let's be charitable and say that he is employing—as he apparently is—able men, even though they are being selected entirely on a political basis," commented Lorena Hickok.[9]

From top to bottom, from administrator to laborer, the early Pennsylvania appointments reflected political influence. During a phone call in early July 1935, when Jones was choosing his district administrators, he praised a prospective Philadelphia appointee. Hopkins inquired, "Is he a good Democrat?" "Oh yes," Jones replied.[10] By early August in Pittsburgh, 289 workers in the area's reclassification division of the State Emergency Relief Board busied themselves looking for "good Democratic" sponsors so they could stay on the payroll when the division

8. *Press,* Sept. 30, 1934; letter, W. I. Ellis to Howe, Jan. 22, 1934, DNC, Pa., File, OF 300, FDRL; letter, M. A. Barr to Howe, Mar. 3, 1935, letter, Howe to Joseph Guffey, Mar. 12, 1935, letter, Guffey to Howe, Mar. 18, 1935, OF 400, FDRL.

9. Letter, Joseph Guffey to Harry Hopkins, June 3, 1935, WPA Record Group 69, Pa. 630, Box 2394 I-K, NA; *PG,* Dec. 12, 1935; Hickok Report File, July 24, 1935, Hopkins mss., FDRL; Charles, *Minister of Relief,* p. 300.

10. It is difficult to evaluate the historical evidence from which this account was taken. In all accounts of the period, Hopkins is generally considered to be a foe of politics in WPA, as was probably the case. Recorded in the transcript of a telephone call, the federal administrator's asking, "Is he a good Democrat?" may have been a sarcastic remark aimed at Jones's political bent. However, the historian, unable to hear the actual voice, must accept the statement at face value.

merged with the WPA at the beginning of October. When Charles W. Scovell, Jr., the area's reclassification supervisor, was quoted by some of the workers as handing out the warning to search for a Democratic godfather, he retorted: "I deny saying that Mayor McNair's signature would be no good on any application. . . . What I told my staff is a matter between the staff and me." John F. Laboon, the district's WPA administrator, corroborated Scovell's denial of political hirings and said all employees and officials supervising WPA work would get jobs on merit alone. However, a few days later, John Fitzgerald, a young nephew of Democratic State Chairman David L. Lawrence, received appointment as paymaster of the Pittsburgh WPA program.[11]

As the 1935 county commissioners' election neared, one observer claimed that Jones actually hesitated in cooperating with the incumbent Republican board for fear that if the program made a good showing, it would work against the Democrats at election time. During the closing days of the campaign, Commissioner C. C. McGovern attacked politics in both the PWA and the WPA, neither of which had yet actually got off the ground. Finding more political "cooperation" than he bargained for, the commissioner charged that the demand of the PWA that the Allegheny County Authority begin work on the Liberty Tunnel plaza by the Monday prior to the balloting was just "another glaring example in which the Democratic State gang is playing politics with human misery." With regard to the WPA, McGovern feared that officials of the federal program would send thirty or forty men a day to various areas of the county regardless of whether the commissioners approved the project and whether materials and tools were on the scene; he maintained that the practice would continue until after the election when proper procedure again would be followed.[12]

Preelection-day activities added fuel to McGovern's fire. Charging that WPA authorities had picked 1,250 Negro voters from Pittsburgh's Third and Fifth Wards for project work outside the city, the irate commissioner held that the Democrats were trying to garner majorities in the two wards.

11. Transcript, telephone conversation between Harry Hopkins, George Earle, and Edward Jones, July 8, 1935, WPA Record Group 69, Pa. 610, Box 2376, NA; *Pittsburgh Sun-Telegraph* (hereafter cited as *ST*), Aug. 15, 1935; ibid., Aug. 21, 1935.

12. John McClellan, assistant regional engineer, to George D. Babcock, acting field representative, Nov. 4, 1935, WPA Record Group 69, Pa. 610, Box 2377, NA; *Press*, Nov. 1, 1935.

The finger of accusation pointed to two Joneses—Edward, the state administrator, and Paul, Negro state workmen's compensation referee—as the masterminds behind the Democratic strategy. Paul F. Murphy, head of the Federal-State Employment Service, which did the hiring for WPA, announced that his office had selected the Hill District residents because WPA authorities could easily arrange rail transportation for them on the conveniently located Pennsylvania and B & O Railroads. John F. Laboon denied all, labelling as ridiculous Republican accusations that the men were rushed out to jobs on Monday, November 4, allowed to loaf all day, and then told to go home and take Tuesday, election day, off. Noting that the operation had been part of the federal agency's master plan, he declared: "Our schedule called for the sending of these men from the Hill District out on a job Monday. We could not upset the efficiency of our office and half our schedule merely because it happened to be the day before the election." Whatever the reason for the step-up in employment, the Democrats carried the Negro Third Ward, but they lost the Fifth—despite the fact that Negroes made up approximately 60 percent of Pittsburgh's unemployed in early 1935.[13]

After the election accusations of political discrimination within the WPA continued. A two-day conference of the Associated Employees of the Pennsylvania Relief Administration, meeting in Pittsburgh, charged favoritism in the federal program and resolved that WPA positions should be filled on an objective merit basis only. The primary problem facing the SERB employees was the fear of losing their jobs as a result of the withdrawal of the federal government from direct relief and its establishment of the WPA. Success of the works program meant a lessening of the direct relief rolls and a cutback in employment of state social workers. As *The Pittsburgh Press* editorialized, "To ask them what they think of W.P.A. is equivalent to asking a discharged employee what he thinks of his successor." The dispute between the social workers and the WPA flared up a month later in December 1935, when Edward Jones accused his social-worker critics of trying to save their jobs by plotting to ruin his program with such tactics as the sabotaging of WPA projects. Jones claimed relief officials "celebrated" the beginning of WPA by shutting down all Local Works Division projects they had in operation and throwing 40,000 out of relief work, whereas in other states the WPA

13. *Press,* Nov. 5, 1935; ibid., Feb. 7, 1935; *PG,* Nov. 4, 1935.

absorbed LWD projects, thereby being provided with a head start. More-over, according to the state administrator, "those eligible for relief were advised not to be in a hurry about reporting to work and assumed they would be kept on relief."[14]

At a tempestuous, wild-eyed meeting held at the Irene Kaufmann Settlement House, just after McNair had capitulated in his showdown with Earle, Congressman Theodore L. Moritz, a follower of the mayor, complained that the organization was handing out WPA jobs through the Democratic ward chairmen. Announcing that he would call for an investi-gation of how the relief money was being spent, the congressman sulked, "Just think, I voted for that five billion dollars and now I can't send any-body down to the W.P.A.—however needy the man—because I'm sup-posed to be outside the organization." Angered by the continuing string of allegations, Paul F. Murphy, the local director of the Federal-State Employment Service, announced that he would ask Mrs. R. Templeton Smith and her sister, Mrs. J. O. Miller, to "pull the cards" that would send the next 2,000 WPA workers to their jobs; both women had sharply cross-examined John F. Laboon before a meeting of their League of Women Voters. Whereas the employment service assigned relief work jobs by chance, administrative nonrelief jobs were filled from names submitted by the WPA's personnel department.[15]

The constant complaints, frequently emanating from and highlighted in the emphatically anti-New Deal *Pittsburgh Post-Gazette*, prompted State Administrator Edward Jones to refuse the newspaper's reporters' access to records and information concerning his agency. When ques-tioned at his Harrisburg office as to whether he had any specific examples of news distortion, Jones merely stated that he based his decision on the *Pittsburgh Post-Gazette*'s attitude. In a wire to Harry Hopkins, the editor of the paper wryly stated: "The paper had criticized W.P.A. administra-tive inefficiency here and politics as exemplified in hiring 1800 day before election when no tools or materials available, paying for two days and dropping day after election. Will continue to [criticize] but want to know whether your office approves effort to deny public information. . . ." He kept his word—he continued to criticize. On December 13, two days after

14. *ST*, Nov. 18, 1935; *Press*, Nov. 18, 1935; ibid., Nov. 19, 1935, editorial page; ibid., Dec. 15, 1935; Jacob Fisher, *The Rank and File Movement in Social Work, 1935–1936* (New York, 1936), pp. 38–39.
15. *PG*, Dec. 9, 1935; ibid., Dec. 13, 1935; *Press*, Dec. 9, 1935.

his wire, he republished photos, which had appeared in the paper's post-election-day issue, of Hill District Negroes sitting around at a WPA project doing nothing.[16]

A few days later, addressing several hundred WPA supervisors summoned by telephone to Pittsburgh's Schenley High School auditorium, Jones and Laboon added ammunition to the already blistering salvos of those attacking politics in WPA. Jones, in a searing blast at the *Pittsburgh Post-Gazette*, in part for its lending encouragement to McNair in his opposition to the federal program, called upon WPA employees to fight back tooth and nail against all attacks on the agency, President Roosevelt, and the New Deal. His Pittsburgh assistant did him one better; answering a question from a WPA worker, Laboon declared: "I'll tell you right now that any W.P.A. worker who is not in sympathy with the W.P.A. program and the Roosevelt administration will be eliminated from W.P.A. payrolls in this district as quickly as I can act. I want you men to report all such cases to me without delay."[17]

Subsequently, Laboon claimed that he had been misquoted. As proof that his operation was free of politics, he pointed to the fact that only 3.8 percent of project employees in his district were nonreliefers, although the law allowed the hiring of 10 percent. Jones declared that Laboon's remarks applied only to recalcitrant supervisors, who by their attitude toward WPA retarded the program, and had been made in answer to a member of the audience who had charged that some supervisors not in sympathy with the program were hindering WPA's efficiency and effectiveness. He contended that the warning did not apply to the average worker taken off the relief rolls, whom he did not hire on to WPA but "merely provided a job for."[18]

The damage, however, had been done. Former Governor Gifford Pinchot, heeding Roosevelt's public invitation to inform him of improper practices in the administration of relief, noted Laboon's comment and asserted that the program in Pennsylvania had "been sold into political bondage." He continued that work relief in Pennsylvania had been clean until WPA took over, but under that "notorious spoilsman Guffey's . . . man Jones, [it] has been degraded into a Democratic pie-counter." More-

16. Telegram, O. J. Keller to Hopkins, Dec. 11, 1935, WPA Record Group 69, Pa. 610, Box 2377, NA; *PG*, Dec. 12, 1935; ibid., Dec. 13, 1935.
17. *PG*, Dec. 18, 1935.
18. *Press*, Dec. 19, 1935; *PG*, Dec. 20, 1935.

over, he claimed that Guffey's henchmen assessed relief workers 3 percent of salaries under $1200 a year and 5 percent of salaries above that figure, and begged the president to "replace them with men worthy of respect, to take work relief out of Guffey's evil domination, and make it clean again." Roosevelt replied that the charges, except for Laboon's quote, "which will be immediately checked," were not specific and were "merely tirades against persons you conceive to be your political enemies. . . ." Guffey, from a vacation retreat in Miami Beach, declared that Pinchot also sought a place in the sun—"the national political sun." He endorsed Jones as doing as fine a job as anyone in the United States. The year ended with Laboon's accepting a job as superintendent of highways for the new Democratic county administration; he no longer served with Pittsburgh's WPA.[19]

Nineteen hundred and thirty-six brought an important change to Pittsburgh; by April, David Lawrence could inform the White House that for the first time since the Civil War the city registered more Democratic voters than Republican. Six months later, when Lorena Hickok took one of her numerous swings through Pennsylvania, she reported of Pittsburgh's WPA situation, "But my Lord, it's political!" She told of how the district director of the women's and professional projects had boasted that she had collected $3,000 from her projects and proudly added, "I didn't give any receipts for it either." Friends of State Administrator Jones told Miss Hickok: "Oh it's plenty political right here in Pittsburgh. Regular ward politics. But the Republicans would do the same thing if they had W.P.A., wouldn't they?"[20]

They did. In areas of Pennsylvania where the GOP controlled the political machinery, it controlled the WPA. Prior to the 1936 election James Farley received reports of such Republican manipulation. In Fayette County the president of the local United Mine Workers reported how Republican control "is crucifying our party and endangering the election of our Congressmen." Nevertheless, the Pennsylvania Democrats, under Guffey, had more than ten thousand nonrelief workers and approximately three thousand administrative officials on the WPA payroll

19. Pinchot to FDR, Dec. 21, 1935, President's Personal File 289, FDRL; *PG*, Dec. 23, 1935; ibid., Dec. 31, 1935.

20. Telegram, Lawrence to Marvin McIntyre, Apr. 14, 1936, OF 300, FDRL; Hickok Report, Oct. 17, 1936, Nov. 1935–Nov. 1936 File, Hopkins mss., FDRL; Charles, *Minister of Relief,* p. 302.

prior to the 1936 election. The assessments continued despite a directive from Jones against soliciting political contributions on federal projects, issued in March after Senator Vandenberg of Michigan complained of such activity in Pennsylvania.[21]

In September 1936 Patrick Fagan, president of Pittsburgh's UMW, wrote to Farley with regard to Republican charges of WPA irregularities. He suggested that rumors of workers' being compelled to purchase Jones's Democratic flyer "We the People" were probably correct. Fagan distrusted Jones as antilabor and emphasized that the state administrator was "a former Republican and has been connected with some very shady Republican administrations in Pittsburgh." Other critics maintained that construction workers were receiving the lowest paying WPA jobs, while inexperienced political ward heelers were receiving supervisory jobs paying up to $240 a month. In October, William Hard, a radio commentator for the Republican National Committee, alleged that the Democrats placed spies in the Pennsylvania WPA ranks to spot Alf Landon supporters and have them discharged, as well as to force all workers to contribute to FDR's campaign. Hopkins denied these allegations, countering that Republicans, posing as newspapermen, had infiltrated the WPA ranks and were trying to wangle stories out of unknowing workers whom they treated to a hot meal. However, the political accusations did not hurt Roosevelt, as indicated by his landslide victory, including the carrying of Pittsburgh and all of Pennsylvania. In the words of Patrick Fagan, who had criticized the administrator, but not the program, "People [knew] W.P.A. and P.W.A. brought salvation and recovery."[22]

As the Democrats began to consolidate their strength in Pittsburgh, the party's mayoralty nomination increased in value. With the summer drawing on, the Democratic organization, backing incumbent Scully, faced a primary fight, as well as widespread accusations that it had become the

21. W. J. Hynes to Farley, Sept. 8, 1936, OF 300, FDRL (see same file for similar letters); Joseph Alsop and Robert Kintner, "The Guffey," *Saturday Evening Post*, CCX (Apr. 16, 1938), 16; Arthur Vandenberg to Hopkins, Feb. 28, 1936, Hopkins press release Mar. 5, 1936, Hopkins mss., FDRL; state administrator's notice no. 99, Mar. 16, 1936, Case no. 37, WPA Record Group 69, Pa. 610, NA.

22. Fagan to James Farley, Sept. 16, 1936, OF 300, FDRL; clippings from *Pennsylvania State Journal* (Pittsburgh), May 6, 1936, William H. Coleman Scrapbook, Archives of Industrial Society, University of Pittsburgh; Richard C. Keller, "Pennsylvania's Little New Deal" (unpubl. Ph.D. diss., Graduate Faculty of Political Science, Columbia University, 1960), pp. 226–27; *New York Times* (hereafter cited as *NYT*), Oct. 9, 1936, p. 21.

new machine. When the Scully campaign formally got under way in June at a glossy testimonial banquet, Councilmen P. J. McArdle and Thomas Gallagher and County Commissioner Kane were conspicuously absent. The filing of nominating petitions bore out the regulars' worst fears— McArdle had filed for mayor. Moreover, in keeping with his role of perennial candidate and gadfly of the organization, former Mayor McNair entered the primary as a third and rather silent candidate for the office he had recently vacated.

The major battle, however, loomed between McArdle and Scully. Commissioner Kane, in a maneuver to gain leadership in the county, strongly backed McArdle, a Republican turned Democrat, using labor as his wedge. Kane had been president of the printing pressmen's union, and McArdle had served five times as head of the Amalgamated Association of Iron, Steel, and Tin Workers. Ironically, however, during the 1933 Republican primary McArdle had the support of the upper-class Citizens League and was considered to be a silk-stocking Republican himself. He received his principal backing at the time from steelman Ernest T. Weir, who later gained national prominence as an opponent of the New Deal and organized labor. Scully, who had been born into a prominent Pittsburgh family, had attended Yale, and travelled in the company of the city's social elite, being himself listed in the Social Register, could not, unfortunately for him, obscure his silk-stocking past.[23]

Although Scully's labor record appeared satisfactory, he had not come up through the ranks. Besides, some factions of organized labor were not satisfied with their treatment at the hands of Lawrence's organization. When Kane had resigned from his council post to become commissioner, the organization had refused to replace him with a union man. Moreover, some organization-controlled state legislators did not fully support labor-endorsed legislation, often changing bills drafted by labor from their original form. Kane succeeded in beating Lawrence to the labor vote by getting the Pittsburgh Central Labor Union's exclusive endorsement of McArdle; but Lawrence, in desperation, was able to persuade the Central Labor Union's president, Patrick Fagan, to declare for Scully. Ultimately, however, Fagan, a CIO supporter, was read out of the CLU when the AF of L chartered body attempted to purge itself of all dissi-

23. *The Bulletin Index,* July 8, 1937, clipping from *Press,* July 26, 1937, newspaper clipping, Aug. 15, 1937, editorial page, 1937 Election File, PD, CL.

dents. At a rump meeting of Labor's Non-Partisan League, ninety-two union locals also swung their support to McArdle.[24]

Not only did Scully and the organization have to contend with a hostile labor faction, but the Republican candidate for mayor, Robert N. Waddell, stated that he had entered his party's primary race "as my part to rid the city of Pittsburgh from the boss-ridden, machine controlled, Democratic misgovernment." He continued his attacks on the Democrats, at one point, proclaiming: "They're building a political machine such as never before existed and I hope never will exist. When the Mayor can't even make an appointment to a $90.00 a month job without consulting the higherups, I say they ought to be put out of City Hall." The mayoralty campaign tactics since 1933 had come full circle.[25]

There was contention within the party itself. Commissioner Kane asserted that the organization depended "on silence from the candidate, the payroll, and coercion of W.P.A. workers . . ." to achieve victory in the primary. McArdle charged that WPA officials high-pressured women working on the program's local sewing project into attending Scully campaign rallies. The city had recently adopted the project to prevent it from being abandoned; and in a letter to James Kessner, Laboon's successor as WPA district administrator, McArdle claimed that James Gallagher, the sewing project's director, told the women that "a certain public officer" was responsible for saving their jobs and urged them to vote for Scully and attend political rallies in his behalf. Moreover, he allegedly agreed to excuse from work early employees attending rallies, to make up for time spent listening to speeches. After an investigation James B. Quinlan, Pittsburgh's assistant administrator of WPA, denied the charges, admitting only that Gallagher did permit workers to leave fifteen minutes early on condition that they make up the time or suffer a deduction in their salaries. Quinlan expressed regret that McArdle's letter had spread "a false rumor damaging to the integrity of the W.P.A. workers."[26]

McArdle also maintained that the sewing project workers had been maced, causing J. Banks Hudson, Edward Jones's successor, to issue quickly a directive warning his staff against pressuring WPA workers into

24. *The Bulletin Index,* July 8, 1937, 1937 Election File, PD, CL; *Press,* Sept. 6, 1937, editorial page; ibid., Sept. 17, 1937.
25. *ST,* Aug. 4, 1937, 1937 Election File, PD, CL; *Press,* Aug. 4, 1937; ibid., Aug. 14, 1937.
26. *Press,* Aug. 10, 1937; ibid., Aug. 14, 1937; ibid., Sept. 11, 1937.

contributing to the Democratic campaign. This did not prevent William L. Blake, a labor leader and Democratic politician allied with the Kane-McArdle faction, from claiming that during the 1936 campaign the organization gave him a list of WPA workers from whom he was to collect from ten to fifty dollars each.[27]

Politics, it appeared, had even infiltrated the WPA's federal music project. During the general election campaign one complainant wrote to the project's supervisor stating that Democrats were making political use of concert and dance units playing at a recreation center, and asked that an orchestra be provided for a dance at Republican headquarters. The supervisor turned down his request.[28]

During the primary the Democratic organization had purged the work-relief rolls of all men who had been sponsored by Commissioner Kane, replacing them with regulars. Once the disputing factions had reconciled after Scully's primary victory, the WPA was aimed as a weapon at the Republicans. During the months of October and November, hundreds of cases found their way from the direct relief rolls to the WPA payroll. The manning of the city streets alone jumped by over one thousand men. Republicans claimed that the county WPA office received orders to suspend all projects on election day, the work to be made up at a future date, so that all WPA appointees could work at the polls, vote, and take other reliefers to cast their ballots for the Democracy.[29]

State Democratic headquarters had issued instructions to "stress the New Deal" during the 1937 election. The Pittsburgh Democrats took the advice, and after Scully's primary and general election victories, Lawrence could tell FDR, "We had a great victory and it was without question a Roosevelt victory, as we emphasized and re-emphasized the New Deal." Some thought control over the WPA aided in the organization's triumph. Although it did not play a significant roll during the primary, it appears to have had a greater impact during the general election. (See table 14.) Many owed their jobs to the organization; one woman wrote to James P.

27. *Press*, Aug. 17, 1937; ibid., Sept. 2, 1937.
28. *Press*, Oct. 12, 1937.
29. U.S. Senate, *Report of Special Committee to Investigate Campaign Expenditures*, 76 Cong., 1 Sess. (1939), p. 214. This evidence is taken from a sworn affidavit of the chief clerk of WPA in Allegheny County, who was dismissed from her job and may have been retaliating against the Democratic organization. The evidence, however, was accepted by the committee and not proved false when investigated.

Kirk, Democratic county leader to congratulate him on Scully's new term and to remark, "Owing to your generous interest for which I am deeply grateful, [I] am still employed by the W.P.A. assigned to City Planning Commission, City-County Building."[30]

As seen in table 14, unlike McNair's 1933 mayoralty vote, Scully's mayoralty vote was related closely to FDR's presidential support. A high association is found when the 1937 Scully general election vote and the 1936 Roosevelt vote are correlated. However, Scully's primary support appears much different from the president's vote and unlike his own in the 1937 general election. The Roosevelt-Democratic coalition was split asunder during the primary only to be pieced together again at the time of the general election. The split was an economic, not an ethnic, one and can be attributed to Commissioner Kane's mobilization of organized labor against the Scully candidacy.

Table 14 also shows that both Scully's and McArdle's primary votes bear a positive, but low relationship to the ethnic elements in Pittsburgh. In fact, there is little difference between the correlations of their votes and the ethnic variable. On the other hand, there is a much greater difference between Scully's and McArdle's support in high-rent areas and among laborers. Of the three primary candidates, McNair, true to form, did best in the high-rent districts; Scully ran second best, and McArdle fared worst. However, Kane's effort to mobilize labor against the Lawrence organization had a great impact. Although McNair, of whom it might be expected because of his policies as mayor, did poorly among laborers, Scully, who had a significantly better labor record than McNair, did worse. In essence, the split was manufactured. When labor voted against the regular organization, it was less a matter of a group voting against its economic interests than of a group following a strong and popular leader, who was engaged in a struggle for political power and who played upon that group's latent discontent.

From the outset the Kane-McArdle forces had aimed their rhetoric at the common man. Early in August the candidate proclaimed: "Our

30. Bulletin no. 1, Democratic State Committee, 1937 Primary Election Publicity File, Allegheny County Democratic Committee Headquarters (hereafter cited as ACDCH); David Lawrence to FDR, Nov. 15, 1937, DNC, Pa., 1933–1945, I-R, File Box 59, OF 300, FDRL; letter, Margot Dardis to James P. Kirk, Nov. 8, 1937, Congratulatory Letters, 1937 General Election File, ACDCH.

TABLE 14
Coefficients of Correlation Between 1937 Election Votes and Both 1936 Roosevelt Vote and Demographic Variables

	FDR '36	Scully '37 Gen'l	Scully '37 Prim.	McArdle '37 Prim.	McNair '37 Prim.
FDR '36	—	.88	.14	.24	−.33
Foreign born '40	.42	.41	.11	.13	−.35
Individuals on WPA '40	.52a	.64	.16	.15	−.57
Median rent '40	−.72	−.62	.09	−.38	.43
Laborers '40	.59	.46	−.26	.37	−.14

SOURCES: Voting statistics were percentaged from returns published in *Pittsburgh Post-Gazette*, Sept. 15, 1937, and *Pittsburgh Press*, Nov. 3, 1937; rankings regarding WPA, laborers, median rent, and foreign born were taken from Bureau of Social Research, Federation of Social Agencies of Pittsburgh and Allegheny County, *Social Facts About Pittsburgh and Allegheny County,* vol. I, *Pittsburgh Wards* (Pittsburgh, 1945); 1936 FDR voting returns were taken from *Pennsylvania Manual,* 1937 ed.
NOTE: Table is based on Wards 1–32. See Appendix F.
a. The correlation for WPA in 1940 and FDR's 1940 vote is an even higher .74.

appeal is not to the members of the Duquesne Club nor to the residents of Fifth Avenue, who have half an acre of ground around their homes. We have picked a ticket that will honestly and fearlessly represent the common man. To the rank and file we appeal for support." However, some contemporary observers viewed Kane's rhetorical appeal to the rank and file as a part of the power struggle between him and Lawrence during the 1937 Democratic primary. Kane fought for McArdle's candidacy in the hope that he would gain control of both city and county patronage and subsequently be in a position to catapult himself into undisputed county and, perhaps, even state leadership.[31]

The organizational cleavage within the party was definitely on a city-county basis. Lawrence controlled the city and state workers, whereas Kane, as county commissioner, controlled the county payroll. Of the fifty-nine public pay-rollers officially listed as having contributed to the Scully war chest, most served the city; of the twenty-four who swelled the McArdle coffers, the majority worked for the county. Many ward organizations split on the basis of payroll politics. A Twentieth Ward committeeman remembered: "In 1937 I was the acting ward chairman during the primary. I supported Scully. The regular ward chairman supported

31. *Press,* Aug. 13, 1937; ibid., Aug. 29, 1937, editorial page.

McArdle. He worked for the county and was a Kane follower; I was with the state at the time." Many of the city pay-rollers who did support the McArdle ticket shifted to county jobs after the primary.[32]

Labor did not support Scully during the primary, but once McArdle lost, labor lent its support to Scully and the Lawrence Democratic organization. John Kane announced that he was a good Democrat and would not support the Republicans. The chairman of the Steel Workers Organizing Committee, Philip Murray, advised his constituency in Allegheny County to vote straight Democratic. The CIO leaders, as well as leaders of the Railroad Brotherhoods, the Street Railway and Motor Coach Union, the Building Trades Council, the Teamsters Joint Council, and other unions, echoed Murray's endorsement of Scully. Although some AF of L support went to the Republican candidate, Robert Waddell, Scully's labor support in the general election improved greatly over his labor vote during the primary. (See table 14.) Thus, the organization maintained its grasp on municipal power by defeating the threat posed by the county commissioner's office with its labor-mass base and then by absorbing labor back into the Roosevelt coalition before the general election.[33]

As for WPA, the relationship between Scully's primary vote by ward and a ranking of the city's wards by individuals on the WPA payroll in 1940 was not high; nor was this relationship high for the McArdle vote. (See table 14.) The potency of the WPA as a payroll weapon for the regular organization during the primary may have been offset by the Kane-McArdle organization's use of the county commissioner's patronage. Once the Democratic rift healed, the WPA weapon grew in potency, and there was a relatively high relationship between the November balloting and individuals on WPA. The Republicans, having no comparable patronage, could not offset the political use of relief. By no means was WPA the only factor involved in the Democratic victory; for instance, one can see a relatively high relationship with the economic variable of rent. However, the number of individuals on WPA per ward was the variable to which Scully's general election vote bore the closest relationship.

By the end of 1937, a total of $69.5 million had been spent on WPA

32. *Press,* Oct. 17, 1937; interviews with committeemen, 20W10, 26W13, 21W7.
33. *Press,* Oct. 4, 1937; ibid., Oct. 24, 1937; ibid., Oct. 31, 1937.

work in Allegheny County, with the federal government providing $62 million and local sponsors $7.5 million. More than 80 percent of the federal funds went for wages. Employment on government projects reached a peak of 47,095 workers, when the St. Patrick's Day flood in March 1936 wreaked havoc on the area's rivers. By the time of Scully's election, WPA had undertaken more than 530 miles of highway improvements; laid 33 miles of waterlines and 71 miles of sewers; built or improved 81 parks, playgrounds, and athletic fields; produced over a million garments and pieces of bedding; taught 2,200 adults to read and write; and constructed, using salvaged stones, massive bear pits for the city's Highland Park Zoo. It accomplished all this and more, with the county benefitting more than the city because of McNair's stubborn opposition. And before the end of the decade WPA would render other achievements, but not before it became thoroughly entangled in the political wars of 1938.[34]

As the 1938 primary for governor approached, the Democratic organization searched for a standard-bearer. David L. Lawrence appeared to be a leading candidate. When one state project engineer in charge of WPA highway construction wrote to the Democratic leader in February, he offered to stir up interest in Lawrence and the Democratic party, as well as in highways. Moreover, the correspondent claimed that most state employees felt that the Pittsburgh politician would be a prime vote-getter. Lawrence replied, "I do not know what the future may hold in the matter, but I appreciate your sentiments." However, after taking a private poll, he felt that he had learned "what the future may hold" and decided not to run. Senator Guffey believed himself a prime candidate, and when Democrats at a political summit meeting took another view, he stormed out. He denied a rumored rift with Lawrence, commenting: "There has been no such quarrel. If there ever is a separation between us it will take place only at the grave. . . ."[35]

The separation came much sooner. Although the White House proposed William C. Bullitt, United States ambassador to France, as its choice for governor, Lawrence and Philadelphia leader Matthew Mc-

34. *Press,* Oct. 28, 1937.
35. Letter, Lester J. Hendershot to Lawrence, Feb. 11, 1938, 1938 Political Endorsement File, ACDCH; Joseph F. Guffey, *Seventy Years on the Red Fire Wagon* (privately published, 1952), p. 103; copy of story from *Washington Evening Post* (D.C.) Feb. 26, 1938, Guffey Correspondence, 1940, Guffey Papers, W & J.

Closkey forced through the nomination of Pittsburgher Charles Alvin Jones; George Earle, who by law could not succeed himself as governor, received the senatorial nomination. However, Guffey bolted, throwing his support for governor to Thomas Kennedy, the incumbent lieutenant governor and a CIO stalwart, and for senator to Philadelphia's mayor S. Davis Wilson. State Attorney General Charles Margiotti further complicated matters when he too declared himself a candidate for governor. Earlier in the nominating battle, Mayor Scully had attempted to push his welfare director, Bryn Hovde, a former University of Pittsburgh professor, as a compromise candidate, because even union people themselves thought Kennedy was too much of a labor man to carry the nonlaboring areas of the state. The mayor, however, failed in his attempt. As a result, when the AF of L endorsed Jones and Earle, the primary took on the coloration of a dispute between that day's two warring labor factions, as well as between Guffey and Lawrence.[36]

All three slates attacked one another vigorously. The Kennedy supporters controlled the WPA, its administration, and its patronage and used this leverage to advance its cause. David Lawrence informed William Bullitt that reports from almost every county in the state indicated that the opposition to Earle and the state committee's ticket was being built around WPA patronage. "Heading up as we do the State Organization here, which is a Roosevelt organization to the core, we are in the awkward position of being beaten to a pulp by the W.P.A. organization and unable to hit back because if we do, we hit the President and the National Administration. This we will not do regardless of how bad the punishment is, as it would only be grist for the Republican mill for them to have Democratic leaders attacking the Federal Agency, which they have constantly picked on," noted the state leader. Lawrence explained that after a talk with the president, in which he anticipated the use of WPA against his regular organization, he warned WPA State Administrator J. Banks Hudson against such activity. Although Hudson at first agreed to keep the works program out of politics, he later reneged on his promise.[37]

36. Guffey, *Red Fire Wagon*, p. 109; Keller, "Little New Deal," pp. 303–07; memo, James H. Rowe to Missy Lehand, Feb. 25, 1938, DNC, Pa., OF, FDRL.
37. Lawrence to Bullitt, Apr. 15, 1938, Hopkins mss., FERA–WPA Confidential Political File, 1933–1938, Box 64, Folder Bo-Bu, FDRL.

Attorney General Margiotti took advantage of the situation by charging both sides with macing. In an accusation that would later deeply wound the party, Margiotti asserted that the payroll of Pennsylvania's highway department had been padded by Lawrence and accused the heads of the Democratic organization of demanding kickbacks totalling $1.2 million from architects on projects sponsored by the General State Authority. With regard to the Kennedy forces, he declared: "Walter L. Miller, personnel director of the W.P.A. at Harrisburg has been given a leave of absence and now is at Kennedy headquarters as the bag man of the ticket. Miller is the chief W.P.A. macer."[38]

Two to three weeks before the May 17 primary, the Assignment Division in Allegheny County, through the influence of Senator Guffey, worked strenuously to place five to six thousand individuals on WPA payrolls. The added force necessitated increased supervision, the bulk of which was supplied by Kennedy-Guffey supporters. Some of the supervisory personnel jumped from laborers earning $726 a year or common labor foremen earning $1020 a year to general foremen bringing in $1800 to $2160 a year. One worker reported that he had been summoned to the Kennedy headquarters in Pittsburgh and promised a raise on the WPA. Although all WPA administrative employees were supposed to receive prior to the primary a notice warning them against manipulation of the payroll, they did not receive it until two days after the contest.[39]

By that time, despite the vigorous opposition, Jones and Earle had triumphed, enabling them to gird themselves for the coming battle against the Republican candidates for governor and senator, Arthur James and incumbent James J. Davis. William Green, president of the AF of L, called the primary vote "a rebuke of the attempt of C.I.O. dictator John L. Lewis, to seize political control of the state." A Lawrence admirer saw in the power struggle a clear-cut victory for the organization and wired, "I guess you are still the BIG BOY in Pennsylvania." However, a more astute analysis of the results of the contest came several months later— after the Democrats had lost the general election. At that time the United States marshal stationed in Pittsburgh wrote to James A. Farley: "The

---

38. *NYT,* Apr. 24, 1938, p. 12; ibid., Apr. 26, 1938, p. 4.
39. U.S. Senate, *Report of Special Committee,* p. 215; letter, Roy Blakely to James P. Kirk, Apr. 30, 1938, 1938 Primary Election File, ACDCH.

primary left some very deep wounds. The feeling was extremely bitter going from the leaders down to the precinct workers."[40]

The rift that developed was exacerbated by the political uses of the WPA. After the primary Harry Hopkins announced that ten WPA workers throughout the state had been dismissed during the campaign for engaging in political activity and eight had been penalized; three of the ten discharged and all eight penalized hailed from Allegheny County. As the county's Assignment Division purged its rolls of the five to six thousand men it had added to WPA, it should have reduced the supervisory personnel as well. Officials, however, wondered whether the recently appointed Kennedy people or the old organization men should be discharged. As a result, for many weeks they carried a supervisory roll far in excess of their needs. Moreover, although the party schism had supposedly been healed, both factions till fought over the WPA patronage. At the request of his predecessor, Edward N. Jones, who had aligned with Guffey and Kennedy during the primary, State Administrator Hudson appointed William Bailey Jones to take over the WPA personnel office in Pittsburgh. The latter Jones had instructions to line up the WPA office against the Lawrence organization. He did just that, causing District Director James Kessner to complain that he had become powerless in personnel matters and that Jones was acting on a purely political basis. Not until after the election in November did control over personnel matters return to district officials.[41]

The atmosphere surrounding the administration of WPA in Pittsburgh prompted state Representative Joseph A. McArdle to inform James Farley before the November contest, "I am extremely fearful that . . . many of the W.P.A. force are still concerned about the results of the last primary fight instead of being concerned about the next general election." Robert Vann was one man still concerned about the results of the primary. The Negro editor claimed that before the May balloting Guffey and Edward Jones had promised Negroes 10 percent of the state's jobs; but when the organization candidates won, David L. Lawrence forced

40. *Press,* May 18, 1938; telegram, Hester M. Frye to David Lawrence, May 18, 1938, Congratulatory Letters, 1938 Primary Election File, ACDCH; John Sloan to Farley, Dec. 22, 1938, OF 300, FDRL.

41. Report, William H. Strong, Jan. 30, 1939, and attached memo, F. H. Dryden to F. C. Harrington, WPA Record Group 69, Pa. 610, Box 2378, Folder Jan. 23–28, 1939, NA; U.S. Senate, *Report of Special Committee,* p. 215; *NYT,* May 21, 1938, p. 2.

them to renege on the pledge. Annoyed at this break of promise and by the fact that he had been replaced by Paul F. Jones, Pittsburgh's state workmen's compensation referee, as patronage dispenser to Negroes, Vann declared for the Republican ticket. In an open letter to Pittsburgh's WPA workers, Vann wrote: "First, you must know that President Roosevelt is the Great White Father of the W.P.A. Second, President Roosevelt made the W.P.A. possible for you. Third, President Roosevelt has said that he does not want you to give one cent of your W.P.A. money to any political party." He went on to stress that their salaries came not from Lawrence, Earle, or Guffey, but from FDR. He asked them to vote for James, who, he claimed, would not abolish WPA, but who would retain it and get rid of the profiteers, racketeers, and macers. His plea, however, fell upon deaf ears.[42]

Whereas Robert Vann thought Negroes received short shrift from the WPA, some white Protestants who had been affected by Pennsylvania's political wars while working on the federal program vented their anger in xenophobic rage. One such individual wrote to the president: "I wish to call your attention to the fact that the American Citizen does not seem to rate as high as the Foreign born class, such as, they hold better jobs than most American Citizens. Not being prejudiced against the Foreign born or Jewish class, but it does seem they are given the preference when it comes to holding W.P.A. jobs."[43]

Others had more legitimate complaints. When the Young Democrats of Pennsylvania held a major campaign rally at the end of August in Hershey, Pennsylvania, approximately forty-six thousand tickets of the 150,000 sold went to WPA employees; probably one thousand to twelve hundred agency employees distributed the tickets. In Pittsburgh complaints of forced purchases ranged far and wide. One distributor, who resigned from WPA in July to promote the sale of tickets on the promise that he would be later reassigned, was never, to his chagrin, returned to the agency's rolls. Early in August a letter, signed by Senator Guffey but actually written by Edward Jones, was sent to all state employees and all WPA workers. Since it asked for campaign contributions, it exacerbated

42. McArdle to Farley, Oct. 28, 1938, OF 300, FDRL; Keller, "Little New Deal," pp. 359–60; copy of letter, Robert Vann to WPA workers, *Pittsburgh Courier*, Oct. 29, 1938, WPA Record Group 69, Pa. 610, Box 2378, NA.

43. Letter, James Hodge to FDR, July 6, 1938, WPA Record Group 69, Pa. 610, Box 2381, NA.

the political pressures applied by the Hershey picnic ticket sellers. Ironically, at this same picnic Governor Earle told his huge audience, "I can think of nothing more contemptible than the present Republican effort to smear hundreds of thousands of self-respecting men and women on relief and W.P.A. by asserting that their votes are being bought."[44]

Complaints of political coercion in Pennsylvania came pouring into the WPA central office in Washington throughout the campaign. Although J. Banks Hudson, at the prodding of Aubrey Williams, issued a directive against such activities at the end of September, they continued. An Allgeheny County resident, writing to Harry Hopkins in mid-October, complained: "Mr. Hopkins, you can believe the racket they are making out of W.P.A. The truckers must actually buy their jobs regardless if they need the work or not, as long as they have the money to pay, they get the work." In Pittsburgh, when the Progressive Voters League Organization chose to endorse the Republican ticket, newspapers published a list of all members of the league who were serving as WPA labor foremen, foremen, and general foremen. When it was learned that most of these men had been Kennedy supporters during the primary, the organization not only brought pressure on them, but reportedly made a canvass of every WPA worker known to have supported Kennedy during the spring contest. A later investigation by the Senate's Committee to Investigate Senatorial Campaign Expenditures, chaired by Morris Sheppard of Texas, found that no one, however, had been discharged. These men apparently had retained their jobs because control over the WPA remained in the hands of the old Kennedy-Wilson supporters, who, although they paid lip service in the general election to the organization choices, still employed WPA patronage to their own advantage.[45]

At the Hershey picnic, Governor Earle had declared to his audience: "Naturally those on relief and W.P.A. fear they will go hungry if a Republican Administration is elected. Why shouldn't they. The Republican

44. U.S. Senate, *Report of Special Committee*, p. 210; J. Banks Hudson to F. H. Dryden, Sept. 1, 1938, and Carl Reisch to FDR, Jan. 16, 1939, WPA Record Group 69, Pa. 610, Case no. 37, Box 2381, NA; *NYT*, Aug. 19, 1938, p. 1; Keller, "Little New Deal," pp. 348–50; speech, George Earle to Young Democrats of Pa., Hershey, Pa., Aug. 27, 1938, Earle Speech Folder, 1938 General Election File, ACDCH.

45. Williams to Hudson, Sept. 17, 1938, ibid., Sept. 18, 1938, Hudson to district directors, Sept. 20, 1938, WPA Record Group 69, Pa. 610, Case no. 37, Box 2380, NA; George Janicik to Harry Hopkins, Oct. 14, 1938, WPA Record Group 69, Pa. 610, Box 2381, NA; U.S. Senate, *Report of Special Committee*, pp. 211–13.

organization in this state has consistently fought against relief and W.P.A." Just before the election, because WPA had become an outstanding issue, Arthur James answered Earle's charges. Asserting that the political bosses repeatedly claimed that he would stop relief, the Republican candidate announced that the bosses were lying, and he promised "to keep relief and W.P.A. just as long as one man or woman in the state needs it. . . ." Apparently, the people of Pennsylvania believed him. The Democrats suffered a severe trouncing throughout the state.[46]

Pittsburgh, however, bucked the trend; both Jones and Earle carried the city.[47] By 1938 the framework for Pittsburgh's political pattern for the next three decades had been set into a rigid Democratic groove. Its consistent voting for the Democratic party resembled its rigid Republicanism in the years prior to Roosevelt's first election to the presidency. Providing a foundation for the new Democratic organizational structure was the politics of WPA. As the organization consolidated its strength, it could look back to the 1930s as the tough and trying good old days— the years of building a payroll and ensuring a continued string of victories.

46. Speech, George Earle to Young Democrats of Pa., Hershey, Pa., Aug. 27, 1938, Earle Speech Folder, 1938 General Election File, ACDCH; copy of James's radio speech, Oct. 31, 1938, 1938 File, ACDCH.
47. Both candidates' votes bore a high relationship to the number of individuals on WPA throughout the city's 32 wards. The coefficients of correlation between both Earle's and Jones's vote and the number of individuals on WPA in 1940 was .81. (See Appendix G.)

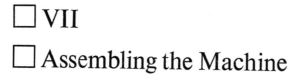

☐ VII

☐ Assembling the Machine

Those who in great cities form the committees and work the machine are persons whose chief aim in life is to make a living by office.

        James Bryce, The American Commonwealth, *vol. II*

☐ With the coming of the New Deal, many observers sounded a death knell for the urban political machine. Despite these advocates of "the Last Hurrah," Pittsburgh, at the end of the depression decade, remained firmly in the grasp of the city's Democratic organization. Politically impotent just a decade earlier, by 1940 the Democratic machine had consolidated its strength in terms of payroll personnel and voting pluralities. A quarter of a century later, it continued to maintain this hold.

The political use of the public payroll is not strange to urban America. David H. Kurtzman has shown that in a year prior to the advent of the New Deal, 1930, 58 percent of Philadelphia's committeemen held public payroll jobs. Harold F. Gosnell found that 59.2 percent of Chicago's committeemen were on the public payroll in 1928 and 48.3 percent held government jobs in 1936. The decrease over the eight-year period is explained by a sharper drop in Republican committeemen on the public payroll than the addition of new Democratic party workers to the payroll. By 1936 three quarters of Chicago's Democratic party workers held government jobs. As the Democratic Kelly-Nash machine began to consolidate its strength, the GOP jobholders suffered greatly—a fate not unlike that of their counterparts in Pittsburgh.[1]

Outside of the big cities the proportion of committeemen holding patronage plums during the New Deal era appears to have diminished. Studying Republican precinct workers in eighteen upstate New York communities in the early 1930s, William E. Mosher found 19 percent of them on the public payroll. This was an average for all cities, with Albany showing a high of 35 percent and Cortland a low of 2 percent. Leon Weaver's investigation of precinct committeemen serving in ten southeastern Illinois rural counties during the last years of the depression decade found "a significantly smaller proportion of public employees than in the Chicago [Gosnell's] group."[2]

Whereas such studies conducted during the New Deal era indicate the proportion of committeemen on the public payroll was smaller outside of large urban centers than within, more recent studies hold that during the years following the New Deal this proportion has dwindled within the major cities as well. These studies indicate that the profit motive has been driven from the temple of grass-roots politics. In a study of Republican committeemen in King County, Washington (Seattle and environs), made during the early 1950s, Hugh A. Bone concluded, "Only a comparatively small number are government employees (13.2%) and few seem motivated by consideration of patronage and economic gain." However, the loose structure of western party politics and the fact that only Republicans were studied may have had some bearing on this finding.[3]

A more broadly based 1960 study of New York County's Democratic, Liberal, and Republican committeemen presents statistical evidence that lends support to "the Last Hurrah" school; it contends that the grass-roots politician has become a middle class, ideologically oriented party worker, uninterested in the material rewards of politics. Finding only 5 percent of the committeemen on the public payroll, the authors held, "The political

1. David H. Kurtzman, "Methods of Controlling Votes in Philadelphia" (Ph.D. diss., Dept. of Political Science, University of Pennsylvania, 1935), table II; Harold F. Gosnell, *Machine Politics: Chicago Model* (Chicago, 1937), pp. 54–56.

2. William E. Mosher, "Party Government and Control at the Grass Roots," *National Municipal Review*, XXIV (Jan. 1935), 17; Leon Weaver, "Some Soundings on the Party System: Rural Precinct Committeemen," *American Political Science Review*, XXXIV (Feb. 1940), 78.

3. Hugh A. Bone, *Grassroots Party Leadership: A Case of King County, Washington*, Bureau of Government Research and Service, report no. 123 (University of Washington, Seattle, 1952), pp. 18–20.

activist views his party organization as an instrument for effectuating policies rather than as a source of personal gain." Moreover, they disagreed with the "classic descriptions of urban politics [which] emphasize the boss-dominated 'machine,' concerned almost exclusively with getting out the vote, getting in the brother-in-law and maintaining itself in power." The study, however, does concede that Manhattan, because of its ethnic and religious composition, as well as its strong reform movement, is not the "typical American community." The authors cushioned this admission by contending: "With regard to urbanization, political structure and processes, Manhattan (as well as the greater New York area) is comparable to urban communities throughout the nation. The present findings, therefore, may well be applicable beyond the confines of Manhattan."[4]

These findings certainly are not applicable to Pittsburgh. In fact, study of the Pittsburgh political organization suggests that rather than bringing about the weakening of machine politics with its extensive use of the public payroll, the New Deal served as a catalyst for the building of a machine. What occurred as a result of the New Deal was a transference of political power from a once solidly entrenched Republican machine to a newly formed Democratic one.

Three methods were employed to investigate the effect of the New Deal on Pittsburgh's machine politics. In order to ascertain information regarding the politics of the era and to obtain personal demographic data about each committeeman, precinct workers active during the New Deal decade were interviewed. This oral history yielded significant data about the politics of WPA. The second method, the comparison of names of committeemen listed in election-return books with listings of the same individuals and their occupations in city directories, permitted an assessment of the change from private to public employment by Pittsburgh Democratic committeemen during the New Deal period. The third technique involved the comparison of the demographic findings obtained from the interviews of New Deal committeemen with similar data gathered from an investigation of Pittsburgh's precinct officials in 1954. A change in the social backgrounds of the committeemen from one period to another could indicate a change in the political environment, whereas no, or little, change in social backgrounds could serve as an indicator of a status quo

4. Robert S. Hirschfield et al., "A Profile of Political Activists in Manhattan," *Western Political Quarterly*, XV (Sept. 1962), 490–91.

within organization politics. In other words, a new style of politics should recruit a new style of political worker. If the background of the political personnel remains the same, one might argue that organization politics has remained the same.

Implementing the first method, interviews regarding 103 Democratic committeemen who served during the 1930s clarified the connection between politics, these precinct officials, and WPA. The 103 Democratic committeemen represented 25 percent of the total elected, with the group being scaled so that each ward was represented by an approximate number of party workers proportionate to the 408 districts in the city. In cases where interviews with committeemen were impossible because of death, relatives were contacted, and they provided the information sought. These interviews, unfortunately, were not as satisfactory as those in which the actual committeemen participated. The committeemen could provide information regarding the politics of the era; their relatives merely supplied demographic information. Names were obtained from the primary-election-return books.

Of the 103 committeemen, one third were on the work-relief rolls at some point during the depression decade, and all but four of them served with the Works Progress Administration. More significant, however, is the fact that a majority of these were foremen or supervisors. A New Deal committeeman from the Thirteenth Ward remarked: "I was laid off from my job as a printer. I got a job as a foreman on WPA. The ward chairman got you the good jobs. Anyone could be a laborer; politics was only needed in the key jobs."[5]

The interviews aided in pinpointing the exact role politics played in the work-relief operation and confirmed many of the written sources. The Pittsburgh Democratic party workers won appointment to the prime positions such as foremen, supervisors, and timekeepers; they found ready acceptance if they had a truck to hire out to WPA, as did one committeeman of the Eighteenth Ward, who recollected: "I got my truck on through politics. I had to go to the ward chairman to get the truck on because twenty other men wanted to do the same." Others advanced their friends to the better positions on work relief through contacts with supervisory personnel and ward chairmen. Moreover, for several of the

5. Interview with committeeman, 13W15. (To maintain anonymity of committeemen, they are listed by ward and district—hence, 13W15 is read 13th Ward, 15th District.)

committeemen, employment with the work-relief agency marked the first rung on a ladder of public employment. The experience of one Eighth Ward party worker is illustrative. An impoverished church sexton during the early years of the depression, he received an appointment as foreman on a WPA project through politics. By 1937 he joined the public payroll as a county deputy sheriff; four years later he went to work in the county treasurer's office; and four years after that he joined the county clerk's office, where, at the time of this study, he still held a high position.[6]

Asked for their motivation in entering politics, the committeemen frequently replied, as did a Third Ward precinct official: "I needed a job. The depression was on; I got a job. I started in politics in 1930 as a Republican, but switched when Roosevelt came in. The Democrats had emergency programs like CWA, WPA." Along with many other committeemen interviewed, this man was still on the public payroll more than thirty years after first entering politics.[7]

The building of the public payroll into a refuge for Democratic party workers occurred continuously throughout the depression decade. During the years following, the process persisted. Although the change in occupation from private to public employment by Pittsburgh's Democratic committeemen seemed to be one logical test of whether or not a machine was being built, a method was sought to document this shift. However, the nature of the party's rank-and-file membership complicated the problem. Committeemen are not among those who get their names mentioned in the newspapers; in fact, they are not even noted in the press on their day of election to office. Nor do these people generally bequeath to history the yarn from which it is most often woven—manuscript material. Thus, the problem became one of securing information regarding the committeemen.

In Pittsburgh committeemen are elected every even year during the spring primary. Mimeographed lists of their names are compiled by the County Board of Elections. However, they are discarded periodically, and the only place where any formal list of these names can be found several decades later is in the original primary-election book where the precinct vote is entered—provided these books are kept by the election

6. Interviews with committeemen, 18W2, 8W2. For job histories similar to 8W2, see Appendix H.
7. Interview with committeeman, 3W4.

officials. Fortunately, in Pittsburgh, they were. These records, however, offered no more information than the precinct, the candidates, and the vote. Having copied the names of these committeemen elected during the New Deal years of 1934, 1936, and 1938, a device was needed to obtain more information about them.

In a plea for the use of new possibilities in the study of American political history, Samuel P. Hays has noted: "Information is available in great abundance about tens and hundreds of thousands of political leaders at the state and local level. City directories indicate the occupation and address of every adult inhabitant; they reveal changes in both occupation and residence within and between generations and therefore demonstrate patterns of social mobility." Thus, the 1927, 1936, and 1940 volumes of R. L. Polk Company's *City Directory of Pittsburgh* were consulted to ascertain the occupation of each committeeman elected in 1934. The study might have selected instead the occupations of those elected in 1928, in 1936, and in 1940 and then compared the proportion on the payroll for each year. However, by using the 1934 list, one can see how the same people were affected over a period of time by the coming to power of the Democrats.[8]

The dates chosen reveal the occupation of this specific group of party workers in a predepression year, at a midpoint of the New Deal, and at a time when Dr. New Deal was fast becoming Dr. Win-the-War. Although the Democratic male committeemen stood as the prime target of the study, investigation of their Republican counterparts served as a control on the findings regarding the fast-growing party of Roosevelt. Since the city's thirty-two wards were composed of 408 districts in 1934, each directory—1927, 1936, and 1940—was consulted 408 times for the

8. Samuel P. Hays, "New Possibilities for American Political History: The Social Analysis of Political Life" (paper delivered at the American Historical Association convention, Dec. 29, 1964), p. 39. This paper also appears in Richard Hofstadter and Seymour Martin Lipset, eds. *Sociology and History: Methods* (New York, 1968). See pp. 210–11. By 1940 the R. L. Polk Company, which has been publishing city directories since the 19th century, issued listings for cities in 45 states and Hawaii, covering approximately 700 local areas in these communities. In addition to other information, these books provide an alphabetical list of names (with occupations); a street and avenue guide; ward boundaries; and city, county, state, and federal offices. Research Publications, Inc., of New Haven has microfilmed for publication almost all the directories listed in Dorothea N. Spear, *Bibliography of American Directories Through 1860* (Worcester, 1961). In 1969 it announced a plan to microfilm directories of the years 1861 through 1901 for selected cities.

occupations of the Democrats and 816 times for the Republicans.[9] In addition, in order to determine the payroll situation in more recent years, the lists of 1962 committeemen—436 Democrats and 872 Republicans— were compared to the 1962 directory. Thus, in total the directories were consulted approximately five thousand times.

Comparing the lists of committeemen elected in 1934, 1936, and 1938 allowed for the sorting out of a hard core of political workers, that is, those chosen in all three election years. This hard core was contrasted to the total group of party workers. Comparing the 1934 Republican list to the 1938 Democratic one permitted the isolation of those Republicans who shifted party during the depression decade and ran for office on the Democratic ticket. Where there was uncertainty regarding the committee- man's name as listed in a directory—often several people had the same or a similar name—the person chosen was the one who lived in the ward in question. Comparison of the name of a wife between directories also provided a check on whether the individual being investigated was the correct one. Unfortunately, the 1927 volume did not publish the spouse's name, although the later ones did.

Finally, the information regarding occupational change was tabulated for each year and percentaged to provide a quantitative measure of this change within the parties. Historian William O. Aydelotte points out, "The principal value of quantification for the study of history, stated in simple terms, is that it provides a means of verifying general statements." Concurring, political scientist Donald R. Matthews has noted: "The quantitative study of large aggregates of people can provide a degree of positive results which the more qualitative studies cannot. When hy- potheses can be expressed in such a way as to be quantitatively tested, this type of research is highly desirable and useful."[10]

9. The Republican number is double that of the Democrats because in each district the former party elects ward executive committeemen as well as county committeemen. Their duties and functions are the same, but the ward executive committeemen can vote for the ward chairman but not for the county chairman. The Democrats elect their county chairman in the primary and through vote of the committeemen. In an interview a Republican party official explained that a major reason for the existence of the ward executive committeemen is to ensure that more Republican workers are active on election day than the Democratic workers. See William G. Willis, *The Pittsburgh Manual: A Guide to the Govern- ment of the City of Pittsburgh* (Pittsburgh, 1950), p. 23.

10. William O. Aydelotte, "Quantification in History," *American Historical*

Table 15 illustrates the impact of the use of the public payroll to build the Pittsburgh Democratic organization during the 1930s—and, to a much greater extent, the continuance of this practice during the early 1960s. Whereas the comparison of the committeemen lists with the 1927 edition of the *City Directory of Pittsburgh* shows only 7.2 percent of those committeemen elected as Democrats in 1934 were on the public payroll in 1927, the 1936 issue of the directory reveals that this figure rose in that year to 19.2 percent for the same people.[11] The interviews establish that at this time, 1935–1936, several of the committeemen obtained work-relief positions and held them generally for a short duration prior to receiving the payroll job. Antiorganization Mayor McNair, still serving during this period, placed a ceiling on the amount of patronage available to the regulars. By 1940 the Democratic organization had consolidated its gains, and almost half of the same individuals elected to committee positions in 1934 occupied a government job. The interviews show that for approximately 10 percent of these men, payroll work was not a new experience; their fathers had served in such jobs.

The payroll had been conquered by the time the New Deal sighed its last breath. Twenty-two years later, at a time when "the Last Hurrah" for machine politics was considered to have been sounded throughout the nation's cities, 77.6 percent of Pittsburgh's Democratic committeemen held a job with city, county, state, or federal government. Moreover, a study of twenty-two of Pittsburgh's thirty-two Democratic ward chairmen in 1960 showed that twenty (91 percent) earned their livelihood by means of a government position. Of twenty Republican chairmen interviewed, only four held government jobs.[12]

Even in the ward with the highest income in the city, the Fourteenth, more than half of the Democratic committeemen were pay-rollers by

Review, LXXI (Apr. 1966), 804; Donald R. Matthews, *The Social Backgrounds of Political Decision-Makers* (Garden City, New York, 1954), p. 21.

11. Of the city's 32 wards, the 29th and the 30th were incorporated into Pittsburgh in 1927, while the 31st and the 32nd joined in the years following 1929. Thus, it is unlikely that the individuals elected from these districts in 1934 were city residents prior to 1927. The city directory at that time provided little information about nonresidents of the city, unless they worked in Pittsburgh. Incorporation dates are from Willis, *The Pittsburgh Manual,* p. xxvi.

12. Milanie Souza, "The Social Backgrounds of Political Decision-Makers: The Ward Chairmen of Pittsburgh" (unpubl. undergraduate tutorial thesis, Chatham College, Pittsburgh, Pa., 1960), p. 32.

TABLE 15
Percentage of Committeemen on Public Payroll

	Committeemen Elected in '34			Committeemen Elected in '62
	'27	'36	'40	
Democratic	7.2%	19.2%	48.2%	77.6%
Republican	18.3	17.6	19.6	5.7

1962, and several of those who were not earned their living as lawyers—
a profession often involved in seeking favors for clients and friends. Although not earning his living at the public trough, the lawyer often looks to municipal government for the tangible rewards of politics. During a factional dispute concerning the 1965 spring primary, the chairman of the Fourteenth Ward forced all committeemen who earned their livelihood as a city or county employee to swear a public loyalty oath to the organization's slate of candidates.[13]

As can be seen in table 16, by 1962 the bulk of Democratic government workers could be found on the city payroll, in contrast to the New Deal years when such jobs were more evenly distributed between the several levels of public service. This fact is another indication of the consolidation of the Democratic organization within the city of Pittsburgh, where the city budget increased from $21,788,341 in 1935 to $65,708,738 in 1965. The assignment of much of these funds to salaries and wages ballooned the organization's patronage powers.[14]

The Republicans, on the other hand, suffered. The proportion of Republican committeemen elected in 1934 and on the payroll during the period from 1927 to 1940 remained relatively stable. (See table 15.) However, whereas the Democratic payroll percentage skyrocketed for those elected in 1962, the Republican figure dipped to less than 6 percent.[15] As shown in table 17, with the decrease in the Republican

13. *Pittsburgh Press,* May 16, 1965.
14. City of Pittsburgh, *Municipal Record,* 1934, vol. 68, p. 322; city of Pittsburgh, Ordinance no. 469, Dec. 28, 1964 (mimeographed copy in possession of the author). Although policemen were barred from holding public or political office in 1950, firemen were not. (City of Pittsburgh, Civil Service Commission, *Digest of General Ordinances, 1939–1960,* Ordinance no. 128, Mar. 25, 1950, p. 50.) An unusual number of firemen served as committeemen in 1962. Since they were engaged in a salary hassle with City Hall, they may have infiltrated the party organization in order to influence municipal budgetary policy.
15. In 1962 the Republicans won the state House for the first time since 1954. They took advantage of the patronage opportunities offered by Harrisburg. A

TABLE 16

Governmental Subdivisions of Public-Payroll Jobs for Committeemen

| | Democratic Committeemen | | | | Republican Committeemen | | | |
| | Elected in '34 | | | Elected | Elected in '34 | | | Elected |
Job	'27	'36	'40	in '62	'27	'36	'40	in '62
City	4.0%	5.2%	16.1%	59.1%	6.8%	7.8%	8.2%	1.0%
County	1.6	7.5	24.3	15.1	10.5	6.5	9.3	3.7
State	0.0	2.6	2.6	2.6	0.6	3.1	1.9	0.6
Federal	1.6	3.6	5.2	0.0	0.4	0.2	0.2	0.4
Others[a]	0.0	0.3	0.0	0.8	0.0	0.0	0.0	0.0
Total gov.	7.2	19.2	48.2	77.6	18.3	17.6	19.6	5.7
(Number)	(18)	(59)	(129)	(294)	(94)	(102)	(101)	(28)

a. Some government jobs could not be classified by governmental level.

proportion of pay-rollers, the Republican ranks of professionals and managers began to swell. There is a smaller jump among the foreman, supervisor and real estate, insurance categories. These figures may indicate that in 1962 a higher occupational class of Republicans served in government in contrast to the Democratic laborers. One caveat must be noted. When comparing the 1962 groups to the 1934 groups, it should be remembered that they are not the same group. The increase in the social status of Republicans in 1962 may merely indicate a change in Republican voters generally and not in the committeemen per se. It is logical that if the city was so overwhelmingly Republican prior to the New Deal, that party would have been comprised of a heterogeneous mass base. If the New Deal polarized politics along economic lines as is currently believed, then the 1962 sample of committeemen may well represent the generally higher income level of the Republican party.

In table 17 laborers stand out as the occupational group that declined most among nonpayroll Democratic committeemen from the depression decade through 1962. However, as noted in table 18, 25 percent of all Democratic precinct workers who served the public did so in the capacity of laborers. Of the total number of Democratic committeemen in 1962— both privately and publicly employed—26 percent were laborers, not

---

breakdown of the patronage dispensed between Jan. 15, 1963, and Mar. 1, 1964, shows that the office of the Republican party chairman, Paul W. Hugus, processed 1,691 state jobs. Pittsburgh's city wards benefitted by 481 state jobs in 436 election districts, while retaining 69 holdovers. Hugus rated this percentage as 1.26 jobs per district. No information was given as to how many of the jobs went to GOP committeemen. (*Pittsburgh Post-Gazette* [hereafter cited as *PG*], Aug. 3, 1964.)

TABLE 17
Occupations of Committeemen

	Democratic Committeemen				Republican Committeemen			
	Elected in '34			Elected	Elected in '34			Elected
Occupation	'27	'36	'40	in '62	'27	'36	'40	in '62
Government	7.2%	19.2%	48.2%	77.6%	18.3%	17.6%	19.6%	5.7%
Laborers[a]	33.2	31.2	15.5	6.9	32.6	33.3	29.4	25.8
Foreman, supervisor	2.4	4.9	2.6	0.0	1.0	1.9	2.5	4.3
Clerk	15.3	13.2	7.1	2.1	15.9	12.3	10.7	5.8
Salesman	4.8	3.3	1.9	1.3	6.2	7.5	7.6	5.8
Real estate, insurance	4.0	2.6	3.8	0.8	2.1	2.6	2.7	3.3
Professional	2.8	3.9	4.1	2.1	1.7	3.2	3.5	10.9
Managerial	3.6	3.6	2.6	0.8	3.9	2.6	1.4	8.0
Other[b]	26.7	10.1	14.2	8.4	18.3	19.0	22.6	30.4
Total percentage	100.0	100.0	100.0	100.0	100.0	100.0	100.0	100.0
(Number)	(248)	(307)	(267)	(379)	(515)	(581)	(514)	(485)

NOTE: All percentages are based on the total number of committeemen minus those names not listed, or for which no occupations are listed, in the directories.
a. Laborer was a broad classification used in the directory. To this was added workmen such as carpenters, plumbers, etc.
b. Other: Includes some proprietors and those not classifiable in groups.

TABLE 18

Occupational Subdivisions of Public-Payroll Jobs for Committeemen

Occupation	Democratic Committeemen				Republican Committeemen			
	Elected in 1934			Elected	Elected in 1934			Elected
	'27	'36	'40	in '62	'27	'36	'40	in '62
Laborers	44%	20%	30%	25%	21%	15%	15%	32%
Foreman, supervisor	0	16	13	14	4	6	3	8
White collar[a]	56	64	57	42	65	76	72	39
Total percentage	79[b]	100	100	100	81[b]	90[b]	97[b]	90[b]
(Number)	(18)	(59)	(129)	(294)	(94)	(102)	(101)	(28)

a. White collar includes clerks, investigators, inspectors, draftsmen, etc.

b. Figures do not add up to 100 percent because some committeemen were listed only as a government worker without additional information as to the type of job. Policemen and firemen were not included, but chiefs and captains were categorized as foremen and supervisors.

much less than the 30 percent Democratic figure in 1940 and the 28 percent figure for Republican committeemen in 1962 employed privately and publicly as laborers. Thus, as the organization strengthened its hold on the city, committeemen-laborers were absorbed into public work, often serving with such agencies as Pittsburgh's Bureau of Bridges, Highways and Sewers. It was not difficult for a laborer to obtain a public job if he knew the right people. Laborers were exempt from the civil service law but were required to file a labor application. Their background was then investigated and references from two Pittsburgh citizens were required to attest to their good character. Nothing said that the citizens could not be local ward and precinct bosses. As one committeeman noted, they often were.[16]

The relative stability of the GOP committeemen on the public payroll during the 1930s may stem from the fact that until 1943 the Republicans controlled the county prothonotary's office (clerk of court of common pleas), which provided work for several of these precinct politicians. Perhaps an even more cogent reason for this stability lies in the fact that some of the Republican workers who were politicians in 1934 may have shifted their party allegiance between 1934 and 1940 for ideological or, more likely, practical reasons, that is, to remain on the payroll. The city somersaulted from a Republican to a Democratic stronghold during the

16. See city of Pittsburgh, Civil Service Commission, *Acts of Assembly and Rules Governing Civil Service of Pittsburgh* (1950), p. 66.

depression decade, increasing the probability that some of these committeemen changed party with the tide.

Although hard to assess for all the Republicans in the 1934 sampling, a comparison of the 1934 Republican and 1938 Democratic committee lists shows that a little more than 6 percent of the 412 Democrats elected as committeemen in 1938 had been elected to the Republican committee in 1934. A comparison of the shifters to the total number of Republicans elected in 1934 shows that whereas 19.6 percent of the total had government jobs in 1940, 46 percent of the shifters served the public during the same year, illustrating the practicality involved in changing one's party registration. In one ward, the Third, more than half the committeemen made this shift, indicating that control of the ward remained in the hands of the same individuals, although their party label had changed. The evidence, however, does not provide information regarding those Republicans who may have changed registration but did not win a committeeman's seat in 1938.

A comparison of the 1934, 1936, and 1938 lists of committeemen shows that 103 Democrats and 163 Republicans won election in all three primaries. These have been designated as the hard core of each party—those individuals who continued to serve throughout the depression. It might be expected that the hard core Democrats did better in obtaining payroll positions than did the committeemen who served for a shorter duration. This assumption proves to be the case; table 19 shows that whereas in 1927 and 1936 these hard-core individuals fared little better at the public trough than their brethren elected once or twice during the New Deal years, by 1940, with the consolidation of the Democratic grip of the city, the hard core had 70.2 percent of its members on the payroll as contrasted to 48.2 percent of the total group. Those who continuously served gained. However, those who remained Republican stalwarts during the era of Democratic growth did little better than the GOP's less persistent workers. In fact, the gap between the Republican hard core and the Republican total, small from the beginning, narrowed as the decade ended.

The third method to determine whether the Roosevelt era helped to build or change Pittsburgh's Democratic organization is carried out by the comparison of the findings regarding the Democratic committeemen who served during the 1930s with those of a similar study undertaken in

TABLE 19
Percentage of Committeemen Elected in 1934 on Public Payroll

Year on	Democratic (103)[a]		Republican (163)[a]	
Payroll	Hard Core	Total	Hard Core	Total
'27	8.5% (59)	7.2%	23.6% (106)	18.3%
'36	24.1 (83)	19.2	19.0 (121)	17.6
'40	70.2 (77)	48.2	20.0 (110)	19.6

a. The figures in parentheses designate the number of committeemen. Each percentage is based on the total minus the number of committeemen not listed or whose occupations are not listed in the directories.

the city during 1954. By analyzing the social backgrounds of the party's grass-roots personnel for the periods during and after the depression decade, one can determine the similarities and the differences between the two groups. A wide difference in background would signify a shift in the type of person attracted to post-New Deal organization politics and would strengthen the case for "the Last Hurrah" thesis; little change in the type of individual serving the party could be taken to indicate that the New Deal had little effect on machine politics.[17]

As seen in table 20, the difference in age between the pre- and post-New Deal committeemen illustrates the fluidity of the Democratic party during the 1930s and its later solidification in terms of personnel. The young people entering politics during the depression decade chose the Democrats; the Democratic organization, previously a weak shadow party in Pittsburgh, accepted them with open arms. The line to political success was short, and an aspiring young, perhaps hungry, politician could rise quickly in the growing organization. Moreover, the older citizens may have been bound more strongly by party tradition, making them reluctant to cut ties with the Republican machine. Whereas the oldsters knew

17. The 1954 study by William J. Keefe and William C. Seyler appeared under the title "Precinct Politicians in Pittsburgh" in *Social Science,* XXXVI (Jan. 1960), 26–32. Although Keefe and Seyler examined both Democrats and Republicans, only the comparison of the Democrats is of value to this investigation. The data regarding the New Deal and the post-New Deal committeemen are not identical: the 1954 study provides figures for both male and female workers, whereas the investigation of those who served in the 1930s concerns only males. Information regarding the 1960 Democratic ward chairmen has been obtained from Souza, "Political Decision-makers." Twenty-two of 32 Democratic chairmen were studied. Pittsburgh's total population figures were taken from U.S. Census of Population reports.

TABLE 20
Age of Total Population, Democratic Committeemen, and Ward Chairmen

Age	'34 New Deal Commn (m.)	'30 Pgh (m.)	'54 Commn (m. & f.)	'50Pgh (m. & f.)	'60 Ward Chmn	'60 Pgh (m. & f.)
20–29	29.1%	16.9%	4.1%	17.0%	—	11.8%
30–39	28.1	16.6	15.5	15.8	4.6	13.2
40–49	32.1	13.7	36.5	13.5	31.8	13.6
50–59	6.8	9.2	29.3	11.6	31.8	12.0
60–69	2.9	4.8	11.8	8.1	22.7	9.6
70+	—	2.4	1.5	4.7	9.1	6.6
Unknown	1.0	—	1.3	—	—	—
Total percentage	100.0	63.6	100.0	70.7	100.0	66.8
(Number)	(103)	—	(665)	—	(22)	—

patronage and good times with the GOP, the young had no such memories; they lived in the future, not the past, and faced unemployment and depression misery.

Of the New Deal committeemen in the study 57.2 percent were under forty years years of age as opposed to 19.6 percent in 1954; 89.3 percent were under fifty years of age during the New Deal's beginning in Pittsburgh, whereas 56.1 percent were younger than fifty years of age two decades later.[18] Although in 1930 there were proportionately more New Deal committeemen under forty than males below that age in the city's total population, by 1954 fewer individuals between twenty-one and forty appeared among the ranks of committeemen than within the entire 1950 Pittsburgh population. By 1954 party lines had solidified; the Democratic organization had been the majority party for almost twenty years, controlling all political power that coincided with its hold on the city and county offices. The younger man found it more difficult to advance himself within the Democratic organization. A 1960 study of Pittsburgh Democratic ward chairmen showed that less than 5 percent were younger

18. In dealing with the figures regarding the age of New Deal committeemen, one must be aware of a built-in bias. Since the interviews were geared to party workers who were still living, a propensity for youth becomes evident. Those respondents still alive would have been 30 years younger during the time of the New Deal, whereas those deceased logically would have comprised a more elderly group of committeemen during the Roosevelt era. However, in the light of the massive shift in party alignment that occurred during the 1930s, the above conclusions are likely to be correct.

TABLE 21
Education of Total Population, Democratic Committeemen, and Ward Chairmen

Education	'34 New Deal Commn (m.)	'40 Pgh (m.)	'54 Commn (m. & f.)	'50 Pgh (m. & f.)	'60 Ward Chmn	'60 Pgh (m. & f.)
1–6	8.7%	21.0%	27.1%	48.0%	18.2%	39.7%
7–8	23.3	37.2				
9–11	19.4	12.8	21.1	17.4	31.8	22.1
Tech., trade	3.9	—	—	—	—	—
H.S. grad.	23.3	12.6	29.5	21.3	27.3	23.4
Col., 1–3	10.8	4.4	12.2	5.1	9.1	5.6
Col. grad.	1.0	6.9	6.0	6.0	13.6	6.4
Grad. School, others	4.8					
Unknown	4.8	0.8	4.1	2.2	—	—
Total percentage	100.0	100.0	100.0	100.0	100.0	100.0
(Number)	(103)	—	(665)	—	(22)	—

than forty and approximately 35 percent were under fifty. The long climb to the powerful position of ward chairman generally took many years, limiting the opportunity for the young. In 1965 a thirty-seven-year-old candidate for the Democratic nomination for sheriff challenged the sixty-nine-year-old organization incumbent, who was seeking his fourth term. The insurgent asserted that the Democratic organization was too old to fight against younger Republican antagonists and argued the necessity of a change in leadership. He lost in the primary.[19]

Table 21 shows a higher education level for the post-New Deal committeemen than for the New Deal party workers. Whereas 39.9 percent of the New Deal committeemen graduated from high school or went on to further schooling, 47.7 percent of the 1954 committeemen did the same. However, as would be expected, the educational level of the entire populace also increased, and the change between the two groups of committeemen who completed high school or beyond (7.8 percent) is less than the change that occurred for the entire city between 1940 and 1950 (8.5 percent).[20] Hence it appears that the difference in social background merely reflects a universal change. In both instances the committeemen's educational level was higher than the population in general; in addition 22.7 percent of the 1960 ward chairmen attended college or went on to graduate

19. *PG*, Feb. 16, 1965.
20. The 1940 figure is for males only; the 1950 figure, for total population.

study, highlighting the educational difference between the leadership level, the grass-roots politicians, and the community at large.

Religion is another important factor in considering social backgrounds. In 1935 a campaign broadside asked, "Does It Pay to Be Too Liberal?" Pointing out that Pennsylvania was 80 percent Protestant and 20 percent Roman Catholic, the County Council of Vigilant Americans asserted that political offices should be apportioned between the two religions in that ratio. The group claimed that of seven top state officials only two, the governor and the United States senator up for election, were Protestants; of five Allegheny County congressmen three practiced Catholicism, one was a Jew, and only one a Protestant; four of six state senators, five of nine Pittsburgh councilmen, and the majority of that year's candidates owed their religious allegiance to Rome. The Vigilant Americans advised, "Demand a Square Deal for Protestants—Use Your Head When You Vote." Four years later, after the Democratic debacle in 1938, millionaire oilman Walter A. Jones told Jim Farley that a basic problem of the Pennsylvania Democracy stemmed from the organization's being too predominantly Roman Catholic.[21]

The figures regarding the religion of Pittsburgh's committeemen tend to bear out Jones's statement of fact, although not necessarily his normative judgment. Table 22 shows that Roman Catholics predominated as Democratic organization workers from the time the Democracy climbed to power during the 1930s. Perhaps the 5 percent increase in Protestant and the same decrease in Roman Catholic committeemen between the 1930s and 1954 reflect the filtering into David Lawrence's organization of former Republican Protestants who, during the two decades in question, decided to grab a piece of the patronage available to Democrats. In both the 1930s and 1954 Roman Catholics predominated in the party. The high proportion of Catholic ward chairmen in 1960 merely mirrors this prevalence, for it seems logical that the party would draw upon its largest group for leadership. That the percentage of Jewish precinct workers remained approximately the same supports the view that little change occurred in party personnel during the years after the New Deal.

Both studies of committeemen, as noted in table 23, found the po-

21. 1935 Publicity Folder, Files of Allegheny County Democratic Committee Headquarters, Pittsburgh, Pa.; Harold L. Ickes, *The Secret Diary of Harold L. Ickes*, vol. II, *The Inside Struggle, 1936–1939* (New York, 1954), 695.

TABLE 22
Religion of Democratic Committeemen and Ward Chairmen

Religion	'34 New Deal Commn (m.)	'54 Commn. (m. & f.)	'60 Ward Chmn
Catholic	68.0%	63.0%	72.7%
Protestant	24.2	29.0	13.6
Jewish	5.9	6.4	9.1
Orthodox	—	—	4.6
Unknown	1.9	1.6	—
Total percentage	100.0	100.0	100.0
(Number)	(103)	(665)	(22)

litically inclined Irish and the Germans to be the two leading ethnic groups involved in Democratic organization politics. Together, these two nationalities had composed half of Pittsburgh's foreign-born population in 1900. Although the Germans had made up 29 percent of the foreign born at the turn of the century and the Irish 21 percent, by 1940 they made up only 12 percent and 9 percent respectively; ten years later they represented 9 percent and 7.4 percent of the population. As they assimilated into Pittsburgh society, they maintained their grasp on organization politics that the head start of early immigration had given them. The Italians, who had held fourth place among New Deal committeemen, stood third in the post-New Deal study. These "new immigrants" who had comprised only 6 percent of the city's foreign born in 1900, had increased to 19 percent in 1940 and 20.7 percent ten years later. As part of the Italians' coming of age, they started to step up their participation in organization politics. As early as 1933, Mayor McNair thought it wise to address a massive campaign rally in Italian. (See Chapter 3.) Following the Italians, the New Deal investigation lists in order precinct officials of Polish and Scottish, Russian, Yugoslav and French backgrounds, whereas the 1954 study, beginning with fifth place, ranks in descending order committeemen of Polish, Austrian, Russian, Scottish, and Czech origins. The Irish-German-Italian combination also held true for the ethnic leadership among ward chairmen in 1960.[22]

22. Figures for foreign born in 1900 and 1940 were taken from "Vital Facts," *The Federator*, XIX (Jan. 1944), 15–16, and "Vital Facts—Countries of Origin of Leading Foreign Born Groups in Pittsburgh," *The Federator*, XIX (June 1944), 19–20; figures for 1950 were taken from table 43, 17th Census of Population, 1950, vol. III (U.S. Bureau of the Census).

TABLE 23
Family Origins of Democratic Committeemen and Ward Chairmen

Family Origin	'34 New Deal Commn	'54 Commn	'60 Ward Chairmen
Irish	27.2%	18%	26.1%
German	22.3	13	18.2
Italian	9.7	9	14.7
English	11.6	A[a]	—
Polish	4.8	B	—
Austrian	1.9	C	—
Russian	3.9	D	9.1
Scottish	4.8	E	4.6
Czech	1.0	F	—
Yugoslav	2.9	—	4.6
Canadian	—	—	2.3
Welsh	1.9	—	—
French	2.9	—	—
Hungarian	1.9	—	—
Lithuanian	1.0	—	—
U.S.	—	—	15.8[b]
Unknown	2.2	—	4.6
Total percentage	100.0	—	100.0
(Number)	(103)	(665)	(22)

NOTE: Since different methods were used to determine ethnic backgrounds, the comparison of the data becomes somewhat impressionistic but does give an idea of the ethnic backgrounds of the committeemen and the chairmen. In the New Deal investigation an individual's ethnic background was determined by ascertaining the nationality of his father's family—regardless of how many generations of the family had been in America. This procedure followed the premise that the influence of ethnic origins on a person's activity and philosophy is not diluted to any great extent by the distance in time from his family's first arrival in this country. The 1954 and 1960 studies arrived at their ethnic findings by determining the birthplace of each individual's grandparents.

a. The 1954 study did not list percentages for the English through the Czechs. Instead these groups were ranked in order from *A* through *F*.

b. Since the study of ward chairmen listed the birthplace of all four grandparents, it included a percentage for the United States.

The last demographic comparison concerns immigrant status. Table 24 shows that there were two and a half times as many foreign-born committeemen in 1934 than there were in 1954. The total percentages of first- and second-generation committeemen are almost identical for the two groups—64.9 percent for 1934 and 61.3 percent for 1954, a majority for both groups. Herein lies the basic continuity between the two groups. Whereas only about 25 percent of the depression decade party workers claimed family standing of third generation or more, 33 percent

TABLE 24
Immigrant Status of Democratic Committeemen

Immigrant Status	'34 New Deal Commn	'54 Commn
Foreign born	9.7%	3.8%
First generation	47.5	NI[a]
Second generation	17.4	[61.3]
Third generation	12.6	
Fourth generation	1.0	33.0
Fifth generation or more	10.8	
Unknown	1.0	1.9
Total percentage	100.0	100.0
(Number)	(103)	(665)

a. NI—no information. The 1954 study gave no other information than the three percentages listed. When that information (total, 38.7 percent) is subtracted from 100 percent, it is found that 61.3 percent were first- and second-generation Americans. The study of ward chairmen gave no exact figures, but noted that none were new immigrants. Most of the chairmen were born in Pittsburgh of foreign-born parents, making them first-generation Americans.

of the 1954 group were at least third-generation Americans. That the latter group includes more individuals of at least third generation can probably be attributed to the passing of two decades.

In general, the background of the Democratic organization personnel did not alter greatly in the New Deal and post-New Deal periods. Where it did vary, it followed the change taken by the general population. The party workers who spanned the two periods witnessed a continuous string of election victories and a consolidation of Democratic voting strength. Whereas Republican registration fell from 95.3 percent in 1930 to 43.9 percent in 1936, Democratic registration jumped from 4.7 percent to 56.1 percent. The election returns illustrate this consolidation. Between 1933 and 1969 the city elected no Republican mayor, and no GOP city official was chosen between 1939 and 1969.

In the national elections of 1932, 1936, and 1940, the mean vote for Roosevelt in Pittsburgh ran well ahead of the mean obtained by the Democratic mayoralty candidates in the elections of 1933, 1937, and 1941. On the other hand, the mayors' means in the general elections from 1945 through 1965—during the post-New Deal era—were slightly higher than those of the Democratic presidents for the races from 1944 through 1964. With a popular candidate like David Lawrence running three times during this period, enough momentum was built up for the local machine to carry on with increased strength, although the national party fared less well in Pittsburgh. (See Appendix I.)

The mean vote received by the Democratic mayoralty candidates in the seven post-New Deal elections exceeded the Democratic mean for the 1933, 1937, and 1941 contests. In only three wards did the Democratic average decline during the post-New Deal period; and two of these, the Seventh and Twenty-sixth, generally voted Republican. Finally, the mean for the organization candidates in the New Deal years' mayoralty primaries was less than for the period following. In every ward of the city, the mean of the organization candidates' vote in the primaries of 1953, 1957, 1959, 1961, and 1965 rated higher than the mean for 1933, 1937, 1941. The voting strength of Pittsburgh's Democratic organization in the years following the depression decade increased and solidified into an instrument of certain victory. (See Appendix I.)

The evidence presented indicates that the New Deal years witnessed the building of a Democratic political machine in Pittsburgh. The interviews with committeemen emphasize the connection between WPA and grass-roots politics during the depression decade; the comparison of the election-return books with the city directories highlights the shift from private to public employment by Pittsburgh Democratic committeemen during the era and illuminates the organization's use of the payroll for the express purpose of building a machine; the demographic data shows there was little significant change in the social backgrounds of party personnel who served before and after the age of Roosevelt—it implies continuity rather than change in the Democratic politics of pre- and post-New Deal Pittsburgh.

The New Deal brought to Pittsburgh and its Democratic committeemen more than Roosevelt's program for recovery and reform. On the municipal level it brought the beginning of an unbroken Democratic voting tradition that extended at least through the 1960s; it also furnished the patronage that served as the initial lubricant for a continually well-oiled machine. For Pittsburgh's Republicans the advent of the New Deal signified "the Last Hurrah"; for the city's Democrats it sounded "the First Hallelujah."

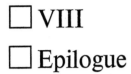

☐ VIII
☐ Epilogue

☐ The death of the urban political machine in post-New Deal America was reported too soon. The corpse has shown traces of life in Pittsburgh and other cities up to the end of the 1960s.

During his quest for the 1964 presidential nomination, Barry Goldwater, in a flourish of political rhetoric, told a convention of Young Republicans that no Democrat could be elected to national office who is "not under deep and unbreakable obligation to the corrupt big city machines." Five years later, in 1968, the nation bore witness to the political machinations of Chicago's Mayor Richard Daley. Television cameras at the Democratic National Convention brought home to the public the image of a politician who ruled "in the personalistic style of a benevolent Irish despot of the wards."[1]

Writing during the early 1960s, journalist William V. Shannon investigated the theory that the welfare state outmoded the political style of bosses such as Boston's James Michael Curley. He commented:

1. *Pittsburgh Post-Gazette* (hereafter cited as *PG*), June 27, 1963; "Dementia in the Second City," *Time,* Asian ed. (Sept. 6, 1968), p. 15.

183

This is sound enough as far as it goes, the welfare state has undoubtedly lessened the dependence of the average voter on the local political leader and the local party machine. This explanation, however, does not account for the durability of the political machine. The operation of the Democratic Party machine in Chicago under Mayor Richard Daley or in Philadelphia under Congressman William Green, Jr., in 1962, are not remarkably different from those of similar machines 30 years ago before the arrival of Roosevelt and the New Deal.

He might well have included David Lawrence's Pittsburgh organization and the New York City party machinery of the early 1960s, to name only two others.[2]

The old-style political organizations clung to life in localities that most resembled those which originally spawned strong local parties in the nineteenth century. Where poverty and the immigrant once served to foster the political machine, poverty and the Negro—at least up until the period of black militancy during the late 1960s—served the same function in mid-twentieth-century America. Immigrants were still pouring into the cities, but during the post-World War II years, instead of coming from County Cork or Bavaria, Sicily, or Galicia, as Charles E. Silberman points out, they arrived in droves from "Jackson, Mississippi and Memphis, Tennessee, and a host of towns and hamlets with names like Sunflower, Rolling Fork, and Dyersburg."[3]

In the twenty-four metropolitan areas with a half-million or more residents, the central cities lost 2,399,000 white residents between 1950 and 1960, a drop of 7.3 percent. They gained 2,641,000 new black residents in the same period, a rise of over 50 percent. By 1960 Negroes accounted for over 20 percent of the population of these cities. The trend continued throughout the 1960s. By 1968 the twelve largest central cities contained over two thirds of the black population outside of the South and one third of the total Negro population in the United States. In six cities (Chicago, Detroit, Cleveland, St. Louis, Milwaukee, and San Francisco), the proportion of Negroes at least doubled; in New York and Los Angeles the

2. William V. Shannon, *The American Irish: A Political and Social Portrait* (New York, 1963), pp. 227–29.

3. Fred I. Greenstein, "The Changing Pattern of Urban Party Politics," *The Annals*, 353 (May 1964), 9; Charles E. Silberman, *Crisis in Black and White* (New York, 1964) pp. 19–20.

proportion probably doubled. In 1968 seven of these twelve cities had more than 30 percent Negro population.[4]

The Negro migrant from Sunflower, as unaware of urban ways as the peasant from a small European village had been seventy years before, found a friend in the local politician. The modern boss could extricate many newcomers from their entanglements with the law, aid them in finding an apartment in a low-cost urban housing project, and direct them to the office dispensing unemployment relief. As Harvey Wheeler has pointed out, the increased government control resulting from the welfare state merely expanded the potential market for influence. Patronage became important not only for its traditional role as a reward to the faithful, but for its furnishing of key points of decision-making leverage. When the modern boss did not offer direct welfare aid, he functioned as an informational conduit between the needs of the poor and the government decision maker who could provide for these needs. Instead of weakening the big city machines, the institution of the welfare state arising out of the depression decade supplied new tools for its development.[5]

4. Silberman, *Crisis in Black and White*, pp. 31–32; *Report of the National Advisory Commission on Civil Disorders* (New York, 1968), pp. 236–49.

5. More than 25 years after the New Deal, during the early months of Lyndon Johnson's "War on Poverty," the Chicago neighborhood centers that were established to carry out the program were, because of political ties to the Daley machine, more aptly described as "little City Halls" (James Ridgeway, "Poor Chicago," *The New Republic*, CLII [May 15, 1965], 18). The mayor was quoted as saying: "There's nothing wrong with politics if it does some good. . . . What's wrong with ward committeemen sending capable men and women for jobs in the poverty program?" (*Chicago Daily News*, Apr. 14, 1965, cited in Peter Yessne, ed., *Quotations from Mayor Daley* [New York, 1969], p. 38).The reference in the text to Harvey Wheeler refers to his article "Yesterday's Robin Hood: The Rise and Fall of Baltimore's Trenton Democratic Club," *American Quarterly*, VII (winter 1955), 335. Wheeler calls this type of boss a "transitional boss," and the article adopts the view, somewhat qualified, that the political machine has declined in America. Writing during the mid-1950s, Wheeler accepts the concept of the "affluent society" resulting from the welfare state, and he also sees a concomitant improvement in race relations. Noting that "even those at the bottom of our economic scale are relatively high," he conjectures that the lower classes, having a stake in American society and its prosperity, will rise up against the transitional bosses. "To the lower class of yesterday the old fashioned political boss was a . . . miraculous, romantic urban Robin Hood, who fleeced the rich and feasted [on] the poor. However, to the well-to-do tax paying 'new lower classes' of today's Welfare State, the man who was yesterday's Robin Hood becomes transformed into today's cancerous social growth" (pp. 341–42). The "discovery" of poverty during the early 1960s and the racial situation at the decade's end make this hypothesis highly questionable. Edward N. Costikyan provides several excellent examples of the contemporary politician's

Yet, for many the New Deal served only as a halfway revolution. Few of America's nonwhites became a part of the affluent society. As late as 1966, 40.6 percent of them (9.3 million people) lived below what was considered to be the poverty level in the United States. Half of these impoverished blacks resided in the major central core cities of the nation. In the American historical and social milieu, unlike the European immigrant, the Negro found it extremely difficult to climb the economic and status ladder. Pointing to this fact in *The Other America: Poverty in the United States*, Michael Harrington remarked that for the son of the immigrant the "experience of breaking the old country tradition and identifying with the great society of America was a decisive moment in moving upward. But the Negro does not find society as open as the immigrant did. He has the hope and the desire, but not the possibility. The consequence is heartbreaking frustration."[6]

In this light it is not surprising to note that in 1964 New York County's Democratic organization (Tammany) proposed a plan to restore to its clubhouses some of the functions of the past by helping Harlem's Negroes and Puerto Ricans find jobs and better housing. Under the plan a party employment expert would process job offers solicited by the party and would forward them to the neighborhood clubhouses. The clubhouses would submit candidates to the headquarters' expert, who would put them in touch with prospective employers. The process of assistance, theoretically at least, had come full circle from Tammany to public welfare agencies and back to Tammany.[7]

---

mediation between his constituents and the official government. See Costikyan, *Behind Closed Doors, Politics in the Public Interest* (New York, 1966), pp. 88–93.

6. For figures on poverty see *Report of the National Advisory Commission*, pp. 258–59. Poverty is defined by the Social Security Administration's poverty level concept as $3,335 or less per year for an urban family of four. Other definitions allow for a higher proportion of poverty in the U.S. than does the Social Security scale. See Conference on Economic Progress, *Poverty and Deprivation in the United States: The Plight of Two Fifths of a Nation* (Washington, D.C., 1962); Michael Harrington, *The Other America: Poverty in the United States* (New York, 1962), p. 77.

7. *New York Times* (hereafter cited as *NYT*), Jan. 12, 1964, p. 1; mimeographed resolution of New York County Democratic Party, Human Relations Committee, Aug. 1964. Ironically, just as the reformers of sixty years before had looked askance at machine efforts to help the immigrants, some of New York County's reform Democratic leaders, who feared the evils of patronage, hamstrung this program. Edward N. Costikyan, who was Tammany leader in 1964, wrote to the author on Nov. 24, 1964: "Unfortunately, it [the plan] was held up for a year while some

Thus, the new urban dweller could now become beholden to the local precinct captains for favors. Since the Negro, unlike the Irish, had not yet priced himself out of the market, low-paying jobs were still appealing, and election-day work for pay drew into the ranks of party workers many otherwise politically passive individuals. In one of Chicago's Negro wards, during the late 1950s, 168 families received free clothing from the local machine before Christmas; about five thousand children were entertained at theater parties; and turkeys were distributed to a large number of needy householders. As late as 1962, a former Pittsburgh committeeman, a Negro himself, who rose to state legislator, gave baskets at Thanksgiving and was constantly busy trying to get his people into a local hospital or a low-rent housing project.[8]

Another committeeman reminisced, "People who wanted to get into public housing always came to me for help." Control over public housing, an outgrowth of the welfare state, apparently aided the party in power. In American cities in recent years, that party has generally been the Democratic party.[9]

Whites, as well as nonwhites, looked to the politician for assistance in finding low-cost residences. Some, like the whites who in 1960 comprised 52.3 percent of Pittsburgh's public-housing tenants and were beholden to the municipality for their shelter and other services, have again assumed the machine-voter obligation for which the advocates of "the Last Hurrah" thesis have long since sounded the death knell. The poverty figures indicate that in 1966, 11.9 percent of the nation's whites (20.3 million people) joined America's nonwhites in living far outside the affluent society. One quarter of these were central core city dwellers. The poor whites were much older on the average than the poor nonwhites,

---

of my leaders wrangled on the nice, esoteric issue of who would have the power to allocate the jobs which they had not yet found. This was merely the expression of a traditional reform attitude about the dangers of patronage, which I do not share but which involved the Committee in a lengthy philosophical discussion all winter, all spring, all summer, and most of the fall. Whether the program will ever get off the ground I do not know."

8. James Q. Wilson, *Negro Politics: The Struggle for Leadership* (Glencoe, Illinois, 1960), pp. 54–56; interview with committeeman, 5W1. (To maintain anonymity of committeemen, they are listed by ward and district—hence 5W1 is read 5th Ward, 6th District.)

9. Interview with committeemen 22W6; see Appendix J for the effect of the housing project vote in New York City and Pittsburgh during the late 1950s and early 1960s.

and many still looked to the politicians for welfare aid and employment opportunity. As a Pittsburgh politician declared in 1963, "Today people are still hunting work. There is unemployment compensation, but they still look for jobs. There is a sense of pride to work."[10]

Even twenty-five years after the New Deal, when an extrapolitical neighborhood group arose in Pittsburgh's Twenty-sixth Ward, the Democratic organization had some connection with it. Although the party officials of the local ward generally shunned the Perry-Hilltop ACTION Housing Association, several of the area's committeemen were members. At least one, the organization's second vice-president, was active. He commented: "Everyone brings complaints to us—like stuffed sewers, opposition to entry of a saloon into the neighborhood, potholes in the street. The usual procedure was to complain to the committeeman. People complain to me. I'm not sure if it's because I'm a committeeman or that I'm in ACTION Housing." In this case his overlapping positions undoubtedly aided the formal party organization, which otherwise might have been undercut in its service function.[11]

Thus, as America passed from New Deal to New Frontier, the need for the urban political machine and its services remained. In many cities the dirge for "the Last Hurrah" went unsung. However, as American cities take on an increasingly darker complexion and are transformed from places of urban control to urban social and environmental crisis, American city politics will become more unpredictable.

Increasingly, the urban caretakers of the New Deal coalition find themselves in political difficulty. Of the thirty-nine mayors named in 1968 to the executive committee and advisory board of the United States Conference of Mayors, a year later almost half were either out of office or in the process of completing their last term—having decided not to run again. Among the more prominent mayors who made their exits were Arthur Naftalin of Minneapolis, Richard C. Lee of New Haven, Jerome P. Cavanagh of Detroit, and Joseph M. Barr of Pittsburgh.[12]

Barr, a product of the Democratic organization that arose with the coming of the New Deal to Pittsburgh, had organized the first Allegheny

10. *Report of the National Advisory Commission,* pp. 258–59 (the measure of poverty is the same as is cited in fn. 6); interview with committeeman 8W2.
11. Interview with committeeman 26W8.
12. *NYT,* June 19, 1969; ibid., July 20, 1969, sec. 4, p. 14. For a discussion of why Naftalin, Lee, and Cavanagh, as well as Ivan Allen of Atlanta were leaving office, see Fred Powledge, "The Flight from City Hall," *Harper's* (November 1969), pp. 69–86.

County Young Democrats in 1933; from 1936 through 1939 he served as manager of the local Democratic County Committee; in 1940, at age thirty-three, he became the youngest man ever to be elected to the Pennsylvania State Senate, where he went on to sponsor much of the legislation leading to Pittsburgh's urban renaissance. When David L. Lawrence became governor of Pennsylvania, Barr inherited the Pittsburgh city machine.[13]

Yet, at age sixty-three, after thirty years in public life, he quit. The result of his decision to retire opened the way for Peter F. Flaherty, a photogenic, forty-three-year-old councilman, who was leader of the entire Democratic ticket four years earlier, to triumph over the organization's candidate in the 1969 mayoralty primary. After three and a half decades, the Pittsburgh Democratic machine put together by David L. Lawrence plummeted to defeat.

Flaherty carried the primary by 17,000 votes, 59 percent of the major candidates' total, and won twenty-four of the city's thirty-two wards. His victory was an individual one, as the organization's entire slate of candidates for city council swept into office. Although some independent council candidates endorsed Flaherty, he endorsed no one in return. Some observers attributed the victory to the "Kennedy image" projected by the antiorganization candidate; others claimed that the organization lost support because tax assessments had been raised in the city during the election year. It was generally agreed that his opponent suffered from not being the incumbent and from running an inept "law and order" campaign.[14]

Others saw fault with the organization itself. The local newspapers conjectured that any organization in control of a party for fifty years and in charge of City Hall for thirty-five years was bound to atrophy. To the chagrin of some of his fellows, one party spokesman proclaimed: "Party leaders will now either have to face up to the new demands of our voters or be replaced by new blood which is ready to be responsive to their workers. . . . The tired old appeals can no longer be used if we expect to be victorious. Voters are demanding us to reject the politics of the past and take a new course—a course where the citizen's interest is paramount."[15]

13. *Pittsburgh Press* (hereafter cited as *Press*), Feb. 22, 1969.
14. *PG*, May 22, 1969; ibid., May 23, 1969; *Press*, May 22, 1969; ibid., May 23, 1969.
15. *PG*, May 23, 1969.

For many the era of the Lawrence Democratic machine appeared to be swiftly drawing to an end. "What was good enough for Pittsburgh yesterday is not good enough today," the *New Pittsburgh Courier* told its black readers. It continued: "We are living in a new age, one marked with rapid social change and social unrest. The Lawrence-Barr regime was not equipped to solve even the simple social problems of yesterday, and there is no evidence that it . . . can solve the more complex social problems of today and tomorrow."[16]

Whether the Democratic organization merely lost a battle or the entire war is still to be seen.[17] However, in either case, the loss cannot be ascribed to the introduction of the merit system, the assimilation of ethnic groups, the full employment and rising national income—or the development of professionalized welfare services under the New Deal. The Pittsburgh machine maintained control until long after these factors came into play in American politics. As the editorial in the *New Pittsburgh Courier* implied, the organization's defeat in the 1969 primary must be considered in the context of the urban crisis of the late 1960s.

The apparent breakdown of the modern American city has taken its toll. The explosive racial situation, urban riots, revenue crises, and strikes make the life of the urban politician a difficult one. For instance, within the span of several months, Mayor Cavanagh's Detroit suffered a police strike, a school strike, an automobile plant strike, and a newspaper strike. An intervening race riot left forty-three dead, hundreds injured, and a city in rubble.

Although Pittsburgh has not suffered from the same degree of turmoil as its Michigan counterpart, its riots and successive revenue crises compounded the miseries of Barr's position. The Pittsburgh politician remarked in his statement of noncandidacy: "To be Mayor of a major city means to be involved in the period of greatest social challenge and change in our nation's history. Never before has there been greater ferment and

16. *New Pittsburgh Courier,* May 17, 1969.
17. In the mayoralty election Flaherty beat his Republican opponent, John K. Tabor, by nearly a two-to-one margin. Although Flaherty refused to endorse the five Democratic council candidates, Barr instructed the party's ward chairmen to work for the recalcitrant candidate. Flaherty denied a Republican charge that he had made a deal with the organization, commenting: "I won it in the primary. They [the organization] couldn't stop me then. If they did support me, it was a pragmatic decision on their part." He went on to attack as "old politics" the use of ward chairmen as links between the mayor's office and the city's neighborhoods. *PG,* Nov. 6, 1969.

social conflict in our urban centers." He later explained the effect of urban turmoil on a mayor: "You are beat like a bag of sand all day. You leave the office and you really feel clubbed. . . ."[18]

The exhausted mayors beat a retreat from their bailiwicks because they cannot contend with the forces of urban change. They cannot meet the eroding tax bases of America's cities; they feel hamstrung by state governments that often impede home rule; they resent the federal government's assignment of priorities to defense and space spending at a time when the defense of urban life in America is weakest, at a time when urban space becomes socially and environmentally polluted. They cannot reconcile the conflict of the races that rips their cities asunder.

Just a century ago, after the Civil War and at a time of burgeoning industrialization, when America's growing cities seemed plunged in crisis, disorder, and breakdown, the boss and his machine aided in restoring order from chaos. Although some contemporary political bosses like Chicago's Mayor Daley may lose contact with their increasing number of black constituents, others, in all likelihood Negroes themselves, might well reestablish the relationship between traditional politics and the urban disadvantaged and bring social, if not environmental, order once again to America's cities.

The era of the black mayor, a logical outgrowth of the changing complexion of America's cities, is upon us.[19] Whether he is supported by

18. *Press*, Feb. 23, 1969; *NYT*, June 19, 1969; ibid, July 20, 1969, sec. 4, p. 14. Before his tenure expired, the mayor's burden increased. In the late summer and early fall of 1969, Barr witnessed the ripping of Pittsburgh by the efforts of a Black Construction Coalition to win more jobs for blacks in the construction industry and the opposition of the white workers to this effort. For a good summary of early events, see John P. Moody, "Monday Report: Anatomy of Black Protest," *PG*, Sept. 15, 1969.

19. Although some American cities in recent years have elected white "law and order" mayors, black mayors have been voted into office in Cleveland, Ohio; Gary, Indiana; and East Orange, New Jersey, where Carl Stokes, Richard Hatcher, and William S. Hart govern respectively. Walter Washington is the appointed mayor of Washington, D.C. In 1969 Atlanta, Georgia, elected Maynard Jackson, a thirty-one-year-old black attorney, as vice-mayor; and in the same city a Negro educator, Horace E. Tate, won 23 percent of the vote for mayor in an eight-man election to place third. Small southern towns like Chapel Hill, North Carolina, and Fayette, Mississippi, have chosen Negro mayors. In Detroit, Negro candidate Richard Austin lost a close contest in his attempt to replace retiring mayor Cavanagh; in Houston, Texas, a young, black state representative, Curtis Graves, polled 31 percent of the vote for mayor. Negro candidates also ran in the primary or general elections in Los Angeles; New Haven and Hartford, Connecticut; Buffalo, New York; and Pittsburgh in 1969, and were seeking to replace Hugh Addonizio in Newark, New Jersey, in 1970. See *Bridgeport Post* (Connecticut), Oct. 9, Nov. 5,

white businessmen as fire insurance against rioting, or is seen as a means of attracting federal government or private foundation money to supplement the decreasing city treasury, or whether he is elected by his black constituency as its only true spokesman, he will have to build a political organization. The persistence of the modern political machine for over a century indicates that it will not die an easy death.

6, 17, 1969. For the view that although the problems of America's cities encompass the question of race, they also transcend it, and that black mayors will provide no easy solutions to America's urban problems, see James F. Barnes, "Carl Stokes: Crisis, Challenge, and Dilemma," in William G. Shade and Roy C. Herrenkohl, eds., *Seven on Black: Reflections on the Negro Experience in America* (Philadelphia, 1969), pp. 117–33.

APPENDIXES, BIBLIOGRAPHIC ESSAY, INDEX

☐ Appendix A
Rank Order Correlations for Votes of Selected Presidential Candidates

Percentages of Votes

Ward	Debs '12	TR '12[a]	Davis '24	La F. '24	La F.-Davis '24	Smith '28	FDR '32
1	6.2%	33.4%	10.0%	48.5%	58.5%	77.3%	63.4%
2	4.5	23.3	6.5	25.8	32.3	74.9	22.1
3	11.6	34.3	4.4	31.3	35.7	46.1	58.4
4	8.0	38.1	10.1	30.0	40.1	51.4	54.0
5	10.7	47.8	5.5	26.8	32.3	38.4	46.6
6	10.5	29.4	4.8	45.5	50.3	57.5	72.2
7	3.0	35.1	12.4	13.8	26.2	35.3	42.6
8	7.6	37.5	14.1	27.9	42.0	52.5	62.2
9	12.0	32.5	6.8	48.2	55.0	63.0	61.9
10	15.8	35.3	8.4	42.6	51.0	56.2	64.4
11	4.5	43.6	10.8	19.5	30.3	35.5	49.1
12	12.4	40.1	8.5	32.4	40.9	56.4	62.9
13	21.5	41.9	9.4	32.6	42.0	36.8	53.9
14	5.1	38.7	11.7	13.7	25.4	35.8	44.1
15	22.6	27.0	7.1	53.1	60.2	54.1	62.2
16	24.1	34.9	7.0	59.6	66.6	71.8	76.9
17	15.1	32.1	5.6	56.9	62.5	63.8	78.6
18	18.4	41.1	6.6	45.6	52.2	46.7	61.8
19	13.7	46.3	9.0	39.2	48.2	44.8	58.1
20	10.0	35.8	8.3	31.4	39.7	44.7	55.4
21	13.6	39.6	6.8	41.3	47.4	47.5	61.4
22	9.0	41.3	8.8	34.2	43.0	44.0	58.3
23	14.0	38.8	6.1	52.4	58.5	57.1	68.4
24	25.7	30.9	5.1	58.0	63.1	60.8	78.3
25	12.8	49.5	6.9	36.1	43.0	36.0	52.2
26	12.1	28.8	7.3	31.8	39.1	35.3	52.9
27	13.9	37.8	8.7	33.8	42.5	47.6	63.1
28	—	—	10.0	26.9	36.9	32.6	47.5
29	—	—	—	—	—	35.4	64.5
30	—	—	—	—	—	44.6	54.5
31	—	—	—	—	—	—	50.6
32	—	—	—	—	—	—	60.2
City	12.8	38.3	8.4	35.9	44.3	48.0	58.0
Co.	15.5	39.6	8.7	31.5	40.2	43.0	55.4
State	6.8	36.6	19.3	14.5	33.8	33.9	47.1
U.S.	6.0	27.5	28.8	16.6	45.4	40.8	59.1

SOURCES: Ward voting returns were computed from *Pennsylvania Manual*, 1913, 1925, 1929, and 1933 eds. Percentages for Pennsylvania and the United States were taken from Svend Peterson, *A Statistical History of American Presidential Elections* (New York, 1963).

a. The Theodore Roosevelt percentage is based on the total of his vote won on three tickets: the Bull Moose party, the Roosevelt Progressive party, and the Washington party.

195

Correlations for La Follette '24

Ward	La Follette '24 Rank	Debs '12 Rank	d	d²	T. Roosevelt '12 Rank	d	d²
1	6	23	17	289	21	15	225
2	24	25	1	1	27	3	9
3	20	16	4	16	20	0	0
4	21	21	0	0	13	8	64
5	23	17	6	36	3	20	400
6	9	18	9	81	25	16	256
7	26	27	1	1	18	8	64
8	22	22	0	0	15	7	49
9	7	15	8	64	22	15	225
10	10	6	4	16	17	7	49
11	25	26	1	1	5	20	400
12	17	13	4	16	9	8	64
13	16	4	12	144	6	10	100
14	27	24	3	9	12	15	225
15	4	3	1	1	26	22	484
16	1	2	1	1	19	18	324
17	3	7	4	16	23	20	400
18	8	5	3	9	8	0	0
19	12	10	2	4	4	8	64
20	19	19	0	0	16	3	9
21	11	11	0	0	10	1	1
22	14	20	6	36	7	7	49
23	5	8	3	9	11	6	36
24	2	1	1	1	24	22	484
25	13	12	1	1	1	12	144
26	18	14	4	16	2	16	256
27	15	9	6	36	14	1	1
28	—	—	—	—	—	—	—
				804			4382

All correlations in this and subsequent appendices were computed by the Spearman rank order formula:

$$R = 1 - \frac{6(\Sigma d^2)}{N^3 - N}$$

where R is the coefficient of correlation, d is the difference between the rankings of a given ward for the variable being measured, and N is the total number of wards included in the particular correlation.[1] For example, in the correlation between La Follette '24 and Debs '12, Ward 1 ranks sixth out of twenty-seven wards in the percentage of votes cast for La Follette and twenty-third in the percentage of votes cast for Debs. The difference (d) between these two ranks is 17; the difference squared (d²) is 289. In the correlation between La Follette '24 and T. Roosevelt '12, Ward 1 ranks sixth out of twenty-seven wards in the percentage of votes cast for La Follette and twenty-first in the percentage of votes cast for Debs. The difference (d) between these two ranks is 15; the difference squared (d²) is 225.

1. F. C. Mills, *Introduction to Statistics* (New York, 1956), pp. 277–79.

Smith '28			F. D. Roosevelt '32			Ward
Rank	*d*	*d²*	*Rank*	*d*	*d²*	
1	5	25	7	1	1	1
2	23	529	28	3	9	2
17	3	9	15	5	25	3
13	8	64	19	2	4	4
21	3	9	25	1	1	5
7	2	4	4	5	25	6
26	1	1	27	0	0	7
12	10	100	10	12	144	8
5	2	4	12	5	25	9
10	0	0	6	4	16	10
25	1	1	23	3	9	11
9	8	64	9	8	64	12
22	6	36	20	4	16	13
24	4	16	26	2	4	14
11	7	49	11	7	49	15
3	2	4	3	2	4	16
4	1	1	1	2	4	17
16	8	64	13	5	25	18
18	6	36	17	5	25	19
19	0	0	18	1	1	20
15	4	16	14	3	9	21
20	6	36	16	2	4	22
8	3	9	5	0	0	23
6	4	16	2	0	0	24
23	10	100	22	9	81	25
27	9	81	21	3	9	26
14	1	1	8	7	49	27
28	5	25	24	1	1	28
		1300			604	

Correlations

La F. '24— Debs '12	La F. '24— TR '12	La F. '24— Smith '28	La F. '24— FDR '32
$R = 1 - \dfrac{6(804)}{19656}$	$R = 1 - \dfrac{6(4382)}{19656}$	$R = 1 - \dfrac{6(1300)}{21924}$	$R = 1 - \dfrac{6(604)}{21924}$
$= 1 - \dfrac{4824}{19656}$	$= 1 - \dfrac{26292}{19656}$	$= 1 - \dfrac{7800}{21924}$	$= 1 - \dfrac{3624}{21924}$
$= 1 - .25$	$= 1 - 1.34$	$= 1 - .36$	$= 1 - .16$
$= .75$	$= -.34$	$= .64$	$= .84$

Correlations for Davis '24

	Davis '24	Smith '28			F. D. Roosevelt '32		
Ward	Rank	Rank	d	d²	Rank	d	d²
1	6	1	5	25	7	1	1
2	21	2	19	361	28	7	49
3	28	17	11	121	15	13	169
4	5	13	8	64	19	14	196
5	25	21	4	16	25	0	0
6	27	7	20	400	4	23	529
7	2	26	24	576	27	25	625
8	1	12	11	121	10	9	81
9	19	5	14	196	12	7	49
10	13	10	3	9	6	7	49
11	4	25	21	441	23	19	361
12	12	9	3	9	9	3	9
13	8	22	14	196	20	12	144
14	3	24	21	441	26	23	529
15	16	11	5	25	11	5	25
16	17	3	14	196	3	14	196
17	24	4	20	400	1	23	529
18	20	16	4	16	13	7	49
19	9	18	9	81	17	8	64
20	14	19	5	25	18	4	16
21	22	15	7	49	14	8	64
22	10	20	10	100	16	6	36
23	23	8	15	225	5	18	324
24	26	6	20	400	2	24	576
25	18	23	5	25	22	4	16
26	15	27	12	144	21	6	36
27	11	14	3	9	8	3	9
28	7	28	21	441	24	17	289
				5122			5020

Correlations

Davis '24—Smith '28

$$R = 1 - \frac{6(5122)}{21924}$$

$$= 1 - \frac{30732}{21924}$$

$$= 1 - 1.40$$

$$= -.40$$

Davis '24—F. D. Roosevelt '32

$$R = 1 - \frac{6(5020)}{21924}$$

$$= 1 - \frac{30120}{21924}$$

$$= 1 - 1.37$$

$$= -.37$$

Correlations for La Follette-Davis '24

	La Follette-Davis '24	Smith '28			F. D. Roosevelt '32		
Ward	Rank	Rank	d	d²	Rank	d	d²
1	5	1	4	16	7	2	4
2	24	2	22	484	28	4	16
3	23	17	6	36	15	8	64
4	19	13	6	36	19	0	0
5	25	21	4	16	25	0	0
6	10	7	3	9	4	6	36
7	27	26	1	1	27	0	0
8	16	12	4	16	10	6	36
9	7	5	2	4	12	5	25
10	9	10	1	1	6	3	9
11	26	25	1	1	23	3	9
12	18	9	9	81	9	9	81
13	17	22	5	25	20	3	9
14	28	24	4	16	26	2	4
15	4	11	7	49	11	7	49
16	1	3	2	4	3	2	4
17	3	4	1	1	1	2	4
18	8	16	8	64	13	5	25
19	11	18	7	49	17	6	36
20	20	19	1	1	18	2	4
21	12	15	3	9	14	2	4
22	13	20	7	49	16	3	9
23	6	8	2	4	5	1	1
24	2	6	4	16	2	0	0
25	14	23	9	81	22	8	64
26	21	27	6	36	21	0	0
27	15	14	1	1	8	7	49
28	22	28	6	36	24	2	4
				1142			546

Correlations

La Follette '24—Smith '28

$$R = 1 - \frac{6(1142)}{21924}$$

$$= 1 - \frac{6852}{21924}$$

$$= 1 - .31$$

$$= .69$$

La Follette '24—F. D. Roosevelt '32

$$R = 1 - \frac{6(546)}{21924}$$

$$= 1 - \frac{3276}{21924}$$

$$= 1 - .10$$

$$= .90$$

Correlation for Smith '28

Ward	Smith '28 Rank	F. D. Roosevelt '32 Rank	d	d²
1	1	7	6	36
2	2	28	26	676
3	17	15	2	4
4	13	19	6	36
5	21	25	4	16
6	7	4	3	9
7	26	27	1	1
8	12	10	2	4
9	5	12	7	49
10	10	6	4	16
11	25	23	2	4
12	9	9	0	0
13	22	20	2	4
14	24	26	2	4
15	11	11	0	0
16	3	3	0	0
17	4	1	3	9
18	16	13	3	9
19	18	17	1	1
20	19	18	1	1
21	15	14	1	1
22	20	16	4	16
23	8	5	3	9
24	6	2	4	16
25	23	22	1	1
26	27	21	6	36
27	14	8	6	36
28	28	24	4	16
				1010

Correlation

Smith '28—F. D. Roosevelt '32

$$R = 1 - \frac{6(1010)}{21924}$$

$$= 1 - \frac{6060}{21924}$$

$$= 1 - .28$$

$$= .72$$

☐ Appendix B

Rank Order Correlations for Ethnic and
Economic Variables and Candidates in 1912,
1924, 1928, and 1932 Elections

Ethnic Percentages and Economic Indicators

Ward	Native Stock '10	Foreign Stock '10	Native Stock '30	Foreign Stock '30	Tenements Occupied '12	Median Rental '30
1	29%	68%	32%	64%	143	$37.82
2	14	84	22	63	159	26.86
3	11	72	7	53	456	30.25
4	34	63	35	60	225	54.78
5	22	53	12	34	192	30.80
6	13	81	22	65	445	21.23
7	56	38	59	35	68	74.83
8	38	58	48	49	109	49.82
9	31	67	34	64	73	29.42
10	25	70	36	56	48	32.90
11	51	43	48	47	121	59.58
12	35	64	32	51	115	40.48
13	54	42	44	42	139	42.72
14	50	47	49	49	41	90.13
15	41	58	38	58	106	35.52
16	18	82	33	65	137	21.66
17	18	82	28	70	260	19.97
18	35	63	45	49	44	35.54
19	42	57	54	45	61	41.78
20	45	54	50	47	59	32.16
21	39	58	41	50	73	29.72
22	52	44	59	35	198	41.56
23	31	67	42	57	420	23.95
24	23	77	44	56	260	22.48
25	47	47	48	42	101	32.44
26	46	52	52	45	59	38.40
27	26	72	38	59	87	32.20
28	—	—	56	41	—	42.10
29	—	—	53	47	—	43.72
30	—	—	57	43	—	45.40
31	—	—	53	46	—	26.33
32	—	—	58	44	—	41.08
City	33	62	41	51	4199	37.06

SOURCES: Percentages of native and foreign stock were computed from 13th Census of Population, 1910 (U.S. Bureau of the Census) and 15th Census of Population, 1930 (U.S. Bureau of the Census). "Most Tenements Occupied, '12" was taken from *Annual Report of the Mayor of the City of Pittsburgh, 1912*, p. 1128; "Median Rental, '30," from Bureau of Social Research, Federation of Social Agencies of Pittsburgh and Allegheny County, *Social Facts About Pittsburgh and Allegheny County*, vol. 1, *Pittsburgh Wards* (Pittsburgh, 1945).

NOTE: For ward percentages for candidates, see Appendix A, p. 195.

Correlation for Foreign Stock '10

Ward	Foreign Stock '10 Rank	T. Roosevelt '12 Rank	d	d^2	Debs '12 Rank	d	d^2
1	9	21	12	144	23	14	196
2	1	27	26	676	25	24	576
3	7	20	13	169	16	9	81
4	13	13	0	0	21	8	64
5	20	3	17	289	17	3	9
6	4	25	21	441	18	14	196
7	27	18	9	81	27	0	0
8	15	15	0	0	22	7	49
9	11	22	11	121	15	4	16
10	8	17	9	81	6	2	4
11	25	5	20	400	26	1	1
12	12	9	3	9	13	1	1
13	26	6	20	400	4	22	484
14	23	12	11	121	24	1	1
15	16	26	10	100	3	13	169
16	3	19	16	36	2	1	1
17	2	23	21	441	7	5	25
18	14	8	6	36	5	9	81
19	18	4	14	196	10	8	64
20	19	16	3	9	19	0	0
21	17	10	7	49	11	6	36
22	24	7	17	289	20	4	16
23	10	11	1	1	8	2	4
24	5	24	19	361	1	4	16
25	22	1	21	441	12	10	100
26	21	2	19	361	14	7	49
27	6	14	8	64	9	3	9
				5316			2248

Correlations

Foreign Stock '10—T. Roosevelt '12   Foreign Stock '10—Debs '12

$$R = 1 - \frac{6(\Sigma d^2)}{N^3 - N}$$

$$R = 1 - \frac{6(5316)}{19656} \qquad\qquad R = 1 - \frac{6(2248)}{19656}$$

$$= 1 - \frac{31896}{19656} \qquad\qquad\quad = 1 - \frac{13488}{19656}$$

$$= 1 - 1.62 \qquad\qquad\qquad\quad = 1 - .69$$

$$= -.62 \qquad\qquad\qquad\qquad = .31$$

Correlations for Foreign Stock '30

Foreign Stock '30		La Follette '24			Smith '28			F. D. Roosevelt '32		
Ward	Rank	Rank	d	d²	Rank	d	d²	Rank	d	d²
1	4	6	2	4	1	3	9	7	3	9
2	6	25	19	361	2	4	16	28	22	484
3	13	20	7	49	17	4	16	15	2	4
4	7	21	14	196	13	6	36	19	12	144
5	28	24	4	16	21	7	49	25	3	9
6	2	9	7	49	7	5	25	4	2	4
7	27	27	0	0	26	1	1	27	0	0
8	17	22	5	25	12	5	25	10	7	49
9	5	7	2	4	5	0	0	12	7	49
10	11	10	1	1	10	1	1	6	5	25
11	19	26	7	49	25	6	36	23	4	16
12	14	17	3	9	9	5	25	9	5	25
13	23	16	7	49	22	1	1	20	3	9
14	16	28	12	144	24	8	64	26	10	100
15	9	4	5	25	11	2	4	11	2	4
16	3	1	2	4	3	0	0	3	0	0
17	1	3	2	4	4	3	9	1	0	0
18	18	8	10	100	16	2	4	13	5	25
19	21	12	9	81	18	3	9	17	4	16
20	20	19	1	1	19	1	1	18	2	4
21	15	11	4	16	15	0	0	14	1	1
22	26	14	12	144	20	6	36	16	10	100
23	10	5	5	25	8	2	4	5	5	25
24	12	2	10	100	6	6	36	2	10	100
25	24	13	11	121	23	1	1	22	2	4
26	22	18	4	16	27	5	25	21	1	1
27	8	15	7	49	14	6	36	8	0	0
28	25	23	2	4	28	3	9	24	1	1
				1646			478			1208

Correlations

Foreign Stock '30— La Follette '24

$$R = 1 - \frac{6(1646)}{21924}$$
$$= 1 - \frac{9876}{21924}$$
$$= 1 - .45$$
$$= .55$$

Foreign Stock '30— Smith '28

$$R = 1 - \frac{6(478)}{21924}$$
$$= 1 - \frac{2868}{21924}$$
$$= 1 - .13$$
$$= .87$$

Foreign Stock '30— F. D. Roosevelt '32

$$R = 1 - \frac{6(1208)}{21924}$$
$$= 1 - \frac{7248}{21924}$$
$$= 1 - .33$$
$$= .67$$

Correlations for Native Stock '10

	Native Stock '10	T. Roosevelt '12			Debs '12		
Ward	*Rank*	*Rank*	*d*	*d²*	*Rank*	*d*	*d²*
1	18	21	3	9	23	5	25
2	25	27	2	4	25	0	0
3	27	20	7	49	16	11	121
4	15	13	2	4	21	6	36
5	22	3	19	361	17	5	25
6	26	25	1	1	18	8	64
7	1	18	17	289	27	26	676
8	12	15	3	9	22	10	100
9	17	22	5	25	15	2	4
10	20	17	3	9	6	14	196
11	4	5	1	1	26	22	484
12	13	9	4	16	13	0	0
13	2	6	4	16	4	2	4
14	5	12	7	49	24	19	361
15	10	26	16	256	3	7	49
16	23	19	4	16	2	21	441
17	24	23	1	1	7	17	289
18	14	8	6	36	5	9	81
19	9	4	5	25	10	1	1
20	8	16	8	64	19	11	121
21	11	10	1	1	11	0	0
22	3	7	4	16	20	17	289
23	16	11	5	25	8	8	64
24	21	24	3	9	1	20	400
25	6	1	5	25	12	6	36
26	7	2	5	25	14	7	49
27	19	14	5	25	9	10	100
				1366			4016

Correlations

Native Stock '10—T. Roosevelt '12

$$R = 1 - \frac{6(1366)}{19656}$$

$$= 1 - \frac{8196}{19656}$$

$$= 1 - .42$$

$$= .58$$

Native Stock '10—Debs '12

$$R = 1 - \frac{6(4016)}{19656}$$

$$= 1 - \frac{24096}{19656}$$

$$= 1 - 1.23$$

$$= -.23$$

Correlations for Native Stock '30

Native Stock '30		La Follette '24			Smith '28			F. D. Roosevelt '32		
Ward	Rank	Rank	d	d²	Rank	d	d²	Rank	d	d²
1	22	6	16	256	1	21	441	7	15	225
2	25	25	0	0	2	23	529	28	3	9
3	28	20	8	64	17	11	121	15	13	169
4	19	21	2	4	13	6	36	19	0	0
5	27	24	3	9	21	6	36	25	2	4
6	26	9	17	289	7	19	361	4	22	484
7	1	27	26	676	26	25	625	27	26	676
8	8	22	14	196	12	4	16	10	2	4
9	20	7	13	169	5	15	225	12	8	64
10	18	10	8	64	10	8	64	6	12	144
11	10	26	16	256	25	15	225	23	13	169
12	23	17	6	36	9	14	196	9	14	196
13	12	16	4	16	22	10	100	20	8	64
14	7	28	21	441	24	17	289	26	19	361
15	16	4	12	144	11	5	25	11	5	25
16	21	1	20	400	3	18	324	3	18	324
17	24	3	21	441	4	20	400	1	23	529
18	11	8	3	9	16	5	25	13	2	4
19	4	12	8	64	18	14	196	17	13	169
20	6	19	13	169	19	13	169	18	12	144
21	15	11	4	16	15	0	0	14	1	1
22	2	14	12	144	20	18	324	16	14	196
23	14	5	9	81	8	6	36	5	9	81
24	13	2	11	121	6	7	49	2	11	121
25	9	13	4	16	23	14	196	22	13	169
26	5	18	13	169	27	22	484	21	16	256
27	17	15	2	4	14	3	9	8	9	81
28	3	23	20	400	28	25	625	24	21	441
				4654			6226			5110

Correlations

Native Stock '30— La Follette '24	Native Stock '30— Smith '28	Native Stock '30— F. D. Roosevelt '32
$R = 1 - \dfrac{6(4654)}{21924}$	$R = 1 - \dfrac{6(6226)}{21924}$	$R = 1 - \dfrac{6(5110)}{21924}$
$= 1 - \dfrac{27924}{21924}$	$= 1 - \dfrac{37356}{21924}$	$= 1 - \dfrac{30660}{21924}$
$= 1 - 1.27$	$= 1 - 1.70$	$= 1 - 1.40$
$= -.27$	$= -.70$	$= -.40$

Correlations for Most Tenements Occupied '12

Ward	Most Tenements Occupied '12 Rank	T. Roosevelt '12 Rank	d	d^2	Debs '12 Rank	d	d^2
1	10	21	11	121	23	13	169
2	9	27	18	324	25	16	256
3	1	20	19	361	16	15	225
4	6	13	7	49	21	15	225
5	8	3	5	25	17	9	81
6	2	25	23	529	18	16	256
7	21	18	3	9	27	6	36
8	15	15	0	0	22	7	49
9	20	22	2	4	15	5	25
10	25	17	8	64	6	19	361
11	13	5	8	64	26	13	169
12	14	9	5	25	13	1	1
13	11	6	5	25	4	7	49
14	27	12	15	225	24	3	9
15	16	26	10	100	3	13	169
16	12	19	7	49	2	10	100
17	5	23	18	324	7	2	4
18	26	8	18	324	5	21	441
19	22	4	18	324	10	12	144
20	24	16	8	64	19	5	25
21	19	10	9	81	11	8	64
22	7	7	0	0	20	13	169
23	3	11	8	64	8	5	25
24	4	24	20	400	1	3	9
25	17	1	16	256	12	5	25
26	23	2	21	441	14	9	81
27	18	14	4	16	9	9	81
				4268			3248

Correlations

Most Tenements
Occupied '12—T. Roosevelt '12

$$R = 1 - \frac{6(4268)}{19656}$$

$$= 1 - \frac{25608}{19656}$$

$$= 1 - 1.30$$

$$= -.30$$

Most Tenements
Occupied '12—Debs '12

$$R = 1 - \frac{6(3248)}{19656}$$

$$= 1 - \frac{19488}{19656}$$

$$= 1 - .99$$

$$= .01$$

Correlations for Median Rental '30

Median Rental '30		La Follette '24			Smith '28			F. D. Roosevelt '32		
Ward	Rank	Rank	d	d²	Rank	d	d²	Rank	d	d²
1	12	6	6	36	1	11	121	7	5	25
2	23	25	2	4	2	21	441	28	5	25
3	20	20	0	0	17	3	9	15	5	25
4	4	21	17	289	13	9	81	19	15	225
5	19	24	5	25	21	2	4	25	6	36
6	27	9	18	324	7	20	400	4	23	529
7	2	27	25	625	26	24	576	27	25	625
8	5	22	17	289	12	7	49	10	5	25
9	22	7	15	225	5	17	289	12	10	100
10	15	10	5	25	10	5	25	6	9	81
11	3	26	23	529	25	22	484	23	20	400
12	10	17	7	49	9	1	1	9	1	1
13	6	16	10	100	22	16	256	20	14	196
14	1	28	27	729	24	23	529	26	25	625
15	14	4	10	100	11	3	9	11	3	9
16	26	1	25	625	3	23	529	3	23	529
17	28	3	25	625	4	24	576	1	27	729
18	13	8	5	25	16	3	9	13	0	0
19	8	12	4	16	18	10	100	17	9	81
20	18	19	1	1	19	1	1	18	0	0
21	21	11	10	100	15	6	36	14	7	49
22	9	14	5	25	20	11	121	16	7	49
23	24	5	19	361	8	16	256	5	19	361
24	25	2	23	529	6	19	361	2	23	529
25	16	13	3	9	23	7	49	22	4	16
26	11	18	7	49	27	16	256	21	10	100
27	17	15	2	4	14	3	9	8	9	81
28	7	23	16	256	28	21	441	24	17	289
				5974			6018			5740

Correlations

Median Rental '30— La Follette '24	Median Rental '30— Smith '28	Median Rental '30— F. D. Roosevelt '32
$R = 1 - \dfrac{6(5974)}{21924}$	$R = 1 - \dfrac{6(6018)}{21924}$	$R = 1 - \dfrac{6(5740)}{21924}$
$= 1 - \dfrac{35844}{21924}$	$= 1 - \dfrac{36108}{21924}$	$= 1 - \dfrac{34440}{21924}$
$= 1 - 1.60$	$= 1 - 1.64$	$= 1 - 1.57$
$= -.60$	$= -.64$	$= -.57$

☐ Appendix C

Rank Order Correlations for 1932 Roosevelt and 1933
McNair Votes and for Ethnic and Economic Variables

Percentages

Ward	Foreign Born '30	Italian Foreign Born '30	Unemployed '34	McNair '33
1	25.3%	9.0%	54.4%	41%
2	25.3	10.0	53.0	8
3	24.6	6.2	56.8	37
4	22.0	2.9	25.6	42
5	14.1	0.6	38.8	48
6	20.0	1.2	40.8	48
7	11.4	0.6	17.0	62
8	14.4	5.4	26.5	59
9	18.7	2.4	33.9	46
10	17.1	1.3	34.0	61
11	16.7	1.8	23.0	60
12	17.2	11.4	38.7	62
13	13.1	5.1	33.3	54
14	16.1	0.7	11.5	61
15	18.3	2.9	30.2	59
16	19.9	0.3	31.4	67
17	21.8	1.3	42.0	62
18	12.7	2.3	33.9	63
19	12.5	3.3	26.8	64
20	13.1	1.9	29.2	60
21	17.0	3.2	38.9	54
22	11.6	1.6	36.4	43
23	18.8	1.3	38.1	54
24	16.9	0.5	31.6	62
25	12.7	2.5	40.7	58
26	11.4	0.9	26.4	63
27	18.7	1.8	32.8	64
28	10.2	1.2	24.5	66
29	11.5	1.1	25.6	72
30	9.9	1.9	26.9	67
31	13.8	4.2	27.4	51
32	10.9	1.5	25.8	70
City	16.3	2.7	31.9	57

SOURCES: Percentages for foreign born and Italian foreign born from Bureau of
Social Research, Federation of Social Agencies of Pittsburgh and Allegheny County,
Social Facts About Pittsburgh and Allegheny County, vol. 1, *Pittsburgh Wards*
(Pittsburgh, 1945). Percentages for 1934 unemployed were taken from J. P. Wat-
son, *Economic Background of the Relief Problem* (Pittsburgh, 1937), p. 46. Per-
centages for the McNair vote were computed from returns in *Pittsburgh Press,*
Nov. 9, 1933.

NOTE: Percentages for F. D. Roosevelt, 1932, and for foreign and native stocks,
1930, can be found in Appendixes A and B, pp. 195 and 201.

Correlation for McNair '33

	McNair '33	Roosevelt '32		
Ward	Rank	Rank	d	d²
1	30	8	22	484
2	32	32	0	0
3	31	17	14	196
4	29	22	7	49
5	25	29	4	16
6	26	4	22	484
7	10	31	21	441
8	18	11	7	49
9	27	13	14	196
10	14	7	7	49
11	16	27	11	121
12	11	10	1	1
13	21	23	2	4
14	15	30	15	225
15	19	12	7	49
16	3	3	0	0
17	12	1	11	121
18	8	14	6	36
19	6	19	13	169
20	17	20	3	9
21	22	15	7	49
22	28	18	10	100
23	23	5	18	324
24	13	2	11	121
25	20	25	5	25
26	9	24	15	225
27	7	9	2	4
28	5	28	23	529
29	1	6	5	25
30	4	21	17	289
31	24	26	2	4
32	2	16	14	196
				4590

Correlation

McNair '33—Roosevelt '32

$$R = 1 - \frac{6(\sum d^2)}{N^3\text{-}N}$$

$$R = 1 - \frac{6(4590)}{32736}$$

$$= 1 - \frac{27540}{32736}$$

$$= 1 - .84$$

$$= .16$$

Correlations for Native Stock '30

Ward	Native Stock '30 Rank	Roosevelt '32 Rank	d	d²	McNair '33 Rank	d	d²
1	26	8	18	324	30	4	16
2	29	32	3	9	32	3	9
3	32	17	15	225	31	1	1
4	23	22	1	1	29	6	36
5	31	29	2	4	25	6	36
6	30	4	26	676	26	4	16
7	1	31	30	900	10	9	81
8	12	11	1	1	18	6	36
9	24	13	11	121	27	3	9
10	22	7	15	225	14	8	64
11	14	27	13	169	16	2	4
12	27	10	17	289	11	16	256
13	16	23	7	49	21	5	25
14	11	30	19	361	15	4	16
15	20	12	8	64	19	1	1
16	25	3	22	484	3	22	484
17	28	1	27	729	12	16	256
18	15	14	1	1	8	7	49
19	6	19	13	169	6	0	0
20	10	20	10	100	17	7	49
21	19	15	4	16	22	3	9
22	2	18	16	256	28	26	676
23	18	5	13	169	23	5	25
24	17	2	15	225	13	4	16
25	13	25	12	144	20	7	49
26	9	24	15	225	9	0	0
27	21	9	12	144	7	14	196
28	5	28	23	529	5	0	0
29	8	6	2	4	1	7	49
30	4	21	17	289	4	0	0
31	7	26	19	361	24	17	289
32	3	16	13	169	2	1	1
				7432			2754

Correlations

Native Stock '30—Roosevelt '32

$$R = 1 - \frac{6(7432)}{32736}$$
$$= 1 - \frac{44592}{32736}$$
$$= 1 - 1.36$$
$$= -.36$$

Native Stock '30—McNair '33

$$R = 1 - \frac{6(2754)}{32736}$$
$$= 1 - \frac{16524}{32736}$$
$$= 1 - .46$$
$$= .54$$

Correlations for Foreign Stock '30

	Foreign Stock '30	Roosevelt '32			McNair '33		
Ward	Rank	Rank	d	d²	Rank	d	d²
1	4	8	4	16	30	26	676
2	6	32	26	676	32	26	676
3	13	17	4	16	31	18	324
4	7	22	15	225	29	22	484
5	32	29	3	9	25	7	49
6	2	4	2	4	26	24	576
7	31	31	0	0	10	21	441
8	17	11	6	36	18	1	1
9	5	13	8	64	27	22	484
10	11	7	4	16	14	3	9
11	20	27	7	49	16	4	16
12	14	10	4	16	11	3	9
13	26	23	3	9	21	5	25
14	16	30	14	196	15	1	1
15	9	12	3	9	19	10	100
16	3	3	0	0	3	0	0
17	1	1	0	0	12	11	121
18	18	14	4	16	8	10	100
19	23	19	4	16	6	17	289
20	21	20	1	1	17	4	16
21	15	15	0	0	22	7	49
22	30	18	12	144	28	2	4
23	10	5	5	25	23	13	169
24	12	2	10	100	13	1	1
25	27	25	2	4	20	7	49
26	24	24	0	0	9	15	225
27	8	9	1	1	7	1	1
28	28	28	0	0	5	23	529
29	19	6	13	169	1	18	324
30	25	21	4	16	4	21	441
31	22	26	4	16	24	2	4
32	29	16	13	169	2	27	729
				2018			6922

Correlations

Foreign Stock '30—Roosevelt '32

$$R = 1 - \frac{6(2018)}{32736}$$

$$= 1 - \frac{12108}{32736}$$

$$= 1 - .37$$

$$= .63$$

Foreign Stock 30—McNair '33

$$R = 1 - \frac{6(6922)}{32736}$$

$$= 1 - \frac{41532}{32736}$$

$$= 1 - 1.27$$

$$= - .27$$

Correlations for Foreign Born '30

	Foreign Born '30	Roosevelt '32			McNair '33		
Ward	Rank	Rank	d	d²	Rank	d	d²
1	2	8	6	36	30	28	784
2	1	32	31	961	32	31	961
3	5	17	12	144	31	26	676
4	3	22	19	361	29	26	676
5	32	29	3	9	25	7	49
6	9	4	5	25	26	17	289
7	31	31	0	0	10	11	121
8	18	11	7	49	18	0	0
9	7	13	6	36	27	20	400
10	16	7	9	81	14	2	4
11	8	27	19	361	16	8	64
12	13	10	3	9	11	2	4
13	19	23	4	16	21	2	4
14	11	30	9	81	15	4	16
15	6	12	6	36	19	13	169
16	10	3	7	49	3	7	49
17	4	1	3	9	12	8	64
18	24	14	10	100	8	16	256
19	22	19	3	9	6	16	256
20	23	20	3	9	17	6	36
21	17	15	2	4	22	5	25
22	21	18	3	9	28	7	49
23	12	5	7	49	23	11	121
24	15	2	13	169	13	2	4
25	25	25	0	0	20	5	25
26	26	24	2	4	9	17	289
27	14	9	5	25	7	7	49
28	27	28	1	1	5	22	484
29	29	6	23	529	1	28	784
30	28	21	7	49	4	24	576
31	20	26	6	36	24	4	16
32	30	16	14	196	2	28	784
				3452			8086

Correlations

Foreign Born '30—Roosevelt '32

$$R = 1 - \frac{6(3452)}{32736}$$
$$= 1 - \frac{20712}{32736}$$
$$= 1 - .40$$
$$= .60$$

Foreign Born '30—McNair '33

$$R = 1 - \frac{6(8086)}{32736}$$
$$= 1 - \frac{48516}{32736}$$
$$= 1 - 1.48$$
$$= -.48$$

Correlations for Italian Foreign Born '30

	Italian Foreign Born '30	Roosevelt '32			McNair '33		
Ward	*Rank*	*Rank*	*d*	*d²*	*Rank*	*d*	*d²*
1	3	8	5	25	30	27	729
2	2	32	30	900	32	30	900
3	4	17	13	169	31	27	729
4	11	22	11	121	29	18	324
5	30	29	1	1	25	5	25
6	23	4	19	361	26	3	9
7	29	31	2	4	10	19	361
8	5	11	6	36	18	13	169
9	13	13	0	0	27	14	196
10	20	7	13	169	14	6	36
11	16	27	11	121	16	0	0
12	1	10	9	81	11	10	100
13	6	23	17	289	21	15	225
14	28	30	2	4	15	13	169
15	10	12	2	4	19	9	81
16	32	3	29	841	3	29	841
17	22	1	21	441	12	10	100
18	14	14	0	0	8	6	36
19	8	19	11	121	6	2	4
20	15	20	5	25	17	2	4
21	9	15	6	36	22	13	169
22	18	18	0	0	28	10	100
23	21	5	16	256	23	2	4
24	31	2	29	841	13	18	324
25	12	25	13	169	20	8	64
26	27	24	3	9	9	18	324
27	17	9	8	64	7	10	100
28	24	28	4	16	5	19	361
29	26	6	20	400	1	25	625
30	25	21	4	16	4	21	441
31	7	26	19	361	24	17	289
32	19	16	3	9	2	17	289
				5890			8128

Correlations

Italian Foreign Born '30—Roosevelt '32   Italian Foreign Born '30—McNair '33

$$R = 1 - \frac{6(5890)}{32736}$$

$$= 1 - \frac{35340}{32736}$$

$$= 1 - 1.06$$

$$= -.06$$

$$R = 1 - \frac{6(8128)}{32736}$$

$$= 1 - \frac{48768}{32736}$$

$$= 1 - 1.48$$

$$= -.48$$

Correlations for Unemployed '34

	Unemployed '34	Roosevelt 32			McNair '33		
Ward	*Rank*	*Rank*	*d*	*d²*	*Rank*	*d*	*d²*
1	2	8	6	36	30	28	784
2	3	32	29	841	32	29	841
3	1	17	16	256	31	30	900
4	27	22	5	25	29	2	4
5	8	29	21	441	25	17	289
6	5	4	1	1	26	21	441
7	31	31	0	0	10	21	441
8	24	11	13	169	18	6	36
9	13	13	0	0	27	14	196
10	12	7	5	25	14	2	4
11	30	27	3	9	16	14	196
12	9	10	1	1	11	2	4
13	15	23	8	64	21	6	36
14	32	30	2	4	15	17	289
15	19	12	7	49	19	0	0
16	18	3	15	225	3	15	225
17	4	1	3	9	12	8	64
18	14	14	0	0	8	6	36
19	23	19	4	16	6	17	289
20	20	20	0	0	17	3	9
21	7	15	8	64	22	15	225
22	11	18	7	49	28	17	289
23	10	5	5	25	23	13	169
24	17	2	15	225	13	4	16
25	6	25	19	361	20	14	196
26	25	24	1	1	9	16	256
27	16	9	7	49	7	9	81
28	29	28	1	1	5	24	576
29	28	6	22	484	1	27	729
30	22	21	1	1	4	18	324
31	21	26	5	25	24	3	9
32	26	16	10	100	2	24	576
				3556			8530

Correlations

Unemployed '34—Roosevelt '32

$$R = 1 - \frac{6(3556)}{32736}$$

$$= 1 - \frac{21336}{32736}$$

$$= 1 - .65$$

$$= .35$$

Unemployed '34—McNair '33

$$R = 1 - \frac{6(8530)}{32736}$$

$$= 1 - \frac{51180}{32736}$$

$$= 1 - 1.56$$

$$= -.56$$

☐ Appendix D
McNair Gains and Losses

Wards Showing McNair Gain Over Roosevelt Vote

Ward	Gain	Roosevelt '32	McNair '33
7	20%	42%	62%
28	19	47	66
14	17	44	61
30	13	54	67
11	11	49	60
26	10	53	63
32	10	60	70
29	8	64	72
19	6	58	64
25	6	52	58
20	5	55	60
5	1	47	48
18	1	62	63
27	1	63	64
31	0.4	51	51
13	0.1	54	54

SOURCES: Percentages for the Roosevelt vote of 1932 were computed from *Pennsylvania Manual*, 1933 ed. Percentages for the McNair vote of 1933 were computed from returns in *Pittsburgh Press*, Nov. 9, 1933.

Wards Showing McNair Loss from Roosevelt Vote

Ward	Loss	Roosevelt '32	McNair '33
6	24%	72%	48%
1	22	63	41
3	21	58	37
17	17	79	62
24	16	78	62
9	16	62	46
22	15	58	43
23	14	68	54
2	14	22	8
4	12	54	42
16	10	77	67
21	7	61	54
10	3	64	61
8	3	62	59
15	3	62	59
12	1	63	62

SOURCES: Percentages for the Roosevelt vote of 1932 were computed from *Pennsylvania Manual,* 1933 ed. Percentages for the McNair vote of 1933 were computed from returns in *Pittsburgh Press,* Nov. 9, 1933.

☐ Appendix E

Rank Order Correlations for Votes of Roosevelt, 1932; McNair, 1933; Gallagher, 1933; and Demmler, 1933

Percentages of Votes

Ward	Gallagher '33 Council	Demmler '33 Council
1	8.2%	7.2%
2	1.8	1.5
3	6.3	6.3
4	8.2	7.9
5	9.3	9.0
6	9.4	8.6
7	11.1	11.2
8	11.6	11.4
9	9.1	9.0
10	12.2	11.8
11	11.0	10.6
12	12.8	13.0
13	11.3	11.2
14	11.0	11.2
15	11.8	11.0
16	13.9	13.2
17	13.0	11.8
18	13.1	12.4
19	12.9	12.2
20	12.2	11.7
21	10.9	11.0
22	8.3	8.1
23	10.9	10.8
24	13.0	12.9
25	11.5	11.4
26	12.6	12.6
27	12.8	13.0
28	12.8	13.4
29	14.0	13.6
30	13.3	12.8
31	10.2	9.9
32	14.2	13.7
City	11.3	11.0

SOURCE: Returns are from *Pittsburgh Press,* Nov. 9, 1933.

NOTE: Percentages represent portion of nine-man total vote that both Gallagher and Demmler received in 1933 city council election. For ward percentages for Roosevelt see Appendix A, p. 195; for ward percentages for McNair see Appendix C, p. 208; for correlation between McNair and Roosevelt see Appendix C, p. 209.

217

Correlations for Gallagher '33

Gallagher '33		Roosevelt '32			McNair '33			Demmler '33		
Ward	Rank	Rank	d	d²	Rank	d	d²	Rank	d	d²
1	29	8	21	441	30	1	1	30	1	1
2	32	32	0	0	32	0	0	32	0	0
3	31	17	14	196	31	0	0	31	0	0
4	30	22	8	64	29	1	1	29	1	1
5	26	29	3	9	25	1	1	25	1	1
6	25	4	21	441	26	1	1	27	2	4
7	19	31	12	144	10	9	81	17	2	4
8	16	11	5	25	18	2	4	15	1	1
9	27	13	14	196	27	0	0	26	1	1
10	13	7	6	36	14	1	1	12	1	1
11	20	27	7	49	16	4	16	23	3	9
12	9	10	1	1	11	2	4	5	4	16
13	18	23	5	25	21	3	9	18	0	0
14	21	30	9	81	15	6	36	19	2	4
15	15	12	3	9	19	4	16	20	5	25
16	3	3	0	0	3	0	0	4	1	1
17	6	1	5	25	12	6	36	13	7	49
18	5	14	9	81	8	3	9	10	5	25
19	8	19	11	121	6	2	4	11	3	9
20	14	20	6	36	17	3	9	14	0	0
21	22	15	7	49	22	0	0	21	1	1
22	28	18	10	100	28	0	0	28	0	0
23	23	5	18	324	23	0	0	22	1	1
24	7	2	5	25	13	6	36	7	0	0
25	17	25	8	64	20	3	9	16	1	1
26	12	24	12	144	9	3	9	9	3	9
27	10	9	1	1	7	3	9	6	4	16
28	11	28	17	289	5	6	36	3	8	64
29	2	6	4	16	1	1	1	2	0	0
30	4	21	17	289	4	0	0	8	4	16
31	24	26	2	4	24	0	0	24	0	0
32	1	16	15	225	2	1	1	1	0	0
				3510			330			260

Correlations

Gall. '33—FDR '32   Gall. '33—McNair '33   Gall. '33—Demm. '33

$$R = 1 - \frac{6(\Sigma d^2)}{N^3 - N}$$

$$R = 1 - \frac{6(3510)}{32736}$$

$$= 1 - \frac{21060}{32736}$$

$$= 1 - .64$$

$$= .36$$

$$R = 1 - \frac{6(330)}{32736}$$

$$= 1 - \frac{1980}{32736}$$

$$= 1 - .06$$

$$= .94$$

$$R = 1 - \frac{6(260)}{32736}$$

$$= 1 - \frac{1560}{32736}$$

$$= 1 - .05$$

$$= .95$$

Correlations for Demmler '33

	Demmler '33	Roosevelt '32			McNair '33		
Ward	*Rank*	*Rank*	*d*	*d²*	*Rank*	*d*	*d²*
1	30	8	22	484	30	0	0
2	32	32	0	0	32	0	0
3	31	17	14	196	31	0	0
4	29	22	7	49	29	0	0
5	25	29	4	16	25	0	0
6	27	4	23	529	26	1	1
7	17	31	14	196	10	7	49
8	15	11	4	16	18	3	9
9	26	13	13	169	27	1	1
10	12	7	5	25	14	2	4
11	23	27	4	16	16	7	49
12	5	10	5	25	11	6	36
13	18	23	5	25	21	3	9
14	19	30	11	121	15	4	16
15	20	12	8	64	19	1	1
16	4	3	1	1	3	1	1
17	13	1	12	144	12	1	1
18	10	14	4	16	8	2	4
19	11	19	8	64	6	5	25
20	14	20	6	36	17	3	9
21	21	15	6	36	22	1	1
22	28	18	10	100	28	0	0
23	22	5	17	289	23	1	1
24	7	2	5	25	13	6	36
25	16	25	9	81	20	4	16
26	9	24	15	225	9	0	0
27	6	9	3	9	7	1	1
28	3	28	25	625	5	2	4
29	2	6	4	16	1	1	1
30	8	21	13	169	4	4	16
31	24	26	2	4	24	0	0
32	1	16	15	225	2	1	1
				3996			292

Correlations

Demmler '33—Roosevelt '32

$$R = 1 - \frac{6(3996)}{32736}$$

$$= 1 - \frac{23976}{32736}$$

$$= 1 - .73$$

$$= .27$$

Demmler '33—McNair '33

$$R = 1 - \frac{6(292)}{32736}$$

$$= 1 - \frac{1752}{32736}$$

$$= 1 - .05$$

$$= .95$$

☐ Appendix F
Rank Order Correlations for Candidates in 1936 and 1937 Elections and for Ethnic and Economic Variables, 1940

Percentage of Votes

Ward	Roosevelt '36	Scully General '37	Scully Primary '37	McArdle Primary '37	McNair Primary '37
1	81%	64%	69%	23%	8%
2	54	48	44	55	9
3	90	86	85	11	4
4	69	63	74	14	12
5	77	66	78	15	7
6	84	62	63	26	11
7	51	45	70	17	13
8	66	53	62	23	15
9	79	63	65	24	11
10	73	61	63	21	16
11	59	49	69	12	19
12	77	65	64	19	17
13	70	50	51	24	25
14	55	41	63	15	22
15	80	62	58	24	18
16	87	64	47	35	18
17	86	69	55	24	21
18	69	57	57	20	23
19	67	52	54	26	20
20	69	52	58	22	20
21	78	65	56	28	16
22	75	62	65	21	14
23	75	58	61	21	18
24	80	57	57	24	19
25	71	59	65	21	14
26	61	47	58	18	24
27	67	51	56	22	22
28	65	49	60	19	21
29	68	49	52	26	22
30	63	49	58	23	19
31	71	59	68	14	18
32	70	50	52	25	23
City	71	57	61	22	17

SOURCES: Roosevelt 1936 percentages were computed from *Pennsylvania Manual,* 1937 ed.; the Scully 1937 general election percentage, from results in *Pittsburgh Press,* Nov. 3, 1937. Primary election results were computed from returns in *Pittsburgh Press,* Sept. 15, 1937.

Ethnic Percentages and Economic Variables

Ward	Foreign Born '40	Individuals on WPA '40	Median Rental '40	Laborers '40
1	21.1%	13.9%	$22.39	5.9%
2	22.9	14.2	17.79	14.4
3	16.6	19.8	19.34	9.3
4	18.8	4.7	36.14	6.6
5	7.2	11.6	24.50	9.5
6	15.1	6.4	16.21	15.8
7	7.7	3.5	45.42	2.4
8	10.8	4.4	33.56	5.3
9	15.4	4.4	21.68	13.6
10	13.0	4.2	24.30	11.4
11	15.2	4.2	39.22	3.1
12	13.9	8.6	32.18	9.8
13	10.2	4.7	35.84	9.0
14	14.8	1.1	60.85	1.6
15	16.1	4.4	31.54	13.8
16	15.0	5.9	17.10	16.4
17	17.2	9.1	16.30	16.8
18	9.4	5.8	25.58	9.1
19	9.7	4.5	33.12	5.8
20	9.4	5.8	24.20	9.9
21	12.3	9.1	20.57	12.8
22	9.7	12.0	21.66	4.8
23	14.5	10.9	17.48	13.6
24	13.4	4.0	17.77	14.9
25	9.3	9.9	23.54	7.1
26	8.7	4.1	36.18	6.7
27	13.9	4.0	31.46	9.9
28	8.5	2.9	31.66	7.6
29	8.1	2.9	33.40	8.1
30	8.3	3.5	33.80	6.9
31	9.8	2.4	25.34	16.8
32	8.1	2.4	36.20	5.8
City	12.6	6.2	24.62	8.9

SOURCE: All statistics were taken from Bureau of Social Research, Federation of Social Agencies of Pittsburgh and Allegheny County, *Social Facts About Pittsburgh and Allegheny County,* vol. 1, *Pittsburgh Wards* (Pittsburgh, 1945).

Correlations for Roosevelt '36

Ward	Roosevelt '36 Rank	Scully General '37 Rank	d	d²	Scully Primary '37 Rank	d	d²
1	5	6	1	1	5	0	0
2	31	29	2	4	32	1	1
3	1	1	0	0	1	0	0
4	19	8	11	121	3	16	256
5	11	3	8	64	2	9	81
6	4	10	6	36	12	8	64
7	32	31	1	1	4	28	784
8	25	19	6	36	15	10	100
9	8	9	1	1	8	0	0
10	14	13	1	1	13	1	1
11	29	27	2	4	6	23	529
12	10	4	6	36	11	1	1
13	17	23	6	36	30	13	169
14	30	32	2	4	14	16	256
15	6	11	5	25	18	12	144
16	2	7	5	25	31	29	841
17	3	2	1	1	26	23	529
18	20	17	3	9	22	2	4
19	24	20	4	16	27	3	9
20	21	21	0	0	19	2	4
21	9	5	4	16	24	15	225
22	13	12	1	1	9	4	16
23	12	16	4	16	16	4	16
24	7	18	11	121	23	16	256
25	15	14	1	1	10	5	25
26	28	30	2	4	20	8	64
27	23	22	1	1	25	2	4
28	26	25	1	1	17	9	81
29	22	26	4	16	28	6	36
30	27	28	1	1	21	6	36
31	16	15	1	1	7	9	81
32	18	24	6	36	29	11	121
				636			4734

Correlations

Roosevelt '36—Scully General '37

$$R = 1 - \frac{6(\sum d^2)}{N^3 - N}$$

$$R = 1 - \frac{6(636)}{32736}$$

$$= 1 - \frac{3816}{32736}$$

$$= 1 - .12$$

$$= .88$$

Roosevelt '36—Scully Primary '37

$$R = 1 - \frac{6(4734)}{32736}$$

$$= 1 - \frac{28404}{32736}$$

$$= 1 - .86$$

$$= .14$$

McArdle Primary '37			McNair Primary '37			Ward
Rank	d	d²	Rank	d	d²	
13	8	64	29	24	576	1
1	30	900	32	1	1	2
32	31	961	31	30	900	3
29	10	100	26	7	49	4
27	16	256	30	19	361	5
4	0	0	27	23	529	6
26	6	36	25	7	49	7
14	11	121	22	3	9	8
8	0	0	28	20	400	9
18	4	16	20	6	36	10
31	2	4	12	17	289	11
23	13	169	19	9	81	12
9	8	64	1	16	256	13
28	2	4	5	25	625	14
10	4	16	15	9	81	15
2	0	0	16	14	196	16
11	8	64	8	5	25	17
22	2	4	3	17	289	18
5	19	361	10	14	196	19
16	5	25	11	10	100	20
3	6	36	21	12	144	21
19	6	36	23	10	100	22
20	8	64	17	5	25	23
12	5	25	13	6	36	24
21	6	36	24	9	81	25
25	3	9	2	26	676	26
17	6	36	6	17	289	27
24	2	4	9	17	289	28
6	16	256	7	15	225	29
15	12	144	14	13	169	30
30	14	196	18	2	4	31
7	11	121	4	14	196	32
		4128			7282	

Correlations

Roosevelt '36—McArdle '37

$$R = 1 - \frac{6(4128)}{32736}$$

$$= 1 - \frac{24768}{32736}$$

$$= 1 - .76$$

$$= .24$$

Roosevelt '36—McNair '37

$$R = 1 - \frac{6(7282)}{32736}$$

$$= 1 - \frac{43692}{32736}$$

$$= 1 - 1.33$$

$$= -.33$$

Correlations for Foreign Born '40

Ward	Foreign Born '40 Rank	Roosevelt '36 Rank	d	d²	Scully General '37 Rank	d	d²
1	2	5	3	9	6	4	16
2	1	31	30	900	29	28	784
3	5	1	4	16	1	4	16
4	3	19	16	256	8	5	25
5	32	11	21	441	3	29	841
6	9	4	5	25	10	1	1
7	31	32	1	1	31	0	0
8	18	25	7	49	19	1	1
9	7	8	1	1	9	2	4
10	16	14	2	4	13	3	9
11	8	29	21	441	27	19	361
12	13	10	3	9	4	9	81
13	19	17	2	4	23	4	16
14	11	30	19	361	32	21	441
15	6	6	0	0	11	5	25
16	10	2	8	64	7	3	9
17	4	3	1	1	2	2	4
18	24	20	4	16	17	7	49
19	22	24	2	4	20	2	4
20	23	21	2	4	21	2	4
21	17	9	8	64	5	12	144
22	21	13	8	64	12	9	81
23	12	12	0	0	16	4	16
24	15	7	8	64	18	3	9
25	25	15	10	100	14	11	121
26	26	28	2	4	30	4	16
27	14	23	9	81	22	8	64
28	27	26	1	1	25	2	4
29	29	22	7	49	26	3	9
30	28	27	1	1	28	0	0
31	20	16	4	16	15	5	25
32	30	18	12	144	24	6	36
				3194			3216

Correlations

Foreign Born '40—Roosevelt '36

$$R = 1 - \frac{6(3194)}{32736}$$

$$R = 1 - \frac{19164}{32736}$$

$$= 1 - .58$$

$$= .42$$

Foreign Born '40—Scully General '37

$$R = 1 - \frac{6(3216)}{32736}$$

$$= 1 - \frac{19296}{32736}$$

$$= 1 - .59$$

$$= .41$$

Scully Primary '37			McArdle Primary '37			McNair Primary '37			Ward
Rank	d	d²	Rank	d	d²	Rank	d	d²	
5	3	9	13	11	121	29	27	729	1
32	31	961	1	0	0	32	31	961	2
1	4	16	32	27	729	31	26	676	3
3	0	0	29	26	676	26	23	529	4
2	30	900	27	5	25	30	2	4	5
12	3	9	4	5	25	27	18	324	6
4	27	729	26	5	25	25	6	36	7
15	3	9	14	4	16	22	4	16	8
8	1	1	8	1	1	28	21	441	9
13	3	9	18	2	4	20	4	16	10
6	2	4	31	23	529	12	4	16	11
11	2	4	23	10	100	19	6	36	12
30	11	121	9	10	100	1	18	324	13
14	3	9	28	17	289	5	6	36	14
18	12	144	10	4	16	15	9	81	15
31	21	441	2	8	64	16	6	36	16
26	22	484	11	7	49	8	4	16	17
22	2	4	22	2	4	3	21	441	18
27	5	25	5	17	289	10	12	144	19
19	4	16	16	7	49	11	12	144	20
24	7	49	3	14	196	21	4	16	21
9	12	144	19	2	4	23	2	4	22
16	4	16	20	8	64	17	5	25	23
23	8	64	12	3	9	13	2	4	24
10	15	225	21	4	16	24	1	1	25
20	6	36	25	1	1	2	24	576	26
25	11	121	17	3	9	6	8	64	27
17	10	100	24	3	9	9	18	324	28
28	1	1	6	23	529	7	22	484	29
21	7	49	15	13	169	14	14	196	30
7	13	169	30	10	100	18	2	4	31
29	1	1	7	23	529	4	26	676	32
		4870			4746			7380	

Correlations

Foreign Born '40—
Scully Primary '37

$$R = 1 - \frac{6(4870)}{32736}$$

$$= 1 - \frac{29220}{32736}$$

$$= 1 - .89$$

$$= .11$$

Foreign Born '40—
McArdle '37

$$R = 1 - \frac{6(4746)}{32736}$$

$$= 1 - \frac{28476}{32736}$$

$$= 1 - .87$$

$$= .13$$

Foreign Born '40—
McNair '37

$$R = 1 - \frac{6(7380)}{32736}$$

$$= 1 - \frac{44280}{32736}$$

$$= 1 - 1.35$$

$$= -.35$$

Correlations for Individuals on WPA '40

Ward	Individuals on WPA '40 Rank	Roosevelt '36 Rank	d	d²	Scully General '37 Rank	d	d²
1	3	5	2	4	6	3	9
2	2	31	29	841	29	27	729
3	1	1	0	0	1	0	0
4	16	19	3	9	8	8	64
5	5	11	6	36	3	2	4
6	11	4	7	49	10	1	1
7	26	32	6	36	31	5	25
8	19	25	6	36	19	0	0
9	18	8	10	100	9	9	81
10	22	14	8	64	13	9	81
11	21	29	8	64	27	6	36
12	10	10	0	0	4	6	36
13	15	17	2	4	23	8	64
14	32	30	2	4	32	0	0
15	20	6	14	196	11	9	81
16	12	2	10	100	7	5	25
17	9	3	6	36	2	7	49
18	13	20	7	49	17	4	16
19	17	24	7	49	20	3	9
20	14	21	7	49	21	7	49
21	8	9	1	1	5	3	9
22	4	13	9	81	12	8	64
23	6	12	6	36	16	10	100
24	24	7	17	289	18	6	36
25	7	15	8	64	14	7	49
26	23	28	5	25	30	7	49
27	25	23	2	4	22	3	9
28	28	26	2	4	25	3	9
29	29	22	7	49	26	3	9
30	27	27	0	0	28	1	1
31	31	16	15	225	15	16	256
32	30	18	12	144	24	6	36
				2648			1986

Correlations

WPA '40—Roosevelt '36

$$R = 1 - \frac{6(2648)}{32736}$$

$$= 1 - \frac{15888}{32736}$$

$$= 1 - .48$$

$$= .52$$

WPA '40—Scully General '37

$$R = 1 - \frac{6(1986)}{32736}$$

$$= 1 - \frac{11916}{32736}$$

$$= 1 - .36$$

$$= .64$$

Scully Primary '37			McArdle Primary '37			McNair Primary '37			Ward
Rank	d	d²	Rank	d	d²	Rank	d	d²	
5	2	4	13	10	100	29	26	676	1
32	30	900	1	1	1	32	30	900	2
1	0	0	32	31	961	31	30	900	3
3	13	169	29	13	169	26	10	100	4
2	3	9	27	22	484	30	25	625	5
12	1	1	4	7	49	27	16	256	6
4	22	484	26	0	0	25	1	1	7
15	4	16	14	5	25	22	3	9	8
8	10	100	8	10	100	28	10	100	9
13	9	81	18	4	16	20	2	4	10
6	15	225	31	10	100	12	9	81	11
11	1	1	23	13	169	19	9	81	12
30	15	225	9	6	36	1	14	196	13
14	18	324	28	4	16	5	27	729	14
18	2	4	10	10	100	15	5	25	15
31	19	361	2	10	100	16	4	16	16
26	17	289	11	2	4	8	1	1	17
22	9	81	22	9	81	3	10	100	18
27	10	100	5	12	144	10	7	49	19
19	5	25	16	2	4	11	3	9	20
24	16	256	3	5	25	21	13	169	21
9	5	25	19	15	225	23	19	361	22
16	10	100	20	14	196	17	11	121	23
23	1	1	12	12	144	13	11	121	24
10	3	9	21	14	196	24	17	289	25
20	3	9	25	2	4	2	21	441	26
25	0	0	17	8	64	6	19	361	27
17	11	121	24	4	16	9	19	361	28
28	1	1	6	23	529	7	22	484	29
21	6	36	15	12	144	14	13	169	30
7	24	576	30	1	1	18	13	169	31
29	1	1	7	23	529	4	26	676	32
		4534			4632			8580	

Correlations

WPA '40—
Scully Primary '37

$$R = 1 - \frac{6(4534)}{32736}$$

$$= 1 - \frac{27204}{32736}$$

$$= 1 - .84$$

$$= .16$$

WPA '40—McArdle '37

$$R = 1 - \frac{6(4632)}{32736}$$

$$= 1 - \frac{27792}{32736}$$

$$= 1 - .85$$

$$= .15$$

WPA '40—McNair '37

$$R = 1 - \frac{6(8580)}{32736}$$

$$= 1 - \frac{51480}{32736}$$

$$= 1 - 1.57$$

$$= - .57$$

Correlations for Median Rental '40

Ward	Median Rental '40 Rank	Roosevelt '36 Rank	d	d²	Scully General '37 Rank	d	d²
1	22	5	17	289	6	16	256
2	27	31	4	16	29	2	4
3	26	1	25	625	1	25	625
4	6	19	13	169	8	2	4
5	18	11	7	49	3	15	225
6	32	4	28	784	10	22	484
7	2	32	30	900	31	29	841
8	9	25	16	256	19	10	100
9	23	8	15	225	9	14	196
10	19	14	5	25	13	6	36
11	3	29	26	676	27	24	576
12	12	10	2	4	4	8	64
13	7	17	10	100	23	16	256
14	1	30	29	841	32	31	961
15	14	6	8	64	11	3	9
16	30	2	28	784	7	23	529
17	31	3	28	784	2	29	841
18	16	20	4	16	17	1	1
19	11	24	13	169	20	9	81
20	20	21	1	1	21	1	1
21	25	9	16	256	5	20	400
22	24	13	11	121	12	12	144
23	29	12	17	289	16	13	169
24	28	7	21	441	18	10	100
25	21	15	6	36	14	7	49
26	5	28	23	529	30	25	625
27	15	23	8	64	22	7	49
28	13	26	13	169	25	12	144
29	10	22	12	144	26	16	256
30	8	27	19	361	28	20	400
31	17	16	1	1	15	2	4
32	4	18	14	196	24	20	400
				9384			8830

Correlations

Median Rental '40—Roosevelt '36

$$R = 1 - \frac{6(9384)}{32736}$$

$$= 1 - \frac{56304}{32736}$$

$$= 1 - 1.72$$

$$= -.72$$

Median Rental '40—Scully General '37

$$R = 1 - \frac{6(8830)}{32736}$$

$$= 1 - \frac{52980}{32736}$$

$$= 1 - 1.62$$

$$= -.62$$

Scully Primary '37			McArdle Primary '37			McNair Primary '37			Ward
Rank	*d*	*d²*	*Rank*	*d*	*d²*	*Rank*	*d*	*d²*	
5	17	289	13	9	81	29	7	49	1
32	5	25	1	26	676	32	5	25	2
1	25	625	32	6	36	31	5	25	3
3	3	9	29	23	529	26	20	400	4
2	16	256	27	9	81	30	12	144	5
12	20	400	4	28	784	27	5	25	6
4	2	4	26	24	576	25	23	529	7
15	14	196	14	5	25	22	13	169	8
8	15	225	8	15	225	28	5	25	9
13	6	36	18	1	1	20	1	1	10
6	3	9	31	28	784	12	9	81	11
11	1	1	23	11	121	19	7	49	12
30	23	529	9	2	4	1	6	36	13
14	13	169	28	27	729	5	4	16	14
18	4	16	10	4	16	15	1	1	15
31	1	1	2	28	784	16	14	196	16
26	5	25	11	20	400	8	23	529	17
22	6	36	22	6	36	3	13	169	18
27	16	256	5	6	36	10	1	1	19
19	1	1	16	4	16	11	9	81	20
24	1	1	3	22	484	21	4	16	21
9	15	225	19	5	25	23	1	1	22
16	13	169	20	9	81	17	12	144	23
23	5	25	12	16	256	13	15	225	24
10	11	121	21	0	0	24	3	9	25
20	15	225	25	20	400	2	3	9	26
25	10	100	17	2	4	6	9	81	27
17	4	16	24	11	121	9	4	16	28
18	8	64	6	4	16	7	3	9	29
21	13	169	15	7	49	14	6	36	30
7	10	100	30	13	169	18	1	1	31
29	25	625	7	3	9	4	0	0	32
		4948			7554			3098	

Correlations

Median Rental '40—Scully Primary '37	Median Rental '40—McArdle '37	Median Rental '40—McNair '37
$R = 1 - \dfrac{6(4948)}{32736}$	$R = 1 - \dfrac{6(7554)}{32736}$	$R = 1 - \dfrac{6(3098)}{32736}$
$= 1 - \dfrac{29688}{32736}$	$= 1 - \dfrac{45324}{32736}$	$= 1 - \dfrac{18588}{32736}$
$= 1 - .91$	$= 1 - 1.38$	$= 1 - .57$
$= .09$	$= -.38$	$= .43$

Correlations for Laborers '40

Ward	Laborers '40 Rank	Roosevelt '36 Rank	d	d^2	Scully General '37 Rank	d	d^2
1	25	5	20	400	6	19	361
2	6	31	25	625	29	23	529
3	16	1	15	225	1	15	225
4	24	19	5	25	8	16	256
5	15	11	4	16	3	12	144
6	4	4	0	0	10	6	36
7	31	32	1	1	31	0	0
8	28	25	3	9	19	9	81
9	9	8	1	1	9	0	0
10	11	14	3	9	13	2	4
11	30	29	1	1	27	3	9
12	14	10	4	16	4	10	100
13	18	17	1	1	23	5	25
14	32	30	2	4	32	0	0
15	7	6	1	1	11	4	16
16	3	2	1	1	7	4	16
17	2	3	1	1	2	0	0
18	17	20	3	9	17	0	0
19	26	24	2	4	20	6	36
20	12	21	9	81	21	9	81
21	10	9	1	1	5	5	25
22	29	13	16	256	12	17	289
23	8	12	4	16	16	8	64
24	5	7	2	4	18	13	169
25	21	15	6	36	14	7	49
26	23	28	5	25	30	7	49
27	13	23	10	100	22	9	81
28	20	26	6	36	25	5	25
29	19	22	3	9	26	7	49
30	22	27	5	25	28	6	36
31	1	16	15	225	15	14	196
32	27	18	9	81	24	3	9
				2244			2960

Correlations

Laborers '40—Roosevelt '36

$$R = 1 - \frac{6(2244)}{32736}$$

$$= 1 - \frac{13464}{32736}$$

$$= 1 - .41$$

$$= .59$$

Laborers '40—Scully General '37

$$R = 1 - \frac{6(2960)}{32736}$$

$$= 1 - \frac{17760}{32736}$$

$$= 1 - .54$$

$$= .46$$

Scully Primary '37			McArdle Primary '37			McNair Primary '37			Ward
Rank	d	d²	Rank	d	d²	Rank	d	d²	
5	20	400	13	12	144	29	4	16	1
32	26	676	1	5	25	32	26	676	2
1	15	225	32	16	256	31	15	225	3
3	21	441	29	5	25	26	2	4	4
2	13	169	27	12	144	30	15	225	5
12	8	64	4	0	0	27	23	529	6
4	27	729	26	5	25	25	6	36	7
15	13	169	14	14	196	22	6	36	8
8	1	1	8	1	1	28	19	361	9
13	2	4	18	7	49	20	9	81	10
6	24	576	31	1	1	12	18	324	11
11	3	9	23	9	81	19	5	25	12
30	12	144	9	9	81	1	17	289	13
14	18	324	28	4	16	5	27	729	14
18	11	121	10	3	9	15	8	64	15
31	28	784	2	1	1	16	13	169	16
26	24	576	11	9	81	8	6	36	17
22	5	25	22	5	25	3	14	196	18
27	1	1	5	21	441	10	16	256	19
19	7	49	16	4	16	11	1	1	20
24	14	196	3	7	49	21	11	121	21
9	20	400	19	10	100	23	6	36	22
16	8	64	20	12	144	17	9	81	23
23	18	324	12	7	49	13	8	64	24
10	11	121	21	0	0	24	3	9	25
20	3	9	25	2	4	2	21	441	26
25	12	144	17	4	16	6	7	49	27
17	3	9	24	4	16	9	11	121	28
28	9	81	6	13	169	7	12	144	29
21	1	1	15	7	49	14	8	64	30
7	6	36	30	29	841	18	17	289	31
29	2	4	7	20	400	4	23	529	32
		6876			3454			6226	

Correlations

Laborers '40—
Scully Primary '37

Laborers '40—
McArdle '37

Laborers '40—
McNair '37

$$R = 1 - \frac{6(6876)}{32736}$$

$$R = 1 - \frac{6(3454)}{32736}$$

$$R = 1 - \frac{6(6226)}{32736}$$

$$= 1 - \frac{41256}{32736}$$

$$= 1 - \frac{20724}{32736}$$

$$= 1 - \frac{37356}{32736}$$

$$= 1 - 1.26$$

$$= 1 - .63$$

$$= 1 - 1.14$$

$$= -.26$$

$$= .37$$

$$= -.14$$

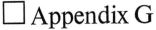
☐ Appendix G
Rank Order Correlations for Democratic Gubernatorial and Senatorial Candidates, 1938, and Individuals on WPA, 1940

Percentages of Votes

Ward	Jones '38	Earle '38
1	64.6%	62.8%
2	83.3	82.7
3	81.9	81.3
4	60.5	58.5
5	66.8	66.2
6	76.8	75.0
7	39.2	36.0
8	51.7	48.5
9	66.3	64.5
10	57.8	55.4
11	48.2	45.8
12	63.8	62.3
13	54.2	51.9
14	39.5	35.1
15	63.1	60.6
16	72.3	70.9
17	72.3	70.6
18	54.7	52.9
19	50.3	47.2
20	51.4	48.9
21	63.7	61.9
22	62.5	61.4
23	63.3	61.8
24	58.6	58.8
25	61.6	59.6
26	45.1	42.6
27	50.5	47.8
28	49.0	46.2
29	49.6	46.0
30	49.6	47.2
31	54.1	52.5
32	49.2	46.5
City	57.0	54.7

SOURCE: Percentages were computed from returns in *Pennsylvania Manual,* 1939 ed.

Correlations for Individuals on WPA '40

Ward	Individuals on WPA '40 Rank	Jones '38 Rank	d	d²	Earle '38 Rank	d	d²
1	3	8	5	25	8	5	25
2	2	1	1	1	1	1	1
3	1	2	1	1	2	1	1
4	16	15	1	1	15	1	1
5	5	6	1	1	6	1	1
6	11	3	8	64	3	8	64
7	26	32	6	36	31	5	25
8	19	21	2	4	22	3	9
9	18	7	11	121	7	11	121
10	22	17	5	25	17	5	25
11	21	29	8	64	29	8	64
12	10	9	1	1	9	1	1
13	15	19	4	16	20	5	25
14	32	31	1	1	32	0	0
15	20	12	8	64	13	7	49
16	12	4	8	64	4	8	64
17	9	5	4	16	5	4	16
18	13	18	5	25	18	5	25
19	17	24	7	49	24	7	49
20	14	22	8	64	21	7	49
21	8	10	2	4	10	2	4
22	4	13	9	81	12	8	64
23	6	11	5	25	11	5	25
24	24	16	8	64	16	8	64
25	7	14	7	49	14	7	49
26	23	30	7	49	30	7	49
27	25	23	2	4	23	2	4
28	28	28	0	0	27	1	1
29	29	25	4	16	28	1	1
30	27	26	1	1	25	2	4
31	31	20	11	121	19	12	144
32	30	27	3	9	26	4	16
				1066			1040

Correlations

WPA '40—Jones '38

$$R = 1 - \frac{6(\Sigma d^2)}{N^3 - N}$$

$$R = 1 - \frac{6(1066)}{32736}$$

$$= 1 - \frac{6396}{32736}$$

$$= 1 - .19$$

$$= .81$$

WPA '40—Earle '38

$$R = 1 - \frac{6(1040)}{32736}$$

$$= 1 - \frac{6240}{32736}$$

$$= 1 - .19$$

$$= .81$$

☐ Appendix H
Job Histories of Selected New Deal Committeemen in Pittsburgh

3W4[1]   This committeeman went into politics for job, obtaining position as WPA Administration aide. In 1937, after supporting Kane-McArdle faction, he was promoted within WPA through Kane's efforts. After Democrats lost state in 1938, 3W4 was dismissed from WPA job. He then went into private business but left it for county job offered by Kane. Job was in works department, where, at the time of this study, he still worked as a lead man.

8W2   See Chapter VII.

8W8   This committeeman claims he joined WPA because of his construction experience, not politics. However, at the time of this study, he had been with City Bureau of Tests for twenty-seven or twenty-eight years. He took civil service test first.

10W4   Steel mill in which this committeeman was employed as a timekeeper shut down. He had served as committeeman prior to that time, but admitted, "I became more interested in politics when I lost my job." He served on WPA as crew foreman, obtaining position through politics. Then he became real estate appraiser for City Board of Assessors and remained in that job.

11W6   This committeeman graduated from Duquesne University in 1927, attended law school for three years, and worked for Dun and Bradstreet for about five years during and after graduation from school. With advent of depression, 11W6 lost his job and eventually obtained WPA foreman's job through politics. In 1936 he obtained city job and then became chief clerk with Bureau of Highways where he remained until 1947 when he went into work for himself.

12W13   This committeeman was laid off from job at Alcoa, but obtained WPA job installing windows in University of Pittsburgh's Cathedral of Learning. "My dad owned the house I lived in, so I couldn't get on relief. Finally, I saw Leo Abernathy at the City-County Building. He sent me to the job." In 1937 John Kane aided him in obtaining county construction job. At time of interview he was serving as county construction supervisor.

13W15   During the depression this committeeman was laid off as printer at *The Pittsburgh Press*. He obtained through politics foreman's job

1. Committeemen are listed by ward and district; therefore, 3W4 signifies 3rd Ward, 4th District.

234

and later timekeeper's job on WPA. After short while in private construction, he served from 1940 to 1943 as deputy constable. He worked in defense plant from 1943 to 1949, after which he became county detective and has held that job ever since. From 1934 to 1950 he served as Democratic committeeman, from 1954 to 1958 as Republican committeeman, and from 1958 to 1962 as Democrat. Each time district attorney's office changed from one party's control to another, he changed registration.

15W6   From 1921 to 1930 this committeeman served as mechanical engineer with Pittsburgh Plate Glass. When depression threw him out of work he became foreman and chief draftsman for WPA. In 1936 he was appointed senior draftsman for county, a post in which he remained until his retirement in 1958.

15W8   After period of unemployment, this committeeman became WPA painter foreman. In 1937 he obtained county job as foreman of bridge painters, which at the time of this study he still held.

15W9   This committeeman worked in contracting business with his father. In 1935, for six to eight months, he served as general foreman on WPA. (Early in McNair's administration he had temporary job in assessor's office as reward for supporting McNair.) After supporting winning candidate for sheriff, he went to work in sheriff's office for four years. During World War II he did electrical wiring on ships for Navy, and after war, from 1946 to 1954, served as head state food agent for western Pennsylvania, a job obtained through politics. At time of interview, 15W9 lived in Tarentum where he owned general store, sold real estate, and served as justice of the peace. In 1946 he became a Republican when local Democrats refused to heed his call for single tax.

15W15   After siege of unemployment, this committeeman obtained general foreman's job on WPA, with aid of Dave Lawrence. In 1936 he went to work for county as bridgeman and in 1945 joined police force, where he was still employed at the time of this study. Once he became policeman, he resigned position as committeeman. However, to protect his interests, his wife served as committeewoman. (Policemen are barred by a 1950 city ordinance from holding a political or public office.)

16W12   This committeeman was laid off from work in steel mill, where he had been employed since 1900. He worked on WPA and prior to that worked for Allegheny County Emergency Relief Board. Once work picked up, he returned to mill until 1950, when he retired. From 1951 through 1961 he obtained a county job, painting white lines on streets. Job was secured

236 □ APPENDIX H

through politics. He claims that he remained with mill until 1950 because of seniority he had accumulated. "Other jobs were insecure."

18W2   This committeeman was in ice business. Refrigerator and depression caught up with him about 1936 or 1937. As result of politics, he got his truck on WPA and did hauling for state. In 1942 he became policeman, position he has held ever since. When he joined force, it was political appendage of Democratic organization.

19W14   This committeeman lost job as master mechanic for firm that repaired heavy construction equipment. In 1935, on day he went to sign up for WPA, he obtained county job as supervising engineer. Although he returned to private industry, from 1950 to 1963 he served again as operating engineer for county.

20W15   When transit system instituted one-man trolley in 1930 and 1931, this committeeman lost his conductor's job. During winter of 1933–1934, he worked on CWA. Although he could not get job under McNair, he did obtain one once Earle was elected governor. When Democrats won county in 1934, 20W15 obtained job as investigator for its law department. He left that job in 1939 and obtained temporary Board of Elections job in 1940. In that same year he was appointed building police guard at County Court House, where he worked until retirement in 1959.

22W6   With coming of depression, this committeeman lost his job as electrician. After working on CWA, he served as foreman and later as supervisor on WPA. He then jumped into job as county deputy sheriff. In 1942 he obtained position of city garage foreman, which at the time of this study he still held. He was leader in Twenty-second Ward until 1963.

26W2   This committeeman lost job in chemical laboratory as result of depression. In 1934 he obtained job with state highway maintenance department and in 1935 joined WPA as supervisor "because," he commented, "I was a committeeman." Since that time he joined Post Office and became supervisor.

26W10   This committeeman was plumber. After serving as labor foreman on WPA, he obtained city job between 1936 and 1937. He returned to private work afterward.

26W7   After this committeeman was laid off as mechanic for International Harvester as result of depression, he served as foreman on WPA until he obtained job as county foreman in Sign and Safety Division. Subsequently, 26W7 became county assessor. His son also entered politics and was city council clerk.

32W3   This committeeman was part-time pharmacist who went on relief rolls as result of depression. He obtained office job on WPA. Subsequently, he served in state inheritance tax office from 1937 to 1943. In latter year he obtained position as investigator for City Law Department, where he was still employed at time of interview.

☐ Appendix I
Percentages of Votes

Democratic Presidential and Mayoralty Means

Ward	Dem. Presidential Mean '44–'64	Dem. Mayoralty Mean '45–'65
1	74.9%	76.4%
2	67.9	78.5
3	85.9	84.1
4	63.1	65.5
5	78.3	77.3
6	81.6	79.0
7	41.3	44.4
8	53.5	56.9
9	76.1	75.9
10	66.2	64.3
11	56.4	58.0
12	66.6	66.8
13	66.1	62.3
14	53.3	54.4
15	71.6	68.6
16	74.6	72.0
17	78.3	73.7
18	61.3	59.4
19	53.0	55.0
20	55.5	55.9
21	71.3	70.4
22	59.6	62.0
23	66.6	66.4
24	59.8	57.7
25	67.3	68.0
26	54.8	46.0
27	55.1	55.7
28	51.5	52.3
29	53.3	54.5
30	55.7	55.8
31	61.0	54.5
32	52.7	51.4
City	61.6[a]	62.1
Co.	55.2	—
State	50.8	—
U.S.	51.0	—

SOURCES: Presidential voting returns for 1944 and 1948 were taken from appropriate editions of *Pennsylvania Manual.* Presidential returns for 1952 through 1964 from Richard M. Scammon, *America Votes,* vols. 1, 2, 4, 7 (Pittsburgh). Author percentaged figures for 1944 and 1948 and averaged figures for all five elections.

Democratic Mayoralty Means

Ward	Dem. Mayoralty Mean '33–'41	Dem. Mayoralty Mean '45–'65
1	57.0%	76.4%
2	47.0	78.5
3	65.0	84.1
4	54.0	65.5
5	61.6	77.3
6	61.0	79.0
7	46.0	44.4
8	52.7	56.9
9	57.3	75.9
10	57.7	64.3
11	51.3	58.0
12	62.7	66.8
13	51.0	62.3
14	45.7	54.4
15	57.0	68.6
16	64.7	72.0
17	65.0	73.7
18	54.3	59.4
19	52.3	55.0
20	52.3	55.9
21	59.0	70.4
22	52.3	62.0
23	56.0	66.4
24	56.0	57.7
25	59.0	68.0
26	48.7	46.0
27	52.3	55.7
28	51.3	52.3
29	53.0	54.5
30	51.9	55.8
31	51.7	54.5
32	53.6	51.4
City	54.9	62.1

SOURCE: Mayoralty vote percentaged and averaged from statistics recorded in office of Nicholas Stabile, budget director of Allegheny County.

Mayoralty vote percentaged and averaged from statistics recorded in office of Nicholas Stabile, budget director of Allegheny County.

a. The unusually disproportionate 75% of the vote won by Lyndon B. Johnson in the 1964 presidential election significantly raises the Democratic presidential mean, thereby lessening the difference between the mayoralty mean, 1945–1965, and the presidential mean, 1944–1964. If the 1964 vote is excluded, the mean for presidential elections, 1944–1960, is 59%.

Democratic Pittsburgh Mayoralty Primary Means

Ward	Organization Candidate Mean '33–'41	Organization Candidate Mean '53–'65
1	75%	88%
2	72	96
3	87	93
4	77	83
5	78	88
6	72	87
7	73	81
8	70	81
9	72	85
10	66	79
11	73	81
12	74	84
13	66	82
14	68	82
15	63	78
16	58	76
17	65	80
18	67	78
19	65	76
20	65	75
21	67	83
22	69	80
23	68	80
24	64	73
25	70	81
26	65	74
27	66	77
28	67	74
29	51[a]	76
30	64	76
31	66[a]	72
32	68	73
City	69	80

SOURCES: Returns for 1933–1941 and 1965 were taken from appropriate post-election-day newspapers; returns for 1953–1961, from files of Allegheny County budget director, Nicholas Stabile. Votes were averaged and percentaged by author.
a. Information for 1933 primary unavailable; mean based on 1937 and 1941.

☐ Appendix J
The Negro, Public Housing, and the Vote

During the 1960 Kennedy-Nixon presidential election, of New York City's seventy-seven election districts where every voter lived in a low-rent housing project, Kennedy won 77 percent of the vote as compared with a citywide average of 63 percent. A sampling of low-rent housing projects in six other cities showed a 79 percent vote for Kennedy. Nationally, he had squeezed through with only 50.1 percent. White project dwellers voted almost as heavily Democratic as the Negroes. Race, however, did play an important role in machine voting, with huge pluralities in Negro wards comprising a sizeable chunk of the organization vote in cities such as New York, Philadelphia, Pittsburgh, Chicago, and Detroit. In the 1961 Democratic mayoralty primary in New York City, Robert F. Wagner, Jr., opposing Tammany Hall, campaigned on a slogan of "Kick out the political bosses." A precinct-by-precinct analysis of the primary vote by Samuel Lubell, however, showed a new kind of political boss, changed in tone but not in substance. Whereas the ancient organization barely turned in twenty precincts of 4,000 by a majority of three-to-one for its candidate, at least thirty-three precincts gave the new-style Wagner machine pluralities of five- and ten-to-one. Many of these were public housing projects. In the general election the voters in the city-controlled housing projects went 70 percent for Wagner, compared to the 52 percent that he drew throughout the city. Predominantly Negro housing projects voted 82 percent for him, the predominantly white projects 63 percent.[1]

Investigation of the vote for mayor in Pittsburgh's public housing developments reveals a similar pattern. Although Pittsburgh's 1960 nonwhite population was 16.8 percent, 47.7 percent of its public housing units were occupied by Negroes. In the city's Bedford Dwellings, a housing project that comprised the Fifth Ward, First Precinct, and was occupied almost completely by Negro tenants, the Democratic candidates for mayor ran consistently ahead of their Fifth Ward total and their city vote in the three mayoralty elections between 1957 and 1961. However, in the Allequippa Terrace development, housing about 50 percent white occupants and comprising the Fifth Ward, Eighteenth and Nineteenth Precincts, the Democratic candidates' votes in the same elections ran consistently behind the mainly Negro ward, but well ahead of the city average.[2]

1. Mimeographed copy of Samuel Lubell, "The People Speak," Apr. 5, 1961, syndicated newspaper column, loaned to author; Lubell, *White and Black: Test of a Nation* (New York, 1964), pp. 129–30.
2. Election returns were taken from files of Nicholas Stabile, budget director of Allegheny County; Information regarding project election districts was taken from

Percentages of Nonwhite Residents and of Votes

	Ward & Pct	Nonwhite		Democratic Vote in Mayoralty Election		
		'57	'60	'57	'59a	'61
Project						
Bedford						
Dwellings	5W1	97.5%	98.4%	83%	89%	86%
Allequippa	5W18	52.3	52.4	68	78	77
Terrace	5W19			72	80	76
Fifth Ward	—	—	84.9	75	82	81
Pittsburgh	—	—	16.8	65	63	67

a. Although Pittsburgh elects a mayor every four years, when David L. Lawrence left office to become governor in 1959, a special mayoralty election was held.

Some observers believe that the true test of a political machine comes during a primary election. If the attainment of 80 percent or more of the primary vote is arbitrarily considered as an indication of strong machine control, Negro support for the organization candidate is evident. This support is seen when comparing the vote in the four Democratic mayoralty primaries between 1953 and 1961 in the precincts of Pittsburgh's two most Negro wards to the vote in the precincts of the city's two most white wards.[3] Of 192 precincts in the most Negro wards, 166—or more than four-fifths—gave the organization candidate at least 80 percent of their vote, whereas, of 70 precincts in the most white wards, only 21—or three-tenths—had more than an 80 percent organization vote.[4]

Registration Board, Allegheny County; Percentages of nonwhite occupants were taken from Pittsburgh Commission of Human Relations, *The Status of Housing of Negroes in Pittsburgh* (May 1962), pp. 22, 24.

3. The 3rd and the 5th Wards contained the highest percentage of Negroes in 1950 and 1960, with 73.2 percent and 78.4 percent nonwhite, respectively, in the former year and 92.4 percent and 84.9 percent, respectively, in the latter. In addition, the 13th Ward's Negro population skyrocketed from 26.9 percent in 1950 to 71.4 percent in 1960. Although its percentage was not calculated for the 1953 vote, the 13th Ward's percentages are included from 1957 on. The wards with the least number of Negroes were the 29th and the 30th. The 29th had 0.1 percent nonwhites in 1950 and 1960, whereas the 30th had 0.3 percent in 1950 and 0.5 percent in 1960. (Pittsburgh Commission on Human Relations, *Population by Color and Ward with Recent Change, Pittsburgh 1950 and 1960*, mimeographed, Mar. 3, 1961.)

4. Election returns from files of Nicholas Stabile, budget director of Allegheny County; Pittsburgh Commission on Human Relations, *Population by Color and Ward with Recent Change, Pittsburgh 1950 and 1960*, mimeographed, Mar. 3, 1961.

☐ Bibliographic Essay

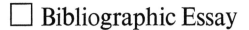

☐ The very nature of the study of urban politics demands that one consult diverse sources ranging from personal interviews to dog-eared manuscripts. Only the most relevant to this work follow.

Aside from the demographic material provided by the interviews with committeemen, city committeemen lists, primary-return books, and city directories described in Chapter 7, statistical information played an important role in probing the working of Pittsburgh's machine politics. The best demographic description of Pittsburgh for the depression decade is *Social Facts About Pittsburgh and Allegheny County*, vol. I, *Pittsburgh Wards*, published in 1945 by the Bureau of Social Research, Federation of Social Agencies of Pittsburgh and Allegheny County. This publication, which distills information from the Fifteenth (1930) and Sixteenth (1940) Censuses of Population of the United States and transforms census tract data into ward data, was a great labor-saving device. When such an aid is not available, the student must transpose the information himself so that he can deal with comparable political and demographic units. When *Social Facts About Pittsburgh* did not provide the appropriate data, the Censuses of 1910 through 1950 were consulted individually. The Special Census of Unemployment: General Report, 1931 (U.S. Bureau of the Census, Washington, 1931) and the *Statistical Abstract of the United States* (U.S. Department of Commerce, Bureau of the Census, Washington, 1934) provided significant demographic data as well.

The best sources for voting returns are the manuals published by most states for their legislature. They frequently provide raw (nonpercentaged) returns for wards and precincts of cities. The *Pennsylvania Manuals* for the years 1913, 1917, 1921, 1925, 1929, 1933, 1937, 1941, and 1945 were consulted for national and state elections in Pittsburgh; the numerical returns were then percentaged by the author. Svend Peterson's *A Statistical History of American Presidential Elections* (New York, 1963) and volumes 1, 2, 4,

243

and 7 of Richard M. Scammon's *America Votes* (Pittsburgh) afforded added election material, although not always in the detail needed by this study. Scammon has also edited *America at the Polls: A Handbook of American Presidential Election Statistics, 1920–1964* (Pittsburgh, 1965), which lists results by state and county. Newspapers often print ward and precinct returns for local as well as state and national elections. The Pittsburgh papers were consulted for this purpose and served as excellent sources. Election-return records on file at the Allegheny County Bureau of Elections proved useful as well. Since the completion of this study. the Archives of Industrial Society, University of Pittsburgh Libraries, has collected over one thousand official manuscript return books for general, municipal, and primary elections in Allegheny County. Consult the compilation by Frank A. Zabrosky, "Allegheny County, Pennsylvania, Voting Records, 1933–1963; A Guide" (Pittsburgh, 1968), which is available from the Archives.

The election-return clipping files maintained by the Pennsylvania Division of the Carnegie Library, Pittsburgh, were most helpful. The Pennsylvania Division is an excellent model for any local history section of a library. Where such a room exists, it should serve as the starting point for research by all students of urban and local history. Nicholas Stabile, budget director of Allegheny County when this study was made, graciously allowed access to his personal return files for Pittsburgh during the years 1945–1961. In the future election-return collection will be facilitated for historians by the election-data archive of the Inter-University Consortium for Political Research at Ann Arbor, Michigan; however, the material is limited to returns for county-level elections for the offices of governor, senator, representative, and president. Urban historians interested in detailed precinct and ward studies of voting behavior will still have to develop their own data.

The problem of election-return analysis and the formation of the New Deal coalition, as discussed in Chapter 2, is receiving increased attention from political scientists and historians. For a review of the literature concerning the issue and a new interpretation, see the article by Jerome M. Clubb and Howard W. Allen, "The Cities and the Election of 1928: Partisan Realignment?" *American Historical Review*, LXXIV (April 1969), 1205–20. The advantages and disadvantages of quantification in the writing of history are discussed in William O. Aydelotte, "Quantification in History," *American Historical Review*, LXXI (April 1966), 803–25.

The minutes of the official proceedings of a city council are important sources for the urban historian. The *Municipal Record*, 1933–1941, vols. 67–75 (city of Pittsburgh, 1933–1941) supplied information sometimes not contained in other sources. *Acts of Assembly and Rules Governing Civil*

Service of Pittsburgh (city of Pittsburgh, Civil Service Commission, 1950) and *Digest of General Ordinances*, 1939–1960 (city of Pittsburgh, Civil Service Commission) aided in the investigation of the machine's use of patronage. William G. Willis's *The Pittsburgh Manual: Guide to the Government of the City of Pittsburgh* (Pittsburgh, 1950) and Edward F. Cooke and G. Edward Janosik's *Guide to Pennsylvania Politics* (New York, 1957) assist in understanding the formal political organization of city and state.

Local politicians, especially those labelled as bosses, are notorious for their lack of record-keeping. Although David L. Lawrence did keep records, the files of the Allegheny County Democratic Committee Headquarters for 1933–1941, maintained at the committee headquarters in Pittsburgh, proved disappointing. Although not providing as much of the inside information as the historian seeks, the letters, memos, speeches, campaign materials, etc., did offer a good insight into the operational workings of the machine. However, some party officials appeared uncomfortable upon seeing an "outsider" peruse the records; whether these files will continue to be available is questionable.

Any student of the New Deal must visit the Franklin D. Roosevelt Library in Hyde Park, New York. Some insight into FDR's relationship with the urban politicians will be found from correspondence with individual city bosses in the President's Personal Files. The Democratic National Committee Files and the Democratic National Committee Women's Division Correspondence for Pennsylvania provide valuable material for the investigation of the link between the Pittsburgh and state organizations and Washington. The Narrative Reports of Lorena Hickok in the Hopkins manuscripts proved especially useful for information regarding politics and relief.

To complete the picture of political influence and relief in Pennsylvania and in Pittsburgh, one should consult the WPA Record Group 69, Pennsylvania 610 collection in the National Archives, Washington, D.C. Searle F. Charles's *Minister of Relief: Harry Hopkins and the Depression* (Syracuse, 1963) provides a general survey of the interaction of politics and relief during the New Deal years. *Pennsylvania Public Assistance Statistics: Summary, 1932–1940*, issued by the commonwealth of Pennsylvania, Bureau of Research and Statistics (Harrisburg, 1940), proved useful in this study for information about relief in Pittsburgh and in the state generally. Equally valuable were two articles by Ralph Carr Fletcher and Katherine A. Biehl, "Trends in Direct Relief Expenditures in Allegheny County, 1920–1937," *The Federator*, XIII (March 1938), 67–72, and "Work Relief and Work Programs in Allegheny County, 1920–1937," *The Federator*, XIII (May 1938), 121–26.

The Joseph F. Guffey Papers, located at Washington and Jefferson College,

Washington, Pa., offer useful information about the formative era of modern Democratic politics in Pennsylvania. Guffey's *Seventy Years on the Red Fire Wagon* (privately published, 1952) supplements this collection. Two manuscript sources of marginal use for this study were the John C. Weaver Social History Collection and the William S. Coleman Papers in the Archives of Industrial Society, University of Pittsburgh, Pittsburgh.

For the day-to-day politics of a city, newspapers provide the most convenient, though not always the most reliable, record. *The Pittsburgh Press*, the anti-New Deal *Pittsburgh Post-Gazette*, and the Hearst *Pittsburgh Sun-Telegraph* were consulted extensively for the decade from 1930 through 1940. The *Pittsburgh Courier* afforded information about the city's Negro politics during the decade, and *Unione* was consulted for the Italian attitude toward the 1933 mayoralty election. The McNair Scrapbooks on file in the Pennsylvania Division of the Carnegie Library, Pittsburgh, facilitated the study of the mayor's career. Walter Davenport's "Mayor's Day in," *Collier's*, XCIII (April 21, 1934), 12–13, offered some further insight into the activities of the mayor.

Although the historian must often be wary of an individual's recall of a past event, interviews can be most helpful in explaining what other evidence leaves unsaid. The value of the oral history interviews with the one hundred and three New Deal committeemen has been discussed in the text. Equally worthwhile were meetings with David L. Lawrence, Emma Guffey Miller, Lorena Hickok, Louis DiNardo, and Thomas Gallagher.

The secondary works concerned with bosses and machines are voluminous. For an introduction to the standard interpretations of the subject, one should consult the following: James Bryce, *The American Commonwealth* (New York, 1924); M. Ostrogorski, *Democracy and the Organization of Political Parties*, vol. II, *The United States*, edited and abridged by Seymour Martin Lipset (Chicago, 1964), especially Chapters 6 and 7 of Part 5; Samuel P. Orth, *The Boss and the Machine: A Chronicle of Politicians and Party Organization* (New Haven, 1919); and Lincoln Steffens, *The Autobiography of Lincoln Steffens* (New York, 1931) and *The Shame of the Cities* (New York, 1957). A delightful handbook for all would-be bosses is William L. Riordan, *Plunkett of Tammany Hall* (New York, 1948).

Harold Zink's *City Bosses in the United States: A Study of 20 Municipal Bosses* (Durham, N.C., 1930); J. T. Salter's *Boss Rule: Portraits in City Politics* (New York, 1935); Harold F. Gosnell's *Machine Politics: Chicago Model* (Chicago, 1937) are good examples of the literature of machine politics that was abundant during the 1930s. Only in recent years has the interest in the topic equalled that of the thirties. The May 1964 issue of *The Annals*,

353, was devoted to the question of bossism in America. With the increasing interest in urban history, historians have turned with relish to the topics of machine politics. The prototype Tweed machine has received attention in Seymour Mandelbaum's analytical study, *Boss Tweed's New York* (New York, 1965) and in Alexander B. Callow, Jr.'s *The Tweed Ring* (New York, 1966). The Urban Life in America series thus far includes three books dealing with urban politics. They are Lyle Dorsett, *The Pendergast Machine* (New York, 1968); Zane L. Miller, *Boss Cox's Cincinnati: Urban Politics in the Progressive Era* (New York, 1968); and Melvin G. Holli, *Reform in Detroit: Hazen S. Pingree and Urban Politics* (New York, 1969). Dorsett's study notes the strengthening effect that New Deal welfare and relief measures had on the Pendergast machine.

Richard C. Wade, in an essay "Urbanization" in C. Vann Woodward, ed., *The Comparative Approach to American History* (New York, 1968), discusses reform and bossism in terms of the periphery of the city versus its center. For a critique of this model as used in Miller's *Boss Cox's Cincinnati*, see Joel A. Tarr's review in the *American Historical Review*, LXXIV (April 1969), 1380–81. Tarr's own interpretation of the phenomenon of bossism can be found in "The Urban Politician as Entrepreneur," *Mid-America*, XLIX (January 1967), 55–67. An especially perceptive model for boss politics can be found by reading Robert K. Merton's *Social Theory and Social Structure* (Glencoe, Ill., 1957). Also see Eric L. McKitrick's "The Study of Corruption," *Political Science Quarterly*, LXXII (December, 1957), 502–14, reprinted in Richard Hofstadter and Seymour Martin Lipset, eds., *Sociology and History: Methods* (New York, 1968). Samuel P. Hays's paper "The Shame of the Cities Revisited: The Case of Pittsburgh," first discussed in a seminar at the University of Pittsburgh, helped to redefine my thinking about the role of machine politics during the progressive era; it has since been published in Herbert Shapiro, ed., *The Muckrakers and American Society* (Boston, 1968). An elaboration on and expansion of the same theme has been published as "The Politics of Reform in Municipal Government in the Progressive Era," *Pacific Northwest Quarterly*, LV (October 1964), 157–69, reprinted in Alexander B. Callow, Jr., ed., *American Urban History: An Interpretive Reader with Commentaries* (New York, 1969).

Nancy Joan Weiss's award-winning undergraduate thesis at Smith College, *Charles Francis Murphy, 1858–1924: Respectability and Responsibility in Tammany Politics* (Northhampton, Massachusetts, 1968), maintains that the difference between the boss and the reformer is not as sharp as once claimed. In this concept she follows the path of J. Joseph Huthmacher's two articles, "Urban Liberalism and the Age of Reform," *Mississippi Valley Historical*

Review, XLIX (September 1962), pp. 231–241, and "Charles Evans Hughes and Charles Francis Murphy: The Metamorphosis of Progressivism," *New York History*, XLVI (January 1965), 25–40. For the view that the boss and his immigrant following were opponents of reform and reformers, see Oscar Handlin, *The Uprooted* (Boston, 1951); Richard Hofstadter, *The Age of Reform* (New York, 1960); and Callow, *The Tweed Ring*. Nathan Glazer and Daniel Patrick Moynihan discuss the immigrant and urban politics in *Beyond the Melting Pot* (Cambridge, Mass., 1963), as does William V. Shannon in *The American Irish: A Political and Social Portrait* (New York, 1963).

Following the tradition of *You're the Boss: The Practice of American Politics* (New York, 1962), which is the memoir of the Bronx New Deal politician Edward J. Flynn, Edward N. Costikyan, a recent head of New York's Tammany Hall, has written a personal account of how the urban political process operates, *Behind Closed Doors: Politics in the Public Interest* (New York, 1966). Harvey Wheeler discusses the effect of the welfare state on urban politics in "Yesterday's Robin Hood: The Rise and Fall of Baltimore's Trenton Democratic Club," *American Quarterly*, VII (winter, 1955), 332–44. Edwin O'Connor's *The Last Hurrah* (New York, 1956) is the classic fictional account of the decline of bossism in recent American life. The book's title has been incorporated into the American political vocabulary.

Information concerning the grass-roots party worker is as important for the study of urban politics as is the material dealing solely with party leadership. Studies that concern themselves with the role of precinct committeemen include the following: Hugh A. Bone, *Grassroots Party Leadership: A Case of King County, Washington*, Bureau of Government Research and Service, report no. 123 (University of Washington, Seattle, 1952); Sonya Forthal, *Cogwheels of Democracy* (New York, 1946); Gosnell, *Machine Politics*; Robert S. Hirschfield et al., "A Profile of Political Activists in Manhattan," *Western Political Quarterly*, XV (September 1962), 489–506; William J. Keefe and William C. Seyler, "Precinct Politicians in Pittsburgh," *Social Science*, XXXVI (January 1960), 26–32; David H. Kurtzman, "Methods of Controlling Votes in Philadephia," (Ph.D. dissertation, Department of Political Science, University of Pennsylvania, 1935); William E. Mosher, "Party Government and Control at the Grass Roots," *National Municipal Review*, XXIV (January 1935), 15–18, 38; Milanie Souza, "The Social Backgrounds of Political Decision-Makers: The Ward Chairmen of Pittsburgh" (unpublished undergraduate tutorial thesis, Chatham College, Pittsburgh, 1960); Leon Weaver, "Some Soundings on the Party System: Rural Precinct Committeemen," *American Political Science Review*, XXXIV (February 1940), 76–84.

The effect of the precinct worker on the electorate has been measured in the following: Phillips Cutright, "Activities of Precinct Committeemen in Partisan and Non-Partisan Communities," *Western Political Quarterly*, XVII (March 1964), 93–108; Cutright and Peter H. Rossi, "Grass Roots Politicians and the Vote," *American Sociological Review*, XXIII (April 1958), 171–79; and Daniel Katz and Samuel J. Eldersveld, "The Impact of Local Party Activity Upon the Electorate," *Public Opinion Quarterly*, XXV (spring, 1961), 1–24.

Finally, two doctoral dissertations are especially helpful in providing summaries of Pennsylvania politics during the decade of the New Deal. They are Samuel J. Astorino, "The Decline of the Republican Dynasty in Pennsylvania, 1929–1934" (University of Pittsburgh, 1962), and Richard C. Keller, "Pennsylvania's Little New Deal" (Columbia University, 1960).

☐ Index

251

Democratic National Convention, 1968, 183

Democratic party: won Allegheny County, 1935, 108; and CWA, 140; and public housing, 187. *See also* Pittsburgh Democratic party

Democratic party, Philadelphia. *See* Philadelphia, Pa.

Democratic registration, Pittsburgh, 147

Democratic voting, Pittsburgh, 51, 52

Democratic ward chairmen, 145, 176–80 passim

Democrats, Pittsburgh. *See* Pittsburgh Democratic party

Denny, Harmar, 87–88

Depression, 10, 52, 109

Detroit, Mich.: and grass-roots party organization, 13; native white population of, 1930, 40; 1960 Negro population in, 184; and Mayor Cavanagh, 188; strikes in, 190; and black mayoralty candidate, 191n19; mentioned, 82

Dunn, Thomas A., 100, 101, 105

Earle, George: and 1934 governorship, 92, 94; and ripper bill, 93, 193; and relief, 127, 129–30, 131; and McNair, 128, 132, 133, 136, 145; and WPA, 129–30, 160; and aid to Pittsburgh, 130–31; and Pittsburgh City Council, 131–32; and political press agent, 142; and secretary of labor, 142; and 1938 senatorial election, 156–57, 161

Economic data, correlated with votes, 79–80

Economic rent: and McNair, 83; law of, 136. *See also* Single tax

Elections, Allegheny County: county commissioner, 1931, 30–31; county commissioner, 1935, 107–08

Elections, Pennsylvania: gubernatorial, 1934, 24; gubernatorial, 1938, 155–61; senatorial, 1938, 155–61

Elections, Pittsburgh: county commissioner, 1931, 30–31; mayoralty primary, 1933, 53–67 passim; mayoralty general, 1933, 68–83 passim; may-

oralty, 1937, 148–54 passim; mayoralty, 1933–1965, 181–82; presidential, 1932–1940, 181–82; mayoralty, 1969, 189, 190n17

Employment, 190

Ethnic groups, 190

Ethnicity, correlated with votes, 79–80, 152–53

Fagan, Patrick: and McNair, 101, 105; condemned Jones's handling of WPA, 148; endorsed Scully, 149

Farley, James A.: as political prototype, 15; and Tammany, 1932, 18; and bossism, 19; visited Pittsburgh, 73; and McNair, 91; and WPA, 147, 148, 158; and 1938 Democratic primary, 157–58; and Catholics in Pennsylvania politics, 178; mentioned, 26

Federal Farm Loan Office, 140–41

Fire, Bureau of, 87, 100

Flaherty, Peter F., 189, 190n17

Flinn, William, 27–28

Flynn, Edward: and perpetuation of machine, 9, 12; and Roosevelt, 19, 20; appointed minister to Australia, 19; and New Deal, 22

Foreign born, Pittsburgh: by wards, 44; and machine politics, 184; and economic and social status ladder, 186

Foreign stock: correlated with votes, 36–37, 39; in Pittsburgh, 40–41, 42, 43; in U.S. cities, 41

Fort Black Community Club, 111

Frank, Ralph H., 28–29

Gallagher, James, 150

Gallagher, Thomas J.: biography of, 81–82; vote analysis of, 81; worked against Republican takeover, 98; and McArdle, 149

Garland, Robert: as Republican president of city council, 95, 98; and O'Keefe amendment, 101; and CWA, 139

Gary, Ind.: study of 1956 presidential vote in, 13, 14, 16; committeemen in, 16; elected black mayor, 191n19

Ardle, 68; on shifts to Herron, 69–70; on Roosevelt and McNair, 78; on McNair and police magistrate, 95; on ripper bill, 101; on McNair poll, 104; on WPA, 145–46

Pittsburgh Press, The: on relief, 65; endorsed McNair, 68–70; praised NRA, 72; criticized Coyne, 74; against McNair, 94–95; on McNair poll, 104; on WPA, 144; mentioned, 53

Pittsburgh Republican party: and control of city, 28; and 1929 mayoralty primary, 29; decline begun, 29–30; members bolt to Democrats, 54; and Negroes, 59; and lack of party workers, 60; and McNair, 61; used relief, 65–66; and vote frauds, 66; damaged by Coleman, 71; and relief organizations, 111; and registration, 147, 181; and WPA, 147; and 1933 primary, 149; mentioned, 26, 29–31. *See also* Republican party

Pittsburgh Sun-Telegraph: on Herron, 69; on McNair, 78; on city manager plan, 95; on McNair poll, 104; mentioned, 64

Pittsburgh wards. *See* Wards, Pittsburgh

Poles: ward concentrations, 41–42, 50; as committeemen, 179; mentioned, 7

Political machine. *See* Machine, political

Politics, urban, 163–64

Poverty: and machine politics, 184; definition of, 186, 186n6; percent of 1966 population living in, 187; Negro and white statistics on, 187

Precinct workers: in Pittsburgh, 15; rewards for, 17; in relief work, 111

Primary elections. *See* Elections, Allegheny County; Elections, Pennsylvania; Elections, Pittsburgh

Progressives, 36–40

Progressive Voters League Organization, 160

Prohibition, 76

Protestants: as committeemen, 178; mentioned, 159

Public housing, Pittsburgh, 187–88

Public payroll. *See* Payroll, public

Public Works Administration (PWA): and McNair, 115; and union labor, 118; and employees in program, 126; and McGovern, 143; and Fagan, 148

Quay, Matthew, 24–25, 27, 92
Quinlan, James B., 150

Rankin, George, Jr., 122–23
Reed, David A., 57, 71
Reform groups, 5, 28
Relief: in Pittsburgh, 33; and politics, 64, 139; appropriation of funds for, 71; and McNair, 85, 116, 118–19; from private to public, 109, 110; administration of, 110
Relief Works Division (RWD), 113, 115
Reno, Samuel J., 63
Rentals, median: correlated with votes, 38, 39; in Pittsburgh, 42, 45, 51, 52
Republican committeemen, 166–80
Republican National Committee: Colored Voters Division of, 33–34; in WPA, 148
Republican party: and ripper bill, 105; and use of relief, 139–40; in control of state until 1935, 139–40; mentioned, 26, 30. *See also* Pittsburgh Republican party
Republican party, Philadelphia. *See* Philadelphia, Pa.
Riots, 190
Ripper bill: had precedent in Pittsburgh, 92; provisions of, 96–97; in House of Representatives, 102; in committee, 107; mentioned, 92–107 passim
Roman Catholic Bishop of Pittsburgh, 112–13
Roosevelt, Franklin D.: and 1936 campaign, 9, 26, 96, 148, 181; and political machines, 12, 18, 20–21; and Guffey, 18, 26; and 1932 campaign, 18, 32–33, 36–41, 51–52, 54, 77–81, 181; and Flynn, 19–20; and political bosses, 19–20, 184; and third term, 20, 181; and Pittsburgh Democratic party, 34, 53, 59, 72–73, 151; and

Vann, 34, 159; and McNair, 59, 61, 68, 78, 82, 84, 103, 116, 138; and NRA, 60; and relief, 65, 113–14, 116; and Coleman, 71; and lower-class voter, 79; and ripper bill, 98–99, 103; and CWA, 113, 140; and WPA, 125–26, 147; and Johnston, 134; compared to Bryan, 136; defended by Jones, 146; mentioned, 31, 135, 161
Roosevelt, Theodore, 29, 36
Russians: ward concentrations, 42, 50; as committeemen, 179

Schnader, William A., 93
Scully, Cornelius D.: claimed election frauds, 67; in McNair's cabinet, 88; replaced McNair as mayor, 95, 138; fired by McNair, 101; and advice to city council, 129; and WPA, 139; as 1937 mayority candidate, 148–55; and Hovde, 156
Single tax: espoused by McNair, 81–82, 86; and city land tax rate, 129; mentioned, 115, 136. *See also* Economic rent
Skeffington, Frank, 6, 18
Smith, Alfred E.: as Tammany's candidate, 18; supported by Hague, 18; and Republican voting tradition, 35; and analysis of vote, 37–40, 80; and Liberty League, 84
Smith, Mrs. R. Templeton: criticized Herron, 63; endorsed McNair, 69–70; political influence of, 91; against ripper bill, 104; selected WPA workers, 145
Smith, Ralph E., 88
Smith, Richard L., 100
Socialist-Labor party, 36
Social Justice, League of, 86, 132
Social workers, 109, 144
South Pittsburgh Water Co., 132–33
Sports, on Sunday, 76
Staley, Austin L., 101, 104
State Emergency Relief Board (SERB), 110, 129–30, 144
State News Service (Pa.), 119
Steele, Squire Tommy, 27
Steffens, Lincoln, 4, 27–28, 65

Succop, Bertram L., 29–30
Sullivan, Tim, 7

Talbot Act, 110
Tammany: and 1932 presidential candidates, 18; in decline, 22; errors of, 27; clubhouses' aid to poor, 186, 186–87n7; mentioned, 4, 16
Tenements, occupied: correlated with votes, 36, 38, 39
Tweed, William Marcy, 4, 27

Unemployment, in Pittsburgh, 41, 42, 46, 51–52
Unione, 62, 75–76, 79
United Mine Workers, 147–48
U.S. Conference of Mayors, 128, 188
U.S. Congress, 98, 116, 128, 160

Van Dyke, Warren, 54, 56
Vann, Robert: and Negro vote, 33, 60–61; as supporter of McNair, 58–59, 78, 85, 93; and Republicans and relief, 65; criticized Coleman, 72; opposed Democratic organization, 88, 159; and threat to his leadership, 89–90; and Negroes and job distribution, 158–59
Vare, William S., 22, 25, 27
Vare machine, 31, 68, 141
Vote frauds, 65–66, 77
Voting machines, 67, 76

Waddell, Robert N., 64, 150, 154
Ward chairmen, 139–40. *See also* Democratic ward chairmen
Wards, Pittsburgh—First Ward: support to Smith in, 38; vote frauds in, 66; chain voting in, 77; 1932–1933 vote analysis in, 80–81
—Second Ward: and Roosevelt, 38, 78; and foreign stock, 40; vote frauds in, 66; and Herron, 67
—Third Ward: and sabotage of voting machines, 30; Negro population in, 42; Negro registration in, 59–60; committeemen shift parties in, 60, 174; carried by Herron, 78; Democratic organization in, 79; 1932–1933 vote analysis in, 80–81; and WPA workers,

DATE DUE

DEC 26 '74			
APR 08 '78			
GAYLORD			PRINTED IN U.S.A.